USNA Life!

Families, Homes, and Treasured Memories of the United States Naval Academy

By

Vicki Escudé, M.A., M.C.C.

Escudé, Vicki H.

USNA Life! Families, Homes, Social Customs and Treasured Memories of the United States Naval Academy

ISBN-13: 978-1466218673

ISBN-10: 1466218673

1. United States Naval Academy. 2. History 3. Annapolis, Maryland 4. Naval History 5. Annapolis, Maryland History 6. Nineteenth Century Social Customs 7. Twentieth Century Social Customs

Cover photo – Navy Juniors at the US Naval Academy near the bandstand, circa 1900. Note: name on the hat of one child – "Kearsa. . ." - is possibly the name of the ship "Kearsarge." The second ship named "Kearsarge" was launched in 1898.

Dedication

This book is dedicated to the spirit of the United States Naval Academy through the ages, and my special family – Leon, Laura and Chandler, who shared the unique and enriching experiences of living there. I am also grateful for the support of Leon in re-writing and revising this book.

Other Books by Vicki Escudé

Getting Everything You Want and Going for More! Coaching for Mastery

Create Your Day with Intention! The 30-Day Power Coach

Fast-Track Leader: First, Master Yourself! (Get to the Point Books, 2011)

The Philosophy and Practice of Coaching – Contributing Author – (Wiley, 2008)

Viva o seu Dia com Intenção! Um Poderoso Coaching de 30 dias (in Portuguese)

ACKNOWLEDGEMENTS

The Author would like to acknowledge the following people who contributed to the completion of this book: Professor Kenneth Hagan – former director of the USNA Museum, who encouraged me to write; Mrs. Jane Price, former Archivist at the USNA; Alice Creighton, Beverly Lyle, and the entire staff of the USNA Archives and Special Collections in the 1990s; Professor Michael P. Parker; Mr. Jim Cheevers, Curator of the USNA Museum; Mrs. Tom Hamilton for encouragement and quotes from her manuscript; Mr. Draper Kaufmann III for the use of his father's memoirs; RADM and Mrs. Randolph King, and to all the people who contributed anecdotes and memories of life at the United States Naval Academy.

Note: Some pictures are courtesy of the USNA Archives, as noted on the picture.

FORWARD

Writing this book has taken many years of research. While living at the Naval Academy from 1991 to 1995, I was fascinated by the history of the old homes, the unique traditions, and the stories that some of the "old timers" would tell.

For three years or so I haunted the Naval Academy Archives, looking at old books, letters, pictures and microfiche. I began requesting information and stories from former residents through various Navy publications, and nearly every day I would receive in my mailbox precious anecdotes from the past. It was clear that the Yard was dear to many people from around the world, and of all ages.

Rear Admiral and Mrs. Randy King sat in my kitchen at 50 Rodgers Road, the same home Randy had lived in 60 years prior during his childhood, and shared wonderful insights, perspectives, and specific details about life on the Yard.

Mrs. Mary Ramsay Sease contacted me from a military retirement home, Vinson Hall, in the Washington, DC area. She was around the age of 94 in 1993 when I visited her there. She shared fascinating stories about early Navy aviators such as her husband, but also about life on the Yard as a child and as the granddaughter of a Superintendent.

Mrs. Thomas Hamilton, Emmie, wrote me from her home in California, and sent me a copy of her book, *Second Fiddle to a Pigskin*, which was full of stories about her husband and her children when they lived at the Academy. Her husband passed away while I was researching the book, was buried at the Academy, and Mrs. Hamilton asked me to attend the funeral and reception.

I met some "characters" who loved to spin some tales – mostly true tales – but who loved the Academy life and had memories to share. Some were octogenarians who lived on the Yard as children! I am deeply grateful and honored to have been the person to listen to and record all the stories that came my way. Some of these raconteurs have passed away now, and here, a few of their memories are preserved.

I published the book in 1995 after leaving the Academy, and went on to other pursuits and interests. I named the book, *150 Yesteryears.* In the early 2000s, I was contacted by a NAWC member who wanted to purchase some of the books to sell to benefit the USNA scholarship fund.

Then, in 2011, I was contacted by Elizabeth (Beth) Rue who was living at the Academy at that time. She had been given a copy of *150 Yesteryears*, and wanted to know how to get more copies for friends. Oddly, I had already been retyping the work, as the original disc and computer files had been lost through the years. I told Beth that I was revising and re-publishing the book.

Through Beth's connections, I was able to request and receive additional twenty-first century stories and updates.

Rereading and revisiting the stories of the Yard made me realize how precious the people, the traditions, and the homes are at the United States Naval Academy. I had the opportunity to be in touch with people who lived there more recently, and I was delighted to include their stories, as well. Nearly 20 years after I lived there, I can still hear the drumbeats for the parades on Worden Field. Here is my new rendition of *USNA Life!*

PS,

If you have stories to share, please send them to me. Who knows, there may be another edition one day!

Vicki@excellentcoach.com

Table of Contents

AN AMERICAN CAMELOT: PROLOGUE

History is made daily at the Naval Academy. Officers and families serve here, then leave, certain that significant values will be upheld and that historic precedents will occur in their absence. Leaving the Yard does not mean one has really "gone." A piece of the heart lingers.

This book recounts the history of the residents and the reminiscences of the people who have played upon the social stage at the Academy. Many of the homes are now listed on the National Historic Register and are within the Annapolis Historic District. Encapsulated by the ancient city of Annapolis, the Academy is entwined in the surrounding community, and shares a mutual past. Though most residents live here only two or three years, there is a continuity and commonality of experience among them, and together they perpetuate the grand traditions on the Yard. Former residents, whose lives of service helped shape future Naval officers, tell their legendary stories of life at the United States Naval Academy.

As the academic year begins again at the United States Naval Academy, brilliantly colored red and golden leaves swirl and dance across the empty Parade Field, as if ghosts from the past are playfully gathering to beckon the turning of a season, the beginning of a new cycle. As magical as the seasonal changes, with origins as mysterious as the beginning of time, the rhythms of life here seem immutable and eternal.

The elderly gentleman drags his bag of raked leaves across the field, stooping from time to time to pick up a stray branch or a piece of paper. His eyes carefully survey the expansive green lawn. He tends the grounds in that timeless, personal way that countless others have for a century and a half before him.

Over one hundred and fifty years ago, in 1845, when the Naval School began, another man offered his services to the "Yard." He did not teach navigation or French, but his presence was an essential fiber in the richly woven tapestry of life here. Only remembered as "Dennis," he worked through the uncertain beginnings of the School, through the Civil War and the Spanish American War, and even past the great reconstruction of the Academy at the turn of the twentieth century. He, too, raked leaves and nurtured this garden-like setting. Taunted by the children living here in the 1800s, who would jump into his carefully stacked pile of leaves, scattering his efforts, he was steadfast in his mission.[1] He provided a backdrop for the on-going social drama played by the thousands of residents who have lived on the "Yard," this Camelot among the walls and waterways surrounding the Naval Academy.

Many individuals shaped the daily life at the Academy, and created the social glue and atmosphere that blend to form a nurturing cradle for midshipmen. Underneath the pomp and circumstance are the personalities who lent their hands to the rocking of that cradle.

PART I: EARLY BEGINNINGS: "SHOW ME THE MAN WHO CAN'T DANCE. . ."

CHAPTER I: BORROWING FROM THE PAST

Eighteen century Annapolis was a jewel, a fair maiden courted by the finest suitors of her day. She was a center of shipping and commerce, a colonial capital, a social gadfly, and an enticing hostess for the fomenting revolutionary ideas. Portly men wearing lace accessories and ladies dressed in high fashion were conveyed in sedan chairs carried by strong shouldered slaves along the streets. The bustling Annapolis harbor beckoned sailing vessels both great and small.[2]

Opulent and stately homes were built in Annapolis in the mid-eighteen century, expressing her social stature – The William Paca House, the Chase-Lloyd House, the Brice House, the Hammond-Harwood House, the Governor's House, and the Sprigg estate on Strawberry Hill. And prior to the building of most of these grand homes, the Daniel Dulany House, a graceful mansion with gardens, was built around 1751 by architect John Duff on land bordered by the Severn River and the Annapolis Harbor to command a view of the Chesapeake Bay. Ships from international ports carried exotic wares past the Dulany House gardens and Windmill Point, site of the best grinding mill in the country, on into Annapolis's busy harbor.[3]

This promontory of land at the juncture of the Severn River and Spa Creek was the site of dramatic activity in the eighteenth century. During Revolutionary times, the windows of the Dulany House reflected the bold blaze of the burning ship, the *Peggy Stewart*, which was run aground and set afire nearby on Windmill Point during the famous "Annapolis Tea Party" in 1774.[4] Nationally known notables passed down Northeast Street, nicknamed "Patriots Walk," or what is now Maryland Avenue, to parlay at the grand Dulany home. The Dulany mansion was rented by Thomas Jefferson and James Madison during the post Revolutionary time when Annapolis was the seat of the Continental Congress, and a meeting place for Revolutionary heroes and statesmen.[5]

In 1808, the Dulany heirs sold their elegant home and property to the government; it was thought that should Annapolis need defending, this commanding spot would be the perfect location for a fortification. The old sturdy stone windmill built in 1760 ceased to grind and was removed, Fort Severn was erected, and Windmill Point became the site of Army barracks, guns and daily military maneuvers. The old Dulany House was kept as the commandant's quarters.

Across the Severn River to the north, two more fortifications were built in response to the War of 1812: Fort Madison, and what was to be known later as Fort Nonsense on a rise above the river. Annapolis never needed defending; a hostile shot was never fired from these forts, yet a military presence became entrenched in the area.

In 1845, Fort Severn in Annapolis was chosen for the establishment of a Naval School, with the encouragement of the Secretary of the Navy, George Bancroft. This new institution was to train young men to become officers proficient in naval sciences, rather than have them solely be instructed aboard ship, as "midshipmen" had been trained before. It was to be the Navy's equivalent to the Army's Military Academy in New York. The nine acres of land formerly known as Windmill Point and Fort Severn were transferred to the Navy for the new school. And a mill of a different sort began to grind and refine the lives of future Naval Officers.

The Dulany mansion was still intact, but by 1845 the landscape had been severely altered with use by the Army. Choosing an undesirable fort in an obscure location, however, assured Bancroft of little opposition to his plan[6]. Historian William Oliver Stevens described the grounds:

> As the visitor sees the modern Naval Academy grounds, it would be hard to picture the smallness and primitive character of the first setting. . . . The grounds were ragged and unattractive. On the Severn side there was a steep bank; between that and the river was a marsh. There was no sea wall. The outstanding landmark, which survived until 1895, was the famous old mulberry tree.[7]

This mulberry tree, which dated from before the Revolutionary period, had long been used as a bearing guide on charts for ships entering the port of Annapolis.[8] It also figured as an important point of reference at the Naval Academy, seen in early maps and photographs, until it became decayed and was removed in 1895.

Annapolis in the mid-1800s was not the enticing maiden of the previous century. Having lost some of her charm and liveliness due to the shifting of commercial interests to Baltimore, she was no longer a cultural drawing card. Naval Surgeon Edmund L. DuBarry refused the position as Naval School physician because it was, he said of Annapolis, "the dullest and most horrible place in the U. States – it is very old, and I do not suppose a house has been built there in 40 years – the place is finished and will not improve."[9] Annapolis was showing her age.

The school began without fanfare – a quiet beginning in a quiet town. "At eleven o'clock on the morning of October 10, 1845, all hands assembled in one of the recitation rooms, and the Superintendent, after a brief but pointed address in which he announced he should exact rigid compliance with all laws, orders, and regulations, declared the School open."[10] Seven days after this inauguration, the *Maryland Republican* casually made note of the opening with the statement that, "' . . . about 40 young gentlemen have already reported themselves, whose handsome appearance and gentlemanly deportment give a cheerful aspect to the quiet streets of [the] City.'"[11] The townspeople of Annapolis seemed to have a singular economic response to this new beginning: "The landlords of Annapolis welcomed the coming of the school by raising rents."[12]

Early Social Foundations and Annapolis Ties

Commander Franklin Buchanan, as the first Superintendent, set the social tone for midshipmen and residents, and provided an inseparable link between the school and the Annapolitans. Buchanan was born in Baltimore, Maryland, some 50 miles north of Annapolis and in 1835 married an Annapolitan, Anne Catherine Lloyd, in historic St. Anne's Church in her home town. Mrs. Buchanan's father, Edward Lloyd, had been a congressman, governor, and U.S. senator. In 1836, Buchanan and his new wife bought a brick house on Scott Street, which later became part of the Naval Academy grounds. According to James Ford from his unpublished manuscript of the nineteenth century, ". . . Buchanan had resided in the town with his family – was a great favorite – intermarried with one of the leading families of the State, the Lloyds – and when he set the example of giving entertainments, it was followed by all the best families in the town and of course the Midshipmen had to return these civilities."[13] Superintendents today, following the course charted by Buchanan, provide social leadership and continue to strengthen the bond with the Annapolis community. Appropriately, the current superintendent's quarters built in the twentieth century and renown as a center for entertaining is known as Buchanan House.

The most significant social event, given in the first academic year at the Naval School during January of 1846, was a ball which included the elite of Annapolis and which punctuated Superintendent Buchanan's social standing among the local people. This event also offered the first introduction of midshipmen as a group to the townspeople. "It was . . . the inauguration of a brilliant campaign in which dozens of the fair maidens of Annapolis were to be won and wed by the wearers of the 'Blue and Gold' of the Navy."[14]

Evidently, the Army soldiers of Fort Severn had little success in wooing Annapolis girls; however, the men of the Navy provided a greater attraction for the maidens. Ford explained:

> . . . [T]he introduction of naval tactics proved more potent in subduing the hearts of the ladies. If they could not be won by sailor's blarney, [they could be influenced with] a lace shawl or a family of canaries from Madeira, a Spanish mantilla, a straw bonnet from Leghorn, a velvet cloak from Genoa, a silk dress pattern from Lyons, a box of gloves from Paris or an amber necklace from Constantinople. . . .[15]

Needless to say, with the promise of such irresistible gifts and chivalrous attentions, balls became a popular yearly tradition. Each year a Winter Ball was held beneath "'Banners and trophies captured in blood.'"[16]

Learning social skills and dancing was part of the curriculum for midshipmen. Rear Admiral Edward Simpson who was one of the rapscallions in the first class of the Naval School, and who later become the first President of Alumni in 1886, emphasized the importance of a well-rounded education by remarking, **"Show me the man who can't dance, and you point to a man who is not up in all branches of his profession."**[17]

Early midshipmen carried their "skills" into the town of Annapolis with varying degrees of success. Professor Lockwood who was assigned to the new Naval School, related an incident involving an anonymous midshipman of dubious decorum and an Annapolis "belle." He wrote:

> Mid[shipman] Blank had heard of the charm and hospitality of a certain Miss X on Cornhill Street, and being out one night he resolved to call on her. Unfortunately, before doing so, he partook of too much wine. He called notwithstanding, was loud and boisterous and very hilarious in his actions, and did not leave till after midnight. The next day, sobered and cool, he reflected on his rude conduct towards Miss S and resolved to call and apologize for the same. On arrival he talked soberly and quietly for some time, when Miss S said, "Why Mr. Bland, what is the matter with you? Last night you were charming but today you are so dull. I think you must be sick."[18]

The midshipmen began to cement liaisons with Annapolis residents by visiting their homes during the first years of the Naval School, a tradition that has endured. As noted by Ford, "Last but not least among the attractions of the old town were the far famed luxuries of the Chesapeake, such as soft-shell crabs, terrapins, canvas-backed ducks, which although overlooked by Secretary Bancroft eclipsed all the other boasted advantages of Annapolis in the eyes of the Midshipmen. They looked forward with much more pleasure to the banquets that awaited them in the hospitable homes of the town than to the feasts of reason to be given within the limits of Fort Severn."[19]

Annapolitans, likewise, began to visit and enjoy this new home of the midshipmen. By 1847, the Naval School, formerly an unattractive place, had become an enticement for townspeople and other visitors, and was becoming a desirable place to educate a son. During Buchanan's time, there were no formal drills or parades to amuse visitors. Still, the grounds and the novelty of the school drew guests to the Yard.[20]

For the first fifteen years before the Civil War, campus festivities were enjoyed by midshipmen, residents, and Annapolitans, but they were infrequent. Admiral George Dewey who graduated from the Naval Academy in 1858, recalled the atmosphere on the Yard during his days as a midshipman. "'The rule was one endless grind of acquiring knowledge.'"[21]

Just as Buchanan of the Navy married a genteel Annapolitan, the Naval Academy itself took Annapolis as a bride, with each mate supporting the other through both calm and turbulent times, encouraging and sometimes chiding each other. It was a union that complemented and enriched the two great entities. And typical of nineteenth century marriages, Annapolis tended the household, preserving her heritage, while the Academy followed a warrior's pursuits.

The First Naval School Residences

Commander and Mrs. Franklin Buchanan, the first Superintendent and his wife, occupied the Dulany mansion, already nearly 100 years old. The Naval School also inherited other structures in addition to the Dulany House. Among several buildings were a row of officers' quarters which were built in 1834 for use by Fort Severn. Commander Buchanan assigned these quarters, later to become known as Buchanan Row to the first staff members of the School.

Professor Lockwood, the first Instructor in Natural Philosophy, tells of the humorous beginnings of his Naval School residency:

> The new Superintendent was very enthusiastic and full of his new office. He had fully solved the problem of how to lodge the expected personnel in the very limited quarters at the fort. Said he, "There are just four houses for you gentlemen – one for the surgeon, one for Lt Lockwood, Marcy and Howison."
>
> "But," said I, "Captain, I shall not be a bachelor after October 1st."
>
> "What's that," he said, "that's unfortunate – I mean for us, not for you."
>
> The matter was arranged by my taking in March and Howison's going into a little closet of a house near the Superintendent's office next door – a one story structure built for a quartermaster's storehouse.[22]

Nineteenth century Naval Academy historian James Ford remarked about this beginning of family life at the Academy: **"So that in the very first week of its history, a prospective bride began to exercise an influence in the new Naval School which in various ways has been maintained by many other fair brides and matrons to this day."**[23] Indeed, the influence of women has been an important factor in the definition of the grand lifestyle maintained at the Naval Academy.

In 1846, the quartermaster's office was expanded and then assigned to Chaplain Jones. This small officer's quarters as mentioned by Lockwood was a brick building which had been built onto the wall of the fort. The residence was known later as 27 Buchanan Row. A wooden cottage constructed near the old mulberry tree and used temporarily as a hospital, was also designated as officer's quarters, and later moved next to Number 27 and known as 28 Buchanan Row. Both small houses with unique origins and which shared a wall with the old fortress wall were still occupied by officers until they were razed in the late 1890s.[24]

Daily Life: Characters, Tricksters and Rascals

The professors and naval officers residing in their new quarters near the Dulany House and the famous old mulberry tree were immediately immersed in campus life. Quite unlike the young, impressionable plebes who report to the Naval Academy today, the first midshipmen were already well-seasoned, and had a few tricks up their sleeves.

> . . . [They] were bearded men, who had seen the world outside the bulwarks of a man-of-war. . . . Some of them had figured in the salons of Paris and London; others had hobnobbed with kings and princes in the East, . . . a few had seen the inside of a Turkish watch-house. . . . It could hardly be expected that such

characters as these would submit to the restraints of academic routine with the pliancy of collegiate freshmen.[25]

Predictably, these "characters" began to sneak out of their quarters to seek nocturnal amusement in the taverns of Annapolis, as well as to provide harassment to the school's residents.

The officers' and professors' quarters, later known as Buchanan Row, were staffed with a man servant and were provided with furniture from government funds. The residents also enjoyed fresh milk daily from their own dairy cows outside each quarters. These cows were sometimes the objects of midshipman mischief. Upon returning late at night from an unauthorized excursion into town, some rambunctious midshipmen lifted Surgeon Lockwood's cow up on a canvas belt into the old mulberry tree. Dr. Lockwood could not find his cow in the morning at milking time. After an extensive search, the watchman on duty heard a plaintive cry from the tree above, and lowered the much distressed cow to the ground. It was reported that she withheld her milk for the remainder of that day.[26]

Other pranks involved the residents' precious bovines. Commander Upshur, the second superintendent of the School, also had to contend with cow capers.

> On one occasion the genial Superintendent and Lieutenant Ward had a serious talk about their respective cows in the presence of two of the [class of] '41s. Ward complained that his cow, well fed on government grass gave only a quart of milk daily, and Upshur lamented a similar falling off in the supply of milk from his cow, Betty, fed on grass, shorts, ship stuff and etc. Neither of them discovered the cause of the trouble until the close of the examination when one of the '41s present at the interview informed them that Walter Jones and other members of the class, milked both cows every night to make milk punches in their quarters.[27]

Lieutenant Ward's cow was also captured several times by the midshipmen and used by them to parody his teaching methods. One of the mids would climb on the cow's back and put her through paces on the parade field to demonstrate tactical maneuvers to a crowd of enthusiasts. After one of these "demonstrations," the old cow struck back, and tossed the haughty mid on the ground.[28]

Lieutenant Ward was one of the early Buchanan Row residents who regularly entertained mids at his quarters, though the students still proved to be rascals under his own roof. The midshipmen would drop by to see Lieutenant Ward in the evenings to discuss and debate his specialty – gunnery. The crafty mids would agree with his point of view, and the genial Professor would offer them his best bourbon, which was the original intent of their visit.[29]

Physicians at the Naval Academy have always been "on call" for sporting injuries. Up until 1850, dueling was one of the midshipmen's more dangerous though forbidden pastimes. Surgeon Lockwood was called out one evening to remove a bullet from a midshipman, which had lodged in his hip "accidentally." Cleverly uncovering the real cause of the injury, he inquired about the accident, "What distance?" The mids in attendance replied quickly, "Ten paces," before they realized that they had implicated themselves as participants in a duel.[30]

Courting Officers' Daughters

Officers' daughters have attracted romantic attentions from midshipmen at the Naval Academy since early days. When Alfred Thayer Mahan was a midshipman from 1855 to 1859, he was smitten by the charms of the Commandant's daughter, Nannie Craven. Commander Craven invited Midshipman Mahan over to the Commandant's quarters for dinner frequently, and would even miss-read his watch so that the two young people could have more time together. Because of such cordial treatment, Mahan stated, "'Damme, if I know which I like best, father or daughter.'"[31] Admiral Mahan became a well known naval historian, and Mahan Hall on campus was named in his honor.

Another evening at the Craven residence, several of the midshipmen came by to serenade some young ladies gathered there. They were rewarded by being walloped with large apples hurled by the girls.[32] Courting at the Naval Academy had its ups and downs.

During the time of Superintendent Blake beginning in 1857, midshipmen were allowed to visit the homes of officers and faculty any time of the day, with the exception of study hour, and many preferred to have supper with a family rather than in the mess hall. Mrs. Blake was especially known for being motherly to the midshipmen, and warmly welcomed them into the Superintendent's Quarters at the Dulany House. Superintendent Blake added his personal touch to the midshipmen's lives by responding personally to over one thousand letters each year from the parents.[33]

Early residents, confined to a small parcel of land with their houses near the midshipmen's quarters, were quickly involved in the lives of the students. The high-spirited group of midshipmen in the first few classes were entertaining and exasperating with their antics. Life at the Naval School was filled with drama and excitement from its very beginning.

Early Expansion of the Naval School

In his brief two years as superintendent, Commander Buchanan established close ties for the Naval School with Annapolis, set social precedents, and began to beautify the grounds. Commander Upshur the second superintendent, who served from 1847 to 1850, continued the vision of a grand establishment by expanding the boundaries. In 1847, land and property were purchased which included several houses from Scott Street, to Northeast Street (now Maryland Avenue) on down to the Severn River. Among these houses were the Judge Joseph Hopper

Nicholson House, the William O'Hara House, and the Franklin Buchanan House. The Buchanan House had been owned by the first superintendent. After the purchase, these houses were used as officer and faculty quarters, and the Nicholson House became quarters for the commandant of midshipmen.[34]

The Nicholson house for which there is now a marker in the park near the bandstand was owned by a relative of Francis Scott Key. It was not only one of the several beautiful mansions of Annapolis that was eventually razed by the Naval Academy, but it was the site of a national treasure for many years. Judge Nicholson's wife was the sister of Mrs. Key. It was Judge Nicholson who first took the famous "Star Spangled Banner" penned by Mr. Key to the printer, and suggested the tune, a well-known air, to make the poem a song. The original copy of the poem was kept in a desk at the Nicholson home, locked up and forgotten from 1814 until 1845, when it was discovered by Judge Nicholson's daughter. It was eventually given for safe-keeping to the Walter's Gallery in Baltimore.[35] Interestingly, Francis Scott Key and Franklin Buchanan were related by marriage – both had wives from the prominent Lloyd family. Thus, the inspiring song which was kept on what is now the Naval Academy grounds near the bandstand, has become our national anthem, and is played with patriotic devotion on the Yard.

The Academy built two more houses near the Nicholson House for officers and faculty. One of these new quarters was home to Professor Seager and his family.[36] Seager was a master in the art of pencil and watercolor drawing, and served as Professor of Drawing at the Academy from 1850 to 1867. For a few years, he served extra duty as swordmaster. Fencing, a gentleman's sport, was required of midshipmen. Professor Seager was awarded the rank of "Professor of Mathematics" by President Abraham Lincoln in 1864.[37]

Seager was a familiar figure around the campus in the early years. An accomplished artist, he sketched many Naval Academy scenes as midshipmen and residents continued their daily activities around him. He designed the school's diploma, which was used from 1854 to 1912, with the exception of the years 1866 to 1868. As a tribute to his considerable talent, exhibitions of his pencil and watercolor landscapes were held over a century later in New York by the Hirschl and Adler Galleries in 1983, and again at the Naval Academy Museum in 1986.[38]

Within a few years, the stately Scott Street homes and the new quarters where Professor Seager lived were torn down. Because of an expansion of the Academy in 1853, sponsored by Superintendent Stribling, these residences would have been in the center of the campus. The materials from these homes were used to build quarters near the newly formed boundary by Gate #3.[39]

The house and grounds of the prominent Pinkney family of Annapolis were sold to the Naval Academy in this 1853 expansion. Located near the present-day Chapel, that house was also used as officer housing until 1860, when it, too, was destroyed.[40]

In the 1840s and 1850s, the Academy was an interesting combination of architectural styles with structures borrowed from the old Fort as well as from the citizens of the town. Its residential areas were, perhaps, not much different from the civilian neighborhoods in Annapolis. The streets on the Yard were lined with fine old homes, each with its own individual personality.

Commander Louis M. Goldsborough built two large double houses just inside Gate #3, where the Officer and Faculty Club now stands. These brick homes, complete in 1857, were later converted into apartments.[41] Officially known as "Goldsborough Row," quarters 14 and 15, these apartments were affectionately nicknamed "The Flats" or "The Corrals."

Captain George S. Blake the next superintendent after Commander Goldsborough oversaw the building of Blake Row, a lovely row of five double houses and one large single house. These homes were placed between the old Chapel and Gate #3. Number One Blake Row, a single house, was designated as quarters for the Commandant of Midshipmen, who had previously resided in the old Nicholson mansion. The midshipmen dubbed this line of quarters as "Rascality Row."[42] The Blake Row homes, numbers one through 11, were completed between 1859 and 1861, the latter being finished only three months before the Academy was transported to Newport, Rhode Island, to weather the Civil War.[43]

The mid-nineteenth century was a time of growth and expansion for the United States. Among the accomplishments of the times were the discovery of gold in California and the development of the telegraph and newspaper. The establishment of the novel Naval School and its progressive study of steam engineering was a mark of considerable progress.[44] **By 1850, the Naval School had become a four-year institution, and was re-named the United Stated Naval Academy.**

Displacement of the Academy During the Civil War

During the Civil War years, from 1861 to 1865, the Naval Academy was moved to Newport, Rhode Island, north of the Mason-Dixon Line, to shelter it from Southern encroachments, and to allow the Union Army once again to defend Annapolis at the old Fort Severn. The months prior to the change-over were filled with uncertainty and sadness for the students and families who resided on the Yard. Not only were midshipmen with their indelible bond and cohesive spirit shattered by different political allegiances, the school itself was physically uprooted from its birthplace in Annapolis. Officers and faculty also had to begin to make a choice of which political side to support. In this atmosphere of deliberation and divisiveness, the gaiety of social interactions gave way to late-night discussions within the homes and dormitories.

In 1860, the families along Blake Row watched out of their windows as a solemn procession of midshipmen passed their houses, arm-in-arm, singing a mournful farewell to a popular honor student whose conscience led him to align with the South. As they passed Number One Blake Row, the Commandant's Quarters, Lieutenant Rodgers came out of his house and inquired:

> "What is the meaning of this rioting on Sunday night?" he demanded sharply.

> "No riot, sir," replied the leader, "we are only bidding our classmate good-by."

> "Go on, gentlemen," said the commandant simply, and the dreary little procession resumed its march.[45]

Thus, the somber group continued on toward the gate. This was the first of many sorrowful departures experienced on the Yard.

One of the professors at the Academy, who was compelled to support the South also staged a dramatic exit from the gate, and demonstrated the high sentiments prevalent during these turbulent and trying times. Mr. William Harwood, owner of the famous Georgian-style Hammond-Harwood mansion on Maryland Avenue, was Professor of English and Ethics at the Academy. Upon reaching a decision to leave the position at the school because of his Southern sympathies, he threw the American flag on the ground at the Main Gate, stomped on it, and railed against President Lincoln and the Union. The guard at the gate did not waste any time with this demonstration; he simply grabbed the professor by the neck and shoved him off the property.[46] Union Army troops arrived at the Academy and began using the property and buildings once again to fortify Annapolis, and Superintendent Blake could no longer maintain the school's regimen. The time to ready for departure arrived on April 24, 1861. The class of 1861, reluctant to leave their comrades, smoked a peace pipe and pledged to care for each other, no matter their allegiances. All the midshipmen, both Northerners and Southerners, listened to the band play "The Star Spangled Banner," after which Commandant Rodgers made a heartfelt plea for Union loyalty. Tears flowed in abundance that day at the Naval Academy, shed in advance of the unforeseen atrocities to follow in the Civil War. Truly the midshipmen were brothers, and as soon as they broke their final embrace that day, some brothers became enemies.[47]

A tug shuttled students to the waiting *Constitution*, and the following day this ship whose namesake is the symbol of our country, our unity and our freedom, sailed down the Chesapeake and headed for Fort Adams in Newport. The *Baltic*, which sailed soon afterward, carried the officers and professors who would be there in Newport during the war to train the future naval officers.[48]

CHAPTER TWO: AFTER THE CIVIL WAR

Homecoming

"Homecoming" for the Naval Academy after the war must have been anticipated with much excitement. A picture of the quiet campus, the lovely shade trees, and graceful, well-cared-for homes was certainly poised in the minds of those who were returning to the school's birthplace. But upon arrival in Annapolis, Academy personnel were instead shocked by the altered landscape. Strides that had been made in the early years of the Academy to make the grounds pleasant and hospitable were entirely lost during the occupation of Fort Severn by the Army troops during the Civil War. Stately Blake Row had just been completed before the war, but for the next four years these lovely homes as well as the midshipmen's quarters were used as hospital wards.   There was apprehension about sending Academy residents back to live in neglected quarters that had been filled with sickness and disease.[49]

Park Benjamin, a Naval historian, described the disheartening scenario which faced the arrival of the Academy staff:

> Whatever beauty the place had ever possessed was gone. The long row of willows which had fringed the bay side had been eaten by the cavalry horses. Deep-rutted wagon roads ran in every direction over the ruined lawns. Where once had been flowers and shrubbery now was bare earth, with perhaps a chomp of rank pasture grass here and there. Sheds had been built on the parade to serve for beer-rooms and sutlers' shops. Even the Superintendent's house had been turned into a billiard-saloon.[50]

Perhaps the only unchanged landmark was that steadfast range guide for ships: the welcoming old mulberry tree.

Porter's Miracles

Superintendent David Dixon Porter had expressed an interest in leading the Naval Academy several years prior to his appointment; he wanted to have a hand in properly molding the future officers of the Navy. A strong disciplinarian and a confident tactician, he seemed just the right captain to set a new course for this much-weakened institution. Discipline and academic standards had suffered during the Academy's hiatus in Newport.[51] In addition, Fort Adams in Newport was small and confining, further dampening the spirits of midshipmen, officers, and faculty assigned there. Superintendent Porter did not inherit a strong naval training program, an inspiring environment, nor enthusiastic players. He inherited the raw material for a new creation, and Porter knew exactly what to do with it.

Designated as Superintendent in September, 1865, and seeing the conditions at the school, Porter immediately began to prepare for the second act in the drama of Naval Academy history. He. . . "set a small army of laborers to work, and by the time the academic year opened in October, 1865, the place was in fair order. . . ."[52] **Knowing that the physical appearance of the campus would reflect in the morale of the residents, Rear Admiral Porter continued throughout his tenure to expand, build and beautify the surroundings.**

Superintendent Porter immediately modified the daily routines of midshipmen at the school. A strict code of discipline was established, and to reinforce this training, drills and dress parades in sharp new uniforms began to make the Academy quite a colorful showcase.

Another even more dramatic departure from the former Academy life was the development of a variety of extracurricular activities for the midshipmen. Clubs and theatricals were introduced. Midshipmen who just one year before had been reprimanded by Superintendent Blake for playing a game of cricket, were now encouraged to engage in any number of structured sports and amusements.[53] Fencing, boxing, baseball, and other athletics were established on campus. Rear Admiral Porter realized that these active young men needed to channel their energy and frustrations in positive ways.[54] With a new, high level of campus involvement, the taverns and brothels nearby in Annapolis probably did not hum with quite as much late-night activity as they had in the early years of the Academy.

Further adding to an uplifting atmosphere on the Yard, Porter introduced a program to promote social graces and cultural entertainment. **"Weekly dancing parties, or hops, as they were called, were held in the lyceum over the mess-hall, which were attended not merely by the midshipmen, but by ladies of Annapolis and of the officers' families."[55]** According to Sweetman, an Academy historian, "Sly references were made to 'Porter's Dancing Academy,' and former Superintendent Goldsborough quipped, 'In my time we educated the head. Now, by Neptune they educate the heels.'"[56]

Lieutenant Commander Edward P. Lull in a report for Vice Admiral Porter in 1869 wrote about the transformations at the Academy. Giving a glimpse into the social life of the times, he stated:

> During the Academic year, Hops are given once a month by the officers, and also by the midshipmen; these occur on Saturday(sic) evenings, and terminate by half past eleven.

> About the eight(sic) of January of each year, a grand ball is given by the graduating class, and on the twenty-second of Febuary(sic), a dress hop by the second class. The Balls and Hops, are given in the Gymnasium, which is very well adapted for the purpose. Great skill and taste, has hitherto been displayed by the midshipmen in decorating the Gymnasium for the balls; using flags, arms, evergreens &c. . . . . These hops, believed to have a very refining influence upon the young gentlemen, are certainly very attractive to officers, and to the guests present.[57]

Under Porter's careful attention even the lackluster and sadly attired band increased in size, obtained handsome and colorful uniforms, and became a symbol of the inspiring, high-spirited experience of living at the Naval Academy.[58] Lull wrote:

> There is an excellent Band composed of twenty-eight musicians, attached to the Academy, which is required to play every morning and evening, for an hour, and also for drills, dress-parades &c; many of the musicians also play on reed and stringed instruments, forming a very fine orchestral band for Hops and Balls.[59]

Superintendent Porter's magical influence was woven into every fiber of life at the Academy. In addition to seeing him at formal events, midshipmen also felt Porter's presence in their everyday lives. From time to time he could be found at the old, round gymnasium, a unique landmark left from Fort Severn times, boxing with the midshipmen.[60] He was a visible and accessible role-model for the students.

Because of the small and close Academy community in the mid-1800s, Porter also was aware of the activities of the midshipmen, and their effects on other residents. Either with humor or rancor, he issued an order about a specific midshipman's annoying habits:

> Order by Porter October 25, 1867
>
> Midshipman Thompson (1st Class) who plays so abominably on a fish horn will oblige me by going outside the limits when he wants to practice, or he will find himself coming out of the little end of the horn.[61]

Despite this uncharitable comment from the Superintendent, Colonel Robert Means Thompson, class of 1868, later became one of the Academy's most generous benefactors. In fact, the former Thompson Stadium once located where Halsey Field House now stands, was dedicated to this man in 1931.

Porter took every opportunity to share the excellence the Academy had attained with visiting dignitaries and politicians, hoping to increase its prestige and the monetary allocations for the institution. Once again, the quiet and almost forgotten town of Annapolis, the eighteenth century hostess to national figures, became a center for visiting politicians and influential citizens. She polished up her social graces along with the midshipmen, and joined in the explosion of fanfare stirring at the Naval Academy. Once again as in years before, a stroll down

Maryland Avenue to "middle gate" or Gate #3, would lend itself to the excitement of seeing the arrival or departure of an important personage.

One of these important visitors was President Grant who travelled from the Capital to visit Superintendent Porter. While on the Yard, Grant experienced firsthand the strictly enforced rules of discipline of the Academy. The President and a friend stepped out onto the grounds for a leisurely stroll and to smoke a cigar. The two gentlemen were stopped by a vigilant watchman who informed them, not knowing who they were, that there was no smoking allowed on the Yard. The President praised the watchman for following orders, and quickly extinguished his cigar.[62] Many years later, in 1907, another distinguished visitor, Mark Twain, made a similar mistake with his cigar, but Mr. Clemens was not as compliant or as gracious as Mr. Grant. He was, however, more witty about the incident.

The atmosphere at the Naval Academy was certainly uplifting and appealing to visitors of all kinds. The romantic and seductive flash of the sword and the emotion-stirring beat of the drum drew onlookers and admirers. Lull noted:

> A very attractive feature in the routine of the Academy is the dress parade, which occurs every evening, during the session except Sundays, and except during the most inclement part of the winter. . . . Numerous visitors from the city of Annapolis, witness these parades, finding in them an unfailing source of attraction.[63]

Porter's tenure as Superintendent at the Naval Academy proved to be a turning point for life not only among midshipmen, but among Academy residents, and among the citizens of Annapolis. A forum was provided for a higher level of social participation, and the citizenry inside and outside the gates rose to the occasion.

Women living at the Naval Academy began to play a more significant role during Porter's incumbency. Through the traditional channels of social activities and motherly pursuits which were open to women of the nineteenth century, their influence became a formidable yet balancing presence. The importance of their contribution to the development of life-style at the school is noted by historian Park Benjamin at the end of the nineteenth century. He stated:

> There were . . . other causes which contributed powerfully, though indirectly, to the success of the new order of things. Those familiar with social life at the Academy at the present time [1900] may find it difficult to realize the condition when the feminine influence was directly and for the first time exerted upon the students and welcomed by the disciplinary authorities. But no history of the School can properly omit at least passing tribute to the civilizing work which was done by that lovely group of wives and daughters which came to reside in the grounds in 1865. They found the Naval Academy a barrack; they filled it with the gracious fragrance which cling about their own homes, and left it with such a host of clinging and tender memories that to the gray-headed youngster of to-day the thought of them, as he returns to the old scenes, is a drought at the fountain of youth.[64]

Perhaps Porter's social successes at the Academy were not so much because of the ladies' cooperation in these activities, but because of their requirement of them. The long and desperate war years were ended. The women eagerly burst out of homes previously darkened by tragedy and uncertainty, and excelled in a manner which was defined by the beliefs and customs of the era. In this new atmosphere of conviviality, a balance was struck between the development of a warrior's skills and the gentler skills of sociability.

After the dire experiences of the Civil War, the pendulum naturally swung in a more festive direction. The Naval Academy was the beneficiary of these changes. Many of the new traditions formed during Porter's time have been perpetuated by succeeding generations of Naval Academy residents.

Post Civil War Expansion

During these heartening and expansive times, Annapolis's townspeople graciously relinquished some of their most cherished properties to the Naval Academy, and a new campaign of building and development was begun. Possibly the most elegant of all the acquisitions made by the Academy was the Old Governor's House and grounds. Conveyed to the school in 1866 and 1869, this property was located near the current Chapel and the Porter Road Homes. The exact date of its erection is not known, but it is believed to have been built before 1750 by a provincial official, the Honorable Edmund Jennings. Governor Horatio Sharpe rented Jennings's house during his term in office and in 1769, Mr. Jennings sold the property to Sir Robert Eden, Maryland's last colonial governor. Sir Robert kept his allegiance with the British during the Revolution, left the colonies for his homeland, and his house and gardens were confiscated by the State of Maryland. All succeeding governors resided there, until its purchase by the Naval Academy.[65]

Behind the graceful mansion were lovely gardens and a lake known as Governor's Pond. In 1769, William Eddis, a surveyor of the customs in Annapolis, wrote about the gardens and the view: " ' . . . Perhaps I may be justified in asserting that there are but few mansions in the most rich and cultivated parts of England which are adorned with such a splendid and romantic scenery.' "[66] Although the elegant mansion is no longer standing, the breathtaking panorama of the Severn River and the Chesapeake Bay is always a poignant reminder of that special inheritance.

Upon its acquisition, the Governor's House was immediately designated as the school's library and the site of the Superintendent's office. Later in the century, architect Ernest Flagg, with an eye for blending historic preservation with his new design for the Academy, intended this house to become the superintendent's residence.

In the late 1860s the Academy, like our growing nation, began looking westward for larger parcels of land. In 1867, ten acres of hilly land sloping down to the water along Dorsey Creek, or what is now known as College Creek were acquired from St. John's College.[67] This property, now the site of the Parade Field Homes, was used in 1781 as an encampment of Continental and French Allied forces en route to report to Lafayette in Yorktown, Virginia.

Strawberry Hill

A final property acquisition during Superintendent Porter's tenure was even farther west, possibly considered far out into the country relative to the center of the Academy. In 1868, sixty-seven acres across Dorsey Creek were purchased, which today includes the land bordered by Prince George Street, Route 450, the Severn River, and College Creek. This property was known as "Strawberry Hill," and a draw bridge was placed across the creek to reach this new acquisition.

Strawberry Hill has as an intriguing a history as its name might conjure. Prior to the Revolutionary War, Strawberry Hill, or what is now Hospital Hill, the Cemetery, and the baseball field, or Lawrence Field, was the site of a beautiful country estate owned by the Sprigg family, and visited by many famous people. George Washington recorded in his diary for September 29, 1773, that he "'dined at Mr. Spriggs and went to the play in the evening.' "[68] The setting must have been lovely: a large mansion surrounded by gardens, overlooking the beautiful Severn River and Robert's Creek, as College Creek was known then.

Mr. Richard Sprigg employed William Buckland as his architect for the Strawberry Hill mansion. Mr. Buckland is the well-known designer of the Hammond-Harwood House in Annapolis, and of the interiors of the Chase-Lloyd House in Annapolis and Gunston Hall in Virginia, all beautiful eighteenth century homes in the Georgian tradition. Mr. Sprigg resided here from 1766 to 1789; in 1785 his daughter, Margaret, married Governor Mercer at the home.[69]

In 1796, the mansion and property were leased by the wealthy Henri Stier of Belgium, who was escaping the unpleasantness of the French Revolution. His daughter, Rosalie Eugenia Stier described Strawberry Hill to her brother in a letter:

> . . . Our new house is so enormously big, four rooms below, three large and two small ones on the second floor besides the staircases, and the finest garden in Annapolis in which there is a spring, a cold bath house well fitted up and a running stream! What more could I wish for?[70]

George Calvert, a Maryland legislator and descendent of the Fifth Lord Baltimore, visited Strawberry Hill often, and eventually wed Rosalie Eugenia.

In the nineteenth century, the property was sold several times. In 1803, Anne Arundel County purchased Strawberry Hill, and until 1823, the mansion was used as an alms house for the poor

– a contrast to its illustrious past.[71]   After a few years, the state of the grounds and house deteriorated while being used as an alms house. Instead of repairing the mansion and restoring the grounds, the county purchased a larger home in 1823, now known as the London Town Publik House on the South River, another old, stately mansion, to house the poor.[72]

Superintendent Porter had the dilapidated mansion razed, and in its place, a large Naval Hospital in the Victorian style was built. The mansion and then the hospital were located on a high knoll beside Prince George Street near the Dorsey Creek bridge. After being used for several years, the edifice was abandoned because of its costly upkeep. Left to decay, the hospital became known around Annapolis as "Porter's Folly," akin to the famous old "Bladen's Folly" at the site of McDowell Hall on campus of St John's College in Annapolis.[73] Clarence and Evangeline White, Annapolitans, recall playing in the old, empty hospital as children.

> Our childhood remembrance of it was, on my husband's part, as a place to run through and be scared away by bats, rats, or an occasional guard. . . . For girls, it was forbidden territory, and it was not hard to keep us away from it because we were afraid it was "spooky" and there were evil things waiting to spring out at us. No doubt there was a real menace lurking in there, and not spooks either.[74]

In 1868, when the Naval Academy purchased Strawberry Hill, plans were immediately laid out for a cemetery on the bluff overlooking the Severn River. A year after its purchase, Lull wrote:

> On a high point of land in this last purchase, has been laid out a Cemetary(sic) for the burial of Officers and Seamen and others belonging to the Navy. Beyond the cemetary(sic) there is a handsome Park. The park and cemetary (sic) consist of alternate wood and lawn, with considerable diversity of level. Winding woods and paths have been laid out in [a] very tasteful manner, making all parts accessible. So attractive are these two places that although the improvements are scarcely yet begun, they have become a very favorite resort for the people in the vicinity, a large number of persons visiting each, every pleasant(sic) day. The woods and paths already completed measure three miles, and it is contemplated to lay out two miles more. These are covered with shells, which have been obtained at an extremely small cost.[75]

The same year as the purchase of the land called "Strawberry Hill," in 1868, a charming wooden house of Gothic Revival design, or "Gingerbread" style, was brought up the Severn River on a barge from uncertain origins possibly to accommodate the cemetery keeper and his family. It was originally placed close to College Creek, near the Academy bridge. In later years the house was occupied by the Foreman Laborer. In 1924, it was moved to the hillside among the bungalows where it is today.

This small home with the gabled roof is the oldest home remaining at the Academy. Because of its billeting since 1967, this house has become known as the "German Officer's House," and the red, gold and black German flag flew boldly to mark the residence of the German Exchange Officer. Because of its early relationship with the cemetery, some residents believe that the conspicuous bumping and scraping heard inside the house on blustery winter nights are from lingering, malcontent ghosts; other ascribe the noises to the antique heating system in the old house.

In addition to serving as a cemetery and a lovely public park for daily strolls and charming vistas of the waterfront, the land across the creek was also used as a garden for raising vegetables and fruit for midshipmen and officers' families who lived at the Academy. Eventually, because of its new use, Strawberry Hill became known as "Government Farm."

Enhancing the Main Campus

Along with the acquisition of land during Porter's tenure came some extensive building. A new chapel was raised in 1868, at the end of Blake Row, near where the Superintendent's house is today. In 1869, the midshipmen's dormitory or "New Quarters" was built facing the central park, and parallel to Maryland Avenue. There is a marker near Leahy Hall and the Museum to indicate its former location.

Another innovative stride was made to facilitate more comfortable living in Annapolis and on the Yard. In 1867, the Annapolis water works was completed, and all living quarters and public buildings on the grounds were supplied with running water.[76] Students were then marched to the bath house regularly. **With access to running water the midshipmen were now required to take one bath a week.**[77]

More officer and faculty housing was erected between 1867 and 1869. Three double houses for six families and a single house for the Board of Visitors were built behind the old Governor's mansion along the original Porter Row, which was located on the current site of Dahlgren Hall. These were known as Quarters 20 to 26, with number 24 being the "Board House." Porter Row was distinguished by having a fountain directly in front of the Board House. There is a marker west of Dahlgren Hall indicating the location of two of these houses.

Superintendent Porter's explosive energy and expansive vision laid the framework for the future of the Academy. Perhaps the changes that have been made since his tenure have been made within the spirit of his vision – that the Naval Academy become a significant seat of higher learning and high ideals, as well as a place of uniform beauty and refinement. By the end of his tenure, residents at the Academy were able to stroll among splashing fountains and well-laid paths, and enjoy the beauty of trees, cultivated shrubs and colorful flowers. Areas that had once been a barren wasteland, such as the swampy lowlands behind the midshipmen's quarters, became instead a delightful showcase. And the unhurried, genteel folk of the nineteenth century had leisure time to enjoy the benefits of living in this garden-like setting.

CHAPTER THREE: CHANGES IN THE LATE 1800s

Not all of the areas abutting the Academy fit into the model of genteel living and physical beauty. Surrounded by the Naval Academy was a section of land and houses by the Severn River known as "Lockwoodsville." The east side of Worden Field, the parade grounds, is now located on this spot. According to Professor William Oliver Stevens, "It was the dirtiest, smelliest and slummiest collection of shacks, brewery, gas house and dumps perched on a knoll of the Severn."[78] And, on the opposite end of the Academy's property, by Gate One and the Annapolis Harbor, was an even more disreputable area known appropriately as "Hell Point."

> The old "grog shops" outside of the gate were dives of vice and rendezvous of the ruffians, murderers and bullies of a rare type. It was the scene of many vicious crimes. The citizens of Annapolis appreciated Uncle Sam's purchase of this unsightly den of iniquity, since transposed into a beautiful park and Thompson Stadium.[79]

Hell Point's proximity was a cause of concern from even the earliest days of the Academy. A midshipman was stabbed by one of the ruffians there during Upshur's time as superintendent.

Lockwoodsville was purchased and razed in 1874, and that peculiar pocket of residences no longer flanked the western portion of the Yard. The other side of the campus, however, remained a rough and tough neighborhood well into the twentieth century. Hell Point was not acquired by the Academy until around 1940.

The Marines

A Marine detachment had been assigned to the Academy to serve as security guards aboard naval training ships since the early days of the school's history. As the role and size of the Marine contingency expanded, the need for adequate quarters also grew, but because of the lack of facilities at the Academy, they were assigned to quarters in a shed by the pier. The Secretary of the Navy described these quarters in 1878:

> At Annapolis, the men are quartered in a shed built on a wharf, and mess on board an old ferry-boat, past repair, which is impossible to keep dry. There are no quarters for officers, who have to live away from the men in Annapolis.[80]

Instead of being given appropriations for new quarters, they were allotted some money to repair the sheds. It was not until 1880 that work was begun on their barracks. In 1882, the Marines moved into a spacious and attractive brick building, a lovely addition to the

Academy's landscape, located by the famous old mulberry tree near the harbor. Morale improved, and living at the Naval Academy became an enjoyable privilege for the Marines.

Captain and later Lieutenant Colonel McLane Tilton served as commanding officer of the Marines for several different tours of duty beginning in 1865, and ending with his retirement around 1896.[81] After retiring, he remained in Annapolis, and became known and loved city-wide for his outrageous eccentricities as well as his social graces.

Colonel Tilton was a resident of the new Marine barracks. In keeping with his eccentric reputation, Tilton liked to alarm his friends with the eerie story that he slept with a coffin underneath his bed. After this rumor was spread about town and eyebrows were sufficiently raised, it was discovered that he kept only a small silver chest filled with memorabilia – not a coffin – in his room.

Colonel Tilton had the peculiar habit of washing his own clothes after they had already been laundered by the maid. One day he was upstairs in his quarters at the Marine barracks, scrubbing his clothes in a tub of sudsy water. The doorbell rang, and he called down to the visitors to come up the stairs. Standing there with his arms dripping with soap suds, he was suddenly face-to-face with the Governor of Maryland and his entourage, formally attired, who had come to make an official visit. The unflappable Colonel dried his arms, put on his shirt, and with sufficient dignity proceeded calmly downstairs to receive the Governor.[82]

New Superintendent's Quarters: The Queen Anne-Style House

The grand old Dulany House built in the mid-eighteenth century maintained its status as the Superintendent's residence on the Academy Yard despite the new building and expansion fervor of Porter's time. In 1883, however, Superintendent Francis M. Ramsay and a commission of officers declared the building to be in disrepair and unsafe, and had the old mansion torn down. A new structure was begun, but, according to historian Elihu Riley, Congress had formerly refused money for the quarters, and as an affront to Ramsay, would not allow the building to be completed. "There it remained until the end of the term of the offending Superintendent, a monument of autocratic independence and congressional indignation."[83]

Finally, in 1886, the new Superintendent's quarters were completed where the Dulany House had been, near where the central area of Bancroft Hall now stands. The residence was a red-brick Victorian, a Queen Anne Revival-style home, of architecture popular in the late 1800s. It had gaslight chandeliers and elaborately decorated mantelpieces for its numerous fireplaces. Midshipmen continued to practice their social graces in this charming home. Only seven superintendents lived in this home during its short fourteen year life-span. It was removed around 1900 to make way for the grand reconstruction of the turn-of-the-century.

There were interesting remedies for birds that were a nuisance around the Superintendent's House in the late 1800s. The *New York Times* had this to say about the daily sights and sounds on the Yard:

> The stranger at twilight in the Academy grounds would be startled by the tolling of a bell at short intervals for up in a maple, followed by the sharp clanging of a gong. These are to drive away the countless swallows that congregate every evening in the trees between the Superintendent's house and the band stand. Formerly powder and shot were used, but this method excited so much condemnation it was abandoned years ago.
>
> The New York Times: July 24, 1892[84]

Social Life in the 1880s

The 1880s were Depression years for our country, and Naval Officers did not experience job security, nor anticipate higher wages. Life for officers' families during those years was filled with uncertainty. Lack of congressional appropriations for the Naval Academy was a cause for concern among not only officers' families, but among faculty and local Annapolitans working on the Yard. Notices in journals reflected the growing consternation felt by the community:

> Several Naval Academy sailors were discharged from the service on Monday in accordance with an order from Washington directing a reduction of the force at the Academy. *Army and Navy Register, January 5, 1884.*

> The wholesale discharge of Naval Academy employes(sic) on account of the failure of Congress to pass the Naval appropriation bill created a good deal of excitement, and will entail additional duties on the officers of the Academy, who may have clerical work to perform. *Army and Navy Register, January 3, 1885.*

In the 1880s, when a career Naval officer did not always have an optimistic future, a Naval Academy "cadet" as midshipmen were known from 1877 to 1902, was not guaranteed a job upon graduation. In fact, only ten out of a graduating class could expect a commission, the rest being given $1000 and their termination papers from the service. There was also a grave lack of promotions among career officers; it was not uncommon for a man to remain a lieutenant for nearly twenty years.[85]

Although times were lean during the 1880s, the Academy still entertained dignitaries, provided interesting events for the community of Annapolis, and continued the social activities for the Academy residents and midshipmen. With Annapolis as Maryland's capital, the state legislature met biennially, and the winter months it was in session promised much social gaiety for Annapolitans and Academy residents.

One of the social customs of the late 1800s through the turn of the century was "calls" made on New Year's Day, both at the larger civilian homes and at some Naval Academy quarters. The ladies would "receive" their guests, and everyone dressed in their finest outfits. The civilian men wore a top hat and frock coat; the officers were attired in a formal "undress B," similar to the frock coat. Spiked eggnog was enjoyed at almost every house.[86]

If a resident was not accepting "calls," a basket was hung outside to collect cards of would-be callers. Journal notices gave a glimpse of this local activity which helped bond the Naval Academy and Annapolis families, as well as provide a look at how the married women, both military wives and civilian wives, were acknowledged by the rank or profession of their husbands.

> January 1, 1885
>
> The custom of paying social visits was observed here today, though not on a very large scale, the weather being unpleasant and disagreeable and the callers few. The absence of Governor McLane from Annapolis prevented the usual reception at the executive mansion, although quite a large number, including many naval officers, called to pay their respects and left their cards in the basket which hung on the outside. The conventional card basket hung on many more residences to-day than is usually the case, those who kept "open house" being very few and scattering. For the most part the receptions at the Naval Academy were confined to few houses, the ladies generally receiving in groups. Mrs. Captain Ramsay was assisted at her reception by Miss Hill, of Washington. Others who received at the Academy were Mrs. Engineer Farmer. . . and Mrs. Captain Tilton. Those who kept open house in the city were . . . Mrs. Dr. Randall, [and] Mrs. Judge Magruder. . . .
>
> Naval cadets generally enjoyed the day, having been given full holiday. Many of them made calls during the day. *Army and Navy Register, January 3, 1885.*

Another attractive social feature of the holidays in those years was the annual New Year's Eve Ball for the cadets, always held in the old round gymnasium. Music was provided for this gala event by the Academy Band. The Ball of 1884 was a popular and well-attended affair. "The bright uniforms of the officers and cadets, mingled with the handsome toilets of the ladies, formed a pleasing scene in the brilliantly lighted ball-room."[87] That year, a giant stocking, six feet tall, held humorous gifts from the young ladies for the cadets, and caused much "merriment." The following year, the New Year's Eve Ball of 1885 had a different venue, but was just as exciting.

> As a happy termination to the hop, at midnight a signal was given for the first-class men to assemble in the centre of the ball room. The class then ushered in the new year by singing a song, the chorus of which consisted of the two words, "eighty five," thrice repeated. A cadet in fancy costume, placarded "1885," was then lowered from the cupola of the gymnasium into the ball room, and another cadet, representing the old year, and dressed in tatters, was hoisted, indicating the passing away of the year 1884. After this the cadets rejoined their partners on the floor, and promenaded to the tune of "Home Sweet Home," closing the entertainment. *Army and Navy Register, January 3, 1885.*

Other than the intermittent hops and balls and some athletics after the evening supper each day, there were not many exciting activities at the Academy for the cadets in the 1880s. According to Stevens, the major event of the year was a Thanksgiving field day, during which the cadets chased a greased pig around a field, and climbed a greased pole for amusement.[88] But daily life in that era had a slower gait, and people did not require the fast-paced stimulation and excitement of today. As noted by Alan Moorehead in his book, *The White Nile*. ". . . in this perhaps – in the calm and leisured use of time – one sees by how much we are divided from the nineteenth century."[89]

The children who lived with families on the Yard found interesting ways to amuse themselves. Superintendent Ramsay had his two teenage sons living with him, and they harassed the cadets with impunity. Superintendent Ramsay's granddaughter, Mary Virginia Ramsay Sease recalled an old family story:

> My father, Martin Ramsay, was a teenager when his father was superintendent. He told me that he and his brother made pests of themselves to the mids. My father, around 15 years old, and my uncle, used to break off branches and twigs, get on their stomachs on the parade grounds, and toss sticks while the mids marched. The mids got graded – marks – on the smoothness of marching. The boys got captured once by the mids because of their pranks. My father dared them to do anything to them, because he told them he would tell his father, the Superintendent.[90]

The society of the early Naval Academy reflected the social customs of the nineteenth century elite. In addition, familial connections among Academy personnel and Academy appointees were common through the years, giving the impression of its being an aristocratic enclave. Annapolitans Clarence and Evangeline White commented about an attitude of exclusiveness they felt was prevalent at the Academy in the nineteenth century:

> Because it was so small as to its personnel, buildings, and general layout, it was very restricted and very restrictive as to its management and setup. Of course its attitude was young and arrogant when all appointments into it came through the government by way of the Secretary of the Navy. Also these appointments were more or less generally given to Naval officers' sons, regardless of whether the appointees wanted to become Naval men – a sort of vocation handed from father to son . . . . So in our youth this Naval Academy was as near an autocracy as it had ever been.[91]

Indeed, in the history of the Academy are names of officers from naval families of several generations. In the 1800s, it was common practice for men of any profession to pass their occupational heritage on to their sons, and a Naval career was no different. Perhaps, too, in a profession that required one to move frequently and relinquish ties to ones old home town, the small Naval community served as a "family" which provided a much-needed bond and continuity.

The residents of Annapolis responded positively to the existence of the Naval Academy in the 1880s, and there seemed to be broad participation in social activities among local civilians and the military families. Elihu Riley, an Annapolis historian, wrote in 1887 that having the Naval Academy in Annapolis had been advantageous to the city's economy, and that the interesting cultural and social events of the school enriched the lives of this already refined community.[92]

Not only were the balls and parties exciting to all participants, but the garden-like setting maintained at the Academy helped to create an inviting atmosphere of quality and excellence. The stately row of senior officers' housing on Blake Row, the cozy brick chapel, the grand library in the old Governor's mansion, the junior officers' quarters on Porter Row , Buchanan Row, and Goldsborough Row, and the centrally located cadets' "New Quarters" were all huddled closely together in a square around the picturesque park, and gave the Naval Academy the sense of a close, intimate community. That the Yard had not only become a place of beauty, but an enjoyable place to live is evident in remarks of residents of the day. A correspondent to the *Army and Navy Register* in May of 1885 speaks in heady terms of the setting given to the most important event of the year – Graduation Day – and of the joys of being stationed in Annapolis. The small class of thirty-six graduates was honored in grand style.

Annapolis, May 29, 1885

It would be extremely difficult to find a more beautiful spot than the U.S. Naval Academy is on the eve of graduation day . . . . Nature seems to have been especially kind this year in contributing so largely to the happy surrounding of the institution, which are truly picturesque and beautiful. Copious showers have clothed the silvery-leaved trees with luxuriant foliage, and have blossomed the flower plants which adorn the front of officers' residences so perceptibly that visitors attracted to the Academy readily inhale the rich fragrance imparted by the potted rose-buds, and cannot fail to enjoy a promenade over the well laid off avenues of the inclosure(sic) . . . . The remark is frequent just now that the Academy never looked in better trim before graduation day. If further evidence on this score were needed the observations of a naval officer who is shortly to leave the institution for other duty, having been stationed here three years, might be quoted, He said: **"I consider the Naval Academy the grandest spot on earth, and would be willing to remain here throughout my entire service. It is nothing short than a paradise on earth."**[93]

The living conditions at the Naval Academy had changed dramatically since Professor DuBarry refused the position as an instructor in 1845.

Rounding Out the Nineteenth Century: Further Acquisitions

Significant growth and expansion was not evident for the twenty years following Superintendent Porter's tenure. The Depression years of the 1880s, along with the lack of monetary support from Congress, left the Academy with few new additions to its physical plant. But with the nineties came a surge of development that picked up the momentum, and brought much of the Academy to its present state by the early twentieth century.

In 1891, twelve more acres of land were purchased from St. John's College, to complete the sweep of land between the main campus and Dorsey Creek or College Creek. This hilly, irregular land known as "New Grounds" eventually became part of the current Parade Field. Evangeline Kaiser White told of her experiences as child on this land before it was developed.

> On King George Street . . . was just a hill sloping down to the Severn River. On this hilltop was our town gas tank, and this was a favorite walk from our home on College Avenue on a Sunday afternoon, when our father and uncle took several children out walking. These Sunday afternoon walks were a real treat to the little children of our . . . family.

> . . . On the side of this gas tank a road now called Wagner Street ran right down to the river, from which point a ferry operated, crossing the river to land on the point which now is the far end of the new Severn River Bridge. This ferry was abandoned when a wooden bridge was built across the river . . . . The old wooden bridge was a real achievement in those days, and opened up all of that area known as Westminster Parish, now St. Margaret's..[94]

"Oklahoma:" The Parade Field Homes

After the purchase of the St. John's tract, the Board of Visitors made the recommendation that more housing be added so that junior officers could be quartered on the grounds. They argued that the senior officers had their quarters provided, but that many of the junior officers, with smaller salaries, had to pay high rents for housing in town. The recognition of this hardship led to the construction of what is now known as the Parade Field Homes. Architect O. von Nerta of Washington, D.C., was employed for the new construction project.

As monuments to naval family life, these large Victorian structures still stand at attention along two sides of the Parade Field, where for over a century midshipmen have marched, dignitaries have reviewed parades, and children from these homes have romped and frolicked on the green, manicured grass. They were built to accommodate large Victorian families, when grandparents were often a part of an immediate family, when eight to twelve people would sit down to a supper meal every day, and when live-in maids and cooks performed a vital role in each household. The houses are comprised of two units, each unit consisting of three floors of living space with around 4000 square feet, with butlers' pantries, two sets of indoor stairs, five fireplaces, and a maid's quarters on the third level. Into the 1990s, the houses, as most quarters on the Yard, were heated by an antique steam-heat system, replete with clanging, hissing pipes. In the hot Annapolis summers, there was no central air conditioning provided.

These Colonial Revival structures are especially harmonious with the eighteenth century red-brick colonial architecture prevalent in historic Annapolis. The design is similar to that of other military quarters built in the late nineteenth century around the country, such as those at Fort Ethan Allen in Colchester, Vermont, which have been preserved as condominiums for private citizens.[95] Also, they are similar to those at Warren Air Force Base, which have won a National Preservation Honor Award from the National Trust for Historic Preservation in 1991.[96]

In 1893, the first two double red-brick houses were occupied on "New Grounds," quarters 31 through 34. In 1895, the new avenue was dubbed "Upshur Row" in honor of the second superintendent, and two larger double houses were added. Ten of these double houses along two avenues were completed by 1899 to total twenty family units. In 1904, the second street which borders College Creek, with numbers 45 through 50, became known separately as "Rodgers Row" named for Christopher R. P. Rodgers, who was superintendent from 1878 to 1881.

The settling of the Upshur Row area reminded observers of the 1889 land rush in Oklahoma. In fact, this new area was called "Oklahoma" by the cadets because it seemed untamed and far from the main campus. The 1903 *Lucky Bag*, the cadets' year book, vividly described the colonizing of this new, foreign territory.

> In the year 1895, the word went forth that several new sets of officers' quarters, known officially as Upshur Row were at last ready for occupancy. So great was the haste on the part of the new settlers to take possession, that several large wagons loaded with household goods were on hand waiting for the opening of the gates. This suggested new settlers in Oklahoma, so Upshur Row was promptly dubbed "Oklahoma," and the name is most appropriate. This magic country consists of ten double sets of quarters, finished between 1890 and 1898, and one large house, finished last summer, used temporarily as the Superintendent's quarters. The ground itself was formerly a sandy waste, with a hill in the middle of what is now the parade ground. This ground was leveled off and sodded(sic), and a beautiful level football field was formed near the water.

The Parade Field Homes have the distinction of being the oldest structures built at the Naval Academy that are still standing, with the exception of the small building opposite the guard house by Gate #3. Of the houses on the Yard, the "German Officer's House" is oldest, but it was brought in on a barge from another locale.

To commemorate the one-hundredth anniversary of when the Parade Field Homes were first occupied, and to honor all the families who have supported the Naval Academy by living in these homes, a Centennial Celebration was held on March 23, 1993, which included a tour of several of the quarters.[97]

Another acquisition in the 1891 "Oklahoma" purchase was an old brewery which was converted into officers' quarters. This residence was referred to as "The Brewery" by its occupants until around 1900, when it was removed.[98]

With the addition of the homes at "Oklahoma," the Naval Academy no longer clustered all of its residences around the small central park. As time began to round the bend into the twentieth century, the Academy took off in a new direction, too.

CHAPTER FOUR: SOCIAL LIFE AND SPECIAL PERSONALITIES BEFORE THE TURN OF THE TWENTIETH CENTURY

Let the Games Begin!

The late 1800s saw the institution of one of the greatest traditional rivalries ever known, and one of the most notable social events ever offered at the Academy – the Army-Navy football game. Begun in 1890, this spirited clash roused to an emotional frenzy the feelings of ardent and loyal fans. From its beginning, the rivalry became so intense that military officers were known to arrange duels over the sport. By 1893, President Grover Cleveland terminated the annual conflict, and it was not re-instituted until 1899, when President Benjamin Harrison allowed the game to resume if the players could agree not to kick or mistreat each other.[99] With such precedents, it is easy to understand the intensity of Army-Navy week prior to the game when pranks, chanting, and emotional release are seen at the Academy these days. Still, there was seriousness about the conflict in the nineteenth century that currently cannot be appreciated. Alan Moorehead says of this era, ". . . [O]ne must remember how complete and steady men's convictions were in Victorian times. The doubts and uncertainties that have overtaken life in the twentieth century through two world wars and a plethora of political and scientific inventions were unthinkable then." [100] And team loyalty ran deep.

Early Army-Navy games were played at the service academies, with Army and Navy alternating years, and must have provided extra excitement for the social life at the Academy when Navy was the host. Seating was scarce, and most fans had to stand for the entire fame, but the enthusiasm was strong. The games eventually became too popular for the modest accommodations at either academy, and they were moved to larger stadiums out of town. Park Benjamin captured the spirit of football games and the social setting at the Academy in the 1890s:

> . . . [O]n Saturdays there are studies and drills only up to dinner. After that meal the afternoon is clear, and the visitors flock in – especially everybody's sister and her friend, - and the colors of the Academy, blue and gold, blaze everywhere, and the battalion groups itself on one side of the gridiron and yells " 'Rah-'Rah-'Rah – Hi-Ho- Ha – U.S.N.A. – Siss-B-o-o-m – A-a-h-Nav-e-e-e-e!" with so much enthusiasm that when a good tackle is made for the Navy side, gray headed and portly gentlemen with gold and silver leaves on the collars of their blouses may be observed suddenly to burst into similar vociferations, and continue them until they catch one another's eye, when they brace up and endeavor to look properly dignified and sedate.[101]

And The Band Plays On

The "Gay Nineties" were a time of stepping out and socializing, looking for lighter amusements and congenial friends. The men were dapper in their derbies and straw boaters, and the women were elegant in long white dresses circumnavigating the streets of Annapolis in their horse-drawn black buggies.

Music and dancing were still the mainstays of social life both on and off of the Academy. In town, the dances were held at the assembly rooms of the Municipal Building on Duke of Gloucester Street, and the music was provided by a string orchestra which was directed by Mr. Schreyer. All of the musicians were members of the Naval Academy Band. **Dances were waltzes, interspersed with the Virginia Reel and the Lancers. The young lady's escort would fill in her program, or dance card, with names of different young gentlemen with whom she would dance that evening. Always at exactly midnight, Mr. Schreyer instructed the orchestra to play "Home Sweet Home," and it was time to leave.**[102] Indicative of the times, the dance card was like the proscribed social life of young people; nothing was left to chance.

The local young ladies also attended the hops, or dances, at the Naval Academy which had a similar venue, with the exception that most of the Academy hops ended at the early hour of ten o'clock. The hops, as noted earlier by Edward Lull, were an important element in the refinement of the midshipmen. But the mids had less than refined names for their dates. **Girls from Annapolis were known as "Crabs," and daughters of naval officers who lived on the Yard were known as "Yard Engines."** No matter what they were called, young ladies from local areas and distant cities were always eager to attend the famous Naval academy hops, a tradition dating from the beginning of the history of the school. Hop dresses of this era, as opposed to earlier, more formal times, were usually very versatile. They were often made of muslin, could be laundered easily, and changed each week by adding a different color ribbon.[103] But, though less formal than before, the dances were still nineteenth century-romantic. Stevens nostalgically recalled dancing from before the turn of the century:

> It should be noted also that dancing then was really an elegant accomplishment. A young officer and gentleman had his hop card adorned with such dances as "Polka," "Schottische," "York," "Lancers," and, above all, the Waltz. Ah, that last Blue Danube Waltz with your One and Only! That was dancing.[104]

Not only did the Naval Academy Band members generously lend their talents to string orchestras in Annapolis but they also formed, with some local musicians, the Cornet Band. This brass band was directed by Professor Charles Zimmerman, the consummate director and professional composer for whom the current bandstand in the Academy Park is dedicated. Zimmerman brought to the Academy and the town a quality of excellence, an abundance of talent and enthusiasm, and a handsome and dignified demeanor. His band served the community with weekly summer parades through the town which ended with a concert in front of the City Hotel on Main Street.[105] The sunset and a golden moon rising over the Annapolis Harbor still framed weekly professional concerts by the Academy Band on the City Dock 100 years later in the 1990s.

It was during Zimmerman's tenure as band director that the Academy began taking a closer look at the organization and upkeep of the band. In 1906, the band members were not enlisted personnel, as they were at the end of the twentieth century. According to the Board of Visitor's report in 1906:

> The band of the Academy is the only one. . . in either service, which is not composed of regularly enlisted men. . . . The musicians are employed under civil-service rules, and their pay is insufficient. It has accordingly to be supplemented by contributions from officers and midshipmen. . . . Some of the musicians are of advanced age and are now barely able to perform their duties.[106]

Through Zimmerman's influence and professionalism, the Academy began to appreciate the significant contribution and inspirational support of the Naval Academy Band which enhances this lifestyle of excellence. Changes were eventually made to increase the status, pay and security of band members. In 1993, when Congressional cutbacks threatened the professional band at the service academies, Academy residents and Annapolitans expressed their concern with an out-pouring of letters to Congress in an attempt to save this musical treasure.

Social Demands

The custom of "Paying Calls" was well-defined and expected at the Academy in the 1890s. The school was so small that all of the residents knew each other, and when a new family moved in, the proper courtesy was to pay a visit, or "call" on them. The newcomers, in turn, were expected to call on their visitors at a later date.

Another ritual developed during the late 1800s at the Academy was that of sending invitations to ranking officers and wives for obligatory dinners. A large round table-top was made available to the residents which could convert their regular dining room table into a larger one. When it was time for a family to have one of these important soirees, the table top could be heard bumping down Upshur Row, or Blake Row, being rolled to the appropriate house. According to Stevens, residents would eagerly rush to the windows when they heard the table passing, to see who was having a party, and to determine if they had been included on the invitations list.[107]

Social rules for women were much more defined in those days. Just as women were often referred to with the rank of their husband, such as "Mrs. Captain Tilton" or "Mrs. Superintendent Ramsay," the women carried that rank into their own social activities. **It was an unwritten law that no one left a ladies' party until after the "ranking lady" bid the hostess "goodbye." Never mind that the younger wives had small children who needed attention at home!**[108]

A Sociable Character

Lieutenant Colonel Tilton, the well-known, unpredictable character from the Marine barracks retired in the late 1890s. He moved just outside Gate #3 to 9 Maryland Avenue, a yellow painted brick house known today as the Loockerman-Tilton House, and continued to delight Academy residents and townspeople with his antics. The Loockerman House itself has an interesting history. Built around 1740, it is one of the oldest homes in Annapolis and was still a private residence into the twenty-first century. It was in this house that Commander Franklin Buchanan met in 1844 with other officers to plan the opening of the Naval School.[109]

Colonel Tilton, retired and widowed, enjoyed entertaining groups of young ladies for breakfast in his Maryland Avenue house. These meals were said to last nearly all day. Between courses he would have the girls hop up from the table, and run around his house to stimulate their appetites. The malleable young ladies happily complied.

Professor Stevens told of the time that he greeted the Colonel on the street, and the Colonel stopped and informed him that his intestines were twenty-eight and one-half feet long. Stevens was embarrassed by this remark which was made in the presence of some ladies, but the Colonel cheerfully ambled down the street, walking in the middle of the road rather than on the sidewalk, remarking as he went, "Yes, that's just how long they are!"[110]

Colonel Tilton was able, it seems, to do and say just about what he wanted, and his charm and good-nature far outweighed his outlandish behavior. He was willing to "be himself" to the delight and amusement of the townspeople.

A Peek into a Private Romance

When Captain Philip Henry Cooper was appointed to be superintendent of the Academy in November, 1894, his sixteen year old son, away in a boarding school, wrote to congratulate him. But typical of teenagers of all eras in military families, he also had personal reasons for resisting the change. Uppermost in his son's mind was the fact that if his family moved to the Academy, he would have to miss a dance already scheduled for that Christmas vacation. The son, Philip Benson Cooper, wrote to his father in a letter:

November 8, 1894

Dear Father,

. . . It [the assignment to Annapolis] only brings one disappointment(sic) to me and that is that I am afraid that it will bar my spending my Xmas vacation in Morristown, which I had hoped most strongly to do. I received an invitation to a dance on the 28th of this month but of course I wrote my regrets. Annapolis has not much attraction to me in vacation time; I do not enjoy the dances and the girls either, and I had such strong friends in Morristown.

. . . I can just imagine Mother's delight to be able to keep you home and have such a fine chance of entertaining as she will have in the Sup's quarters down there.[111]

But as the years passed while Superintendent Cooper served at the Academy, young Philip began to mingle with the other families on the Yard, and he met Miss Eleanor May Burnham. "Nell," as she was called, lived with her uncle and aunt, Professor and Mrs. W. W. Hendrickson in quarters 10 Blake Row. Romance developed along Lover's Lane in the Academy's park, and while he was away at school, Philip wanted to have his father, the superintendent, exert some control over young Nell's activities.

Dear Father,

. . . I am worried to death. It is about informal fencing class those miserable girls have gotten up. It has made me miserable – I don't care a hang what the other girls do, but I would rather have had Nell ride a wheel than take that up. . . . She is not the girl for that sort of thing. I wish you could find some sort of excuse for preventing it. Give Corbesier [the sword master] more work or anything. I don't think he has any right to give lessons out of time due to the Government. I never could stand girls doing anything connected with gymnasiums or anything masculine. Nell had intended not to join but that blessed Aunt of hers thought it would be a nice thing for her to do, because she knew I didn't want Nell to do anything like that. It has made me very unhappy.

Won't you speak to Nell. You know how delicate she is. And fencing is severe work. I shall be miserable all the while it goes on. It is so unnecessary. It has completely upset me.[112]

From subsequent letters, it appears that the delicate Nell foiled her opponents, won a bout for feminine self-determination, and continued practicing in the sword master's classes.

Of course Philip had more concerns for his "belle" than her unorthodox athletic interests. He also wanted his father to keep an eye on her social opportunities at this institution for young men. He wrote:

Dear Father,

. . . Now don't you ever let any of those hops stay up late because that will keep Nell up late too. Under Nellie's guidance she seems to be quite a cadet-girl.[113]

Despite their early differences, Philip and Nell became engaged to marry. At "Aunt Nell's" insistence, their engagement lasted three years. The wedding, finally set for June 7, 1899, was held in the Academy Chapel, with the reception afterwards at the Professor's home on Blake Row. Captain Cooper, who was no longer the Superintendent, could not attend his son's wedding. He was again out to sea as he had been for much of young Philip's life.

Philip wrote that he missed his father. With a touching show of sentiment, he had his father's portrait hung in the front parlor of Professor Hendrickson's house for the wedding reception, so that his father's presence could be felt at the momentous occasion. Afterwards, Philip arranged for the portrait to be moved to the sitting room in his new home, "so that you will welcome us back" after the honeymoon.

The *Evening Capital* reported on June seventh, that the wedding was a "Brilliant Affair." Even during those times of slower transportation, 300 guests arrived for the nuptials, and, according to the newspaper, "The company was gathering and occupied main rows of benches, representing the leading families of Annapolis and the families resident in the Naval Academy." After the solemn ceremony, during which Nell "disclosed a sweet, perturbed face," the bride and groom rode by carriage from the small chapel to the Professor's house, to celebrate under the watchful portrait of Captain Cooper.[114]

The young Cooper family set up housekeeping, and right away produced twins also named Eleanor and Philip. Their family eventually grew to five children in Annapolis. Philip played a vital role in upcoming architectural changes at the Academy, as well as used his talents for many of the well-known buildings and projects of the early 1900s in the city. "Crabtown," as Annapolis was known, became their beloved hometown.[115]

Those Gallant Spanish Sailors

The townspeople and the Academy residents in the 1890s were heartily entertained by an unusual group of visitors – prisoners from the Spanish-American War. In 1898, Spanish officers were captured at the Battle of Santiago, and on July 16th, they arrived as prisoners of war to be interned at the Naval Academy. These disconsolate officers arrived in tatters; many of them had fled from burning or sinking ships.

On the afternoon of their arrival by ship, the Academy gates were closed to visitors and curiosity-seekers. **The ladies of the Yard, however, gathered for this historic moment in the Academy Club House, and discreetly watched the sad but**

proud procession as the Spanish senior officers made their way by carriage first to meet with Superintendent McNair and then to be jailed.

To their surprise, Rear Admiral Don Pascual Cervera y Topete and his men were led to one of the finest officer's quarters on the base – 17 Buchanan Row. In addition, they found that the mantelpieces and table tops were decorated with fragrant flowers. They became even more amicable when they discovered that their charm and old-world, courtly manners were welcomed by the local residents. These "captured" prisoners, most of whom were aristocratic noblemen, soon turned the tables on their fate by captivating instead the attentions and favor of the women of Annapolis. The ladies of the Academy, who were lacking in male companionship because many naval officers were off to war, were especially charmed.

Rear Admiral Don Pascal Cervera y Topete and his senior officers had pleasant quarters on Buchanan Row. His junior officers lived on Stribling Row near the midshipmen. They were allowed to roam around Annapolis unattended by guards. In fact, after arriving on a Saturday evening, the following Sunday morning they made their way through the Annapolis streets to attend mass at St. Mary's Church. On subsequent Sundays, a formation of Spanish officers going to church became a familiar sight to the people of Annapolis. Helen Childs Corner, who lived on Duke of Gloucester across from the Municipal Building as a child, remembered seeing the officers march by her house to reach St. Mary's. One day, the tall and dignified Admiral stopped to greet all the children who were watching them from the porch, which left special memories for the local youngsters.[116]

When the officers arrived their clothes were in disrepair, and the Spanish government sent them gold as currency to purchase new outfits. The Naval Academy officials arranged for Ridout Brothers, a clothing store in town, to bring some of their supplies to the Officers' Club on Stribling Row where the prisoners could shop. Mrs. Evangeline Kaiser White recounted a story told by her husband, who worked as a clerk for the Ridouts at that time:

> All payments for the purchases were made with Spanish gold, and that was weighty money to carry home. Mr. White remembers carrying in his trouser pocket eight hundred dollars of this Spanish gold from one day's sales – quite a sizable sum in those days – which nearly dragged his trousers off him, suspenders and all.[117]

Soon these dashing and charming men were invited into homes both on the Academy grounds and in town. They could be found regularly in the homes along Blake Row, Upshur Row, and Porter Row, having dinner, listening to music, and enjoying companionship if not fluent conversation in the hot summer evenings at the Academy.

Even with the kind attentions of the local people, defeat and captivity weighed heavily on Admiral Cervera. Daily the Academy residents watched the silhouette of this proud man silently strolling along the grounds, wearing his dark blue civilian suit and carrying his umbrella, looking out toward the Severn River.

One of the Spanish Marine officers had an unusual habit of appearing each day on the porch of the last house on Upshur Row near the bridge over College Creek, just in time to wistfully watch the daily train lumber on its way toward Baltimore. It was explained by one of the officer's compatriots that he longed to be free to leave on the train, so that he could go home to Spain to be with his family.

The Spanish officers were fascinated with the relative freedom of the American girls here, in comparison with their Spanish counterparts who led more restricted social lives. **Romances blossomed, and one officer's daughter was captivated by the attentions of a gallant lieutenant named Luis.** Luis' mother back in Spain got wind of this international liaison, and wrote to Admiral Cervera to "Send Luis home immediately!" Being a prisoner here, Admiral Cervera certainly was not in a position to send him home right away.

But as lovely as the moonlit walks around the Academy, as gracious as the hospitality, and as intriguing as the young women of the States were to the Spaniards, there was not a lasting relationship formed, and eventually the ladies of Annapolis tearfully bid the men good-bye. In late August, the prisoners were "released," and the men boarded a ship which transported them back to their homeland. Of course, regrets from the people of the Academy and Annapolis were marked, but perhaps the popular Spaniards also missed aspects of their stay. Before leaving for Spain, Admiral Cervera penned a letter to Superintendent McNair expressing his sentiments about the Academy residents:

> The courteous and sympathetic welcome given to all of us by the distinguished families living in the Academy is one more title to our gratitude, and Your Excellency may rest assured that it will never be effaced from our memories. . . .[118]

After leaving the Academy on September 5, Admiral Cervera courteously wired a note to Superintendent McNair to thank him for his kind hospitality:

> On leaving this country, allow me to greet you, wishing you all kinds of prosperity.[119]

Naval officers returned to the Academy after the harsh conflict of war to find that their wives and daughters had been entertaining "the enemy" in their homes! Stories of this brief but interesting interlude with the Spanish officers still entertain visitors to historic Annapolis a century later. On the corner of Blake Road and Buchanan Road, by the Superintendent's House, is a rapid-fire gun captured in 1898 from the *Maria Teresa*, which was the flagship of Admiral Cervera at Santiago, a lasting reminder of the Spanish-American conflict, and of the charming prisoners who so nobly endured their captivity on Buchanan and Stribling Rows.

A Fine Feathered Fanatic

One Spanish captive did stay for an extended time at the Academy, and made his home in an officer's quarters in 42 Upshur Row. During the Battle of Santiago, a midshipman granted a dying Spanish officer's last wish that the mascot of the ship, the *Cristobal Colon*, be taken into safe-keeping. The parrot, who became known as "Cristobal Colon" to the Americans, was vicious toward the midshipman, but to honor the request, he sent the bird to his girlfriend in Annapolis, Claudia Miles, who enjoyed keeping animals. Because her parents had died several years earlier, Claudia and her brother lived with their uncle, Commander Hugo Osterhaus, in the newly built quarters on Upshur.[120]

"Da me un besito!" "Give me a kiss!" the parrot would demand, but visitors soon realized his manner was not as friendly as his words. Even with Claudia's care, Cristobal Colon was always unhappy, biting the fingers of anyone who tried to befriend him, or the lips of anyone who tried to kiss him. However, one day before the prisoners departed for Spain, one of Admiral Cervera's men passed by the officer's house and the bird became excited. The man, a former cook on the captured Spanish ship, used to feed Cristobal. Showing genuine affection for this countryman, Cristobal nuzzled him, and made no attempt to bite. Instead, loud and obnoxious kissing noises could be heard from the cage on the verandah. However, remaining patriotic to his homeland, the parrot continued to display nothing but disdain for his American hosts.

The Department of the Navy refused to let the feathered captive return to Spain with the Spanish officers, much to the regret of his compatriots and the American caretakers. Cristobal Colon lived for another decade, ready to bite anyone who did not speak his native tongue. As a mascot with an unusual temperament, he never failed to amuse the midshipmen and residents with his orneriness. He became one of the Academy's most famous residents, and after his death in 1908, he was eulogized in none other than the New York *Herald*.[121]

A Self-Imposed Captive

The Spaniards were prisoners, yet they admirably overcame the bleakness of captivity during their stay at the Naval Academy. Another gentleman, who was here for many years of his own volition, felt that he was the wrongful captive, a man in surroundings unworthy of his status. Next door to the Osterhaus family, where many a Spanish prisoner came to spend time with Miss Miles while her beau was away fighting in the war, lived Professor Marshall Oliver. And the aristocratic Professor Oliver was extremely distrustful of the Spanish officers. He warned other residents to be careful of being out after dark with the prisoners here, and the Spaniards, knowing his sentiments, avoided his company. Yet this talented and refined man had much in common with the Europeans; they all loved music. Many a night the Spanish captives gathered on the porches of nearby neighbors on Upshur Row to listen to the melodious sounds wafting through the Olivers' open windows during that steamy, hot summer.

> Violin, piano, and voice; music to the Oliver family was not an accomplishment, but the breath of daily life.[122]

Professor Oliver, who taught drawing at the Academy, was a character as eccentric as Colonel Tilton, but without the Colonel's cheerful countenance. His neighbors might have described him as having a short temper and an exaggerated opinion of himself; he haughtily described himself as "a nightingale in a hencoop." Monocle in one eye, one hand held affectedly behind his back, he would stride about the Yard as an aristocratic lord surveying his subjects. Yet, the Professor, with all his airs and not well-liked, was respected for his work at the Academy as a linguist, for his knowledge of literature, and for his talents as an architect. He also contributed to the Annapolis community by helping to design a new St. Anne's Church. Though he held the Navy in disdain, he was buried with full military honors on the same grounds where he lived as a self-imposed captive.[123]

Seeds of Change

Captain Philip Henry Cooper was superintendent of the Academy from 1894 to 1898. He missed the excitement of the Spanish prisoners since his post was transferred to Captain McNair the day before their arrival, but much happened during his tenure that set the course for the grand and irrevocable changes at the Academy to come at the turn of the century.

Although social life for residents at the Academy in the "Gay Nineties" was upbeat and lively, a quiet discontent with living conditions was growing during Cooper's tenure. Unlike the very contained, clearly defined outlines of the Academy today with its sturdy seawalls and brick and wire fences, the visible boundaries of the nineteenth century Yard were more random and changeable. In 1894, the Board of Visitors minutes describes the constant battle with the sea and erosion:

> Roads are washed out with every high tide and storm combined, and the undermining of the sea wall has become a very serious matter.[124]

Nineteenth century standards of sanitation affected the quality of life at the Academy, and were beginning to be questioned by the end of the 1800s. Raw effluent from Naval Academy quarters and from Annapolis was flushed into the Severn River and the Annapolis Harbor, causing a stench, and becoming a health hazard. In 1895, the Board of Visitors noted that the sewerage system was grossly defective, and that its modernization was imperative for the health of the institution. Again, in 1899, the Board stated

that the sewerage system was still not complete.[125] Even as late as 1908, the pollution problem
had not been solved:

> In the opinion of the Board a mistake has been made in discharging the academy sewerage into the
> Severn, which also receives the waste of the city of Annapolis, of the marine barracks, and the Naval
> Hospital. Under certain conditions, at high tide, the sewerage backs up into the service pipes in the
> basement of Bancroft Hall, and this should receive the immediate attention of sanitary engineers, as likely
> to produce improper conditions under which the food of the midshipmen is prepared.[126]

With the exception of the new quarters in "Oklahoma," many of the other buildings and houses
around the campus were becoming dilapidated. The Board of Visitors became concerned about
the appearance and safety of the old structures. In 1895, Colonel Robert Means Thompson, the
former midshipman who during Porter's time wielded the offensive fish horn, engaged Ernest
Flagg to design a new, more harmonious Academy. Flagg, an architect from New York, was
graduated from the École des Beaux-Arts in Paris. The Singer Building in New York, and the
Corcoran Art Gallery and Naval Hospital in Washington are attributed to this man of
considerable talents.

In 1897, the Board of Visitors, still justifying the need for new construction argued:

> Unhappily, there is much to condemn in the present condition of several of [the] structures. Instead of
> something that approaches a system in architecture and arrangement of the various buildings, one sees
> buildings of varied design that have apparently but little relation to each other. A few may be pronounced
> good, others passably good, while at least three or four are so badly constructed and so wholly unsuitable
> that they deserve only to be torn down forthwith.[127]

And torn down they were! Space was made for a new Academy, and for a new century.
Groundwork was laid to accommodate the changes that the twentieth century would bring –
electricity, telephones, and motorized vehicles. In 1897 and 1898, the Marine Barracks, barely
fifteen years old, and the Porter Row Homes built during Porter's tenure, were
unceremoniously razed to make way for the first of Flagg's creations, the Armory, or Dahlgren
Hall. In 1901, the Superintendent's Queen Anne-style house built only fourteen years before,
and Buchanan Row, the handsome homes dating from Fort Severn times, were removed. In
1903, the Blake Row Homes were demolished, and the Commandant, who lived in Number 1,
was housed temporarily in 50 Rodgers Row. Stribling Row, a residence for junior officers, was
taken down in 1905. Goldsborough Row Homes, or "The Corrals" were removed around 1908.
Ironwork from several of the old structures can be seen in Annapolis these days around
windows and as garden fences.

The last reminder of the old Academy, the unique, round Fort Severn where the Army was
prepared to defend Annapolis, where Superintendent Porter boxed with midshipmen, and
where many a romance began at a hop, succumbed to the full-scale demolition in 1909. Even

the famous Governor's House, which Flagg had intended to save for its historic value and to be used as the Superintendent's quarters, was leveled.

In 1895, during Cooper's tour as Superintendent, the Board of Visitors envisioned a new physical appearance for the Academy. In 1895, Ernest Flagg proposed an architectural plan for that transformation. **And, also in 1895, the old mulberry tree, that one constant landmark, bowed to the changes to come. It symbolically made way for the new order, became decayed like the man-made structures on the Yard, and died. The landmarks of the future were to become less personal, and less earth-bound.** Appropriately, Memorial Hall which shelters the memories of the Academy's past, now stands above the roots of the ancient guidepost.

The only continuity between the death and reincarnation of the structure of the Naval Academy was the well-kept appearance of the grounds.

> Board of Visitors' Minutes, 1897
>
> The handsome grounds of the Academy, with its walks and trees, are a credit to the country. As might be expected, they are kept in an exemplary condition. The neatness and perfect cleanliness everywhere apparent attests fidelity on the part of those to whom the care of the grounds has been committed. The appearance of the grounds, while a source of pleasure to the visitor, is a factor of no small value in the moral effect upon the young gentlemen whose daily life at a formative period is passed here.[128]

Dennis, employed at the Academy in 1845, still working for several decades into the twentieth century, was a reminder of the Academy's earliest beginnings. Piling and hauling dead sticks, raking leaves from under the ornamental trees, tending this garden spot by the Severn, the years swirled past him like so many red, yellow and golden autumns. Through inconceivable changes, at the turn of the century he was still doing his job as grounds keeper. What changes he must have seen! What bewilderment he must have experienced!

PART II: THE EARLY TWENTIETH CENTURY
". . . Shuffle and jiggle [with] the best of them."

CHAPTER ONE: THE NEW ACADEMY

It was as if the Academy needed a new set of clothes, and could not bear to be introduced to the twentieth century without a whole new wardrobe. A mere cosmetic change was not enough. The alterations transformed the Yard into a new, unrecognizable persona; the community was no longer a provincial flower, but an international gem. The Naval Academy rose to a higher standard, and daily life was elevated to higher social demands.

In 1899, construction began under Ernest Flagg's direction. And Flagg hired the soon-to-be wed Philip Benson Cooper, son of the former superintendent, as his Clerk of the Works. Philip Cooper, through letters, kept his absentee father informed of the project which was initiated during his father's tenure. On April 25, 1899, Philip reported that Admiral McNair, the current superintendent, broke the first clod for the Armory, later to become Dahlgren Hall, and afterwards they enjoyed a "champagne spread." "Tomorrow we start dredging for the sea wall. Also, we start the Armory. . ."[129]

A train load of Italians arrived to begin the work and the row of trees – "only horse chestnut trees" along Porter Row were removed.[130] Number 28 Buchanan Row, the cottage attached to the old fort wall formerly used as officer's quarters, became the office for contractors. And, everyone on campus gossiped and tittered about old Flagg marrying a much younger wife.

So, among the celebrations marking the laying of cornerstones, and speculations about Mr. Flagg's private affairs, the residents at the turn of the century kept socially active while the construction slowly ensued.

Gray Granite, Gray Stone

The individualistic old structures gave way to the new plans. Originally, Flagg intended the façade of the buildings to be of red brick, in keeping with the Georgian theme of Annapolis, however, a Congressman from New England agreed to back the reconstruction plans only if gray granite from New Hampshire were used. Thus, the United States Naval Academy took on a decidedly European look with its French Renaissance architecture to accommodate the more formal materials. Scaffolding, board fences, trains of supplies, laborers, piles of gray granite, and the clanging sounds of change marked the days now at the formerly quiet community. Virtual giants slowly replaced the intimate old buildings, like a well-meaning Gulliver stepping among the bewildered Lilliputians.

The Superintendent's Parade Field Quarters

After the Superintendent's Queen Anne-style house was removed, new quarters were built on the east end of the Parade Field. Number 29 Upshur Row was added to the row of red-brick houses ten years after the adjacent quarters made their debut in "Oklahoma." In 1902, these newer quarters were erected to temporarily accommodate the Superintendent's family. Because of social responsibilities and status, this house was larger and more elegantly appointed than other homes on the field. The Flagg-designed quarters intended for the Superintendent were completed in 1906. However, because of the sentiment of the Board of Visitors at the time, it looked as if the "temporary quarters" on Upshur Row might house Superintendents permanently. For a few years, the center of social life at the Academy shifted away from the small park near Blake Row and the Chapel.

Beginning with Rear Admiral Willard H. Brownson, four superintendents and their families lived at 29 Upshur Row, from 1902 to 1909. The *Army and Navy Register* (30 August, 1902, p. 14) recorded in 1902 that "The Superintendent's house being now in "Oklahoma" . . . present[ed] a very stately and attractive appearance."[131] The Brownsons and their daughter, Caroline, enjoyed taking their horses around town, and being entertained in Annapolis homes with the popular social event of the day – musicals.

The second family to live in these spacious quarters was that of Rear Admiral James H. Sands. Entertaining internationally known dignitaries was a well-known aspect of the life of Mrs. Sands. However, on one occasion she skillfully navigated a potentially explosive social encounter. She single-handedly was able to soothe the irascible Mark Twain by superseding the rules of the Yard.

Samuel Clemens (Mark Twain) author and humorist, was visiting Annapolis and requested a tour of the Naval Academy on May 11, 1907. At that time there was a no-smoking rule strictly enforced here, and Mr. Twain, like President Grant in the 1860s, was asked several times by reluctant Marine guards to extinguish his cigar. Later in the afternoon the eminent visitor, accompanied by Governor Warfield of Maryland, was approached by Mrs. Sands who was riding by in her fashionable barouche. The visitors were invited to review a parade in Twain's honor from the Superintendent's verandah at 29 Upshur Row. Once on the porch, he asked again to smoke, and this time received permission from Mrs. Sands, defying the regulations once again. Newspapers of the time delighted in reporting his comments about and resistance to the strict Naval Academy no-smoking rule.

A *New York Times* reporter was told by Mr. Clemens how he was "almost arrested" at the Naval Academy:

> "Mine was no ordinary offense," he insisted. "When I affront the law I choose to do so in no obscure, insignificant, trivial manner. Mine was a crime against nothing less than the Federal Government. . . . I was charged with smoking a cigar within a Government reservation. In fact, I was caught red-handed. I

came near setting a stone pile on fire." He went on to say that if Governor Warfield had not introduced him as one of the greatest men in the world that the marines would have had him arrested for his crime. Modestly, he added that he did not know if he deserved the compliment from Governor Warfield, "but who am I to contradict the Governor of Maryland?"[132]

The special "Teddy Bears" marched that day for Clemens, the same midshipman group chosen as guards for President Theodore Roosevelt for the Jamestown Tercentennial Exposition of 1907.[133] After a day replete with comedic material, Mark Twain told the *Times* reporter that he was "much impressed by the Naval Academy. I was all over it, and now it is all over me. I am full of the Navy. I wanted to march with them, but they didn't think to ask me . . ."[134] Instead, he was seen marching-in-place to the beat of the drum and bugle corps while victoriously puffing his cigar from the verandah on Upshur Row.

The Superintendent's New Quarters

Another grand structure, built to blend with the regal quality of the French Renaissance architecture of the midshipmen's quarters and the armory, the Superintendent's Quarters were completed in 1906. This home was of a style and grandeur Flagg thought necessary to entertain heads of state and distinguished citizens. The esteemed Board of Visitors in 1906 did not agree:

> Superintendent's House: This is unfortunately located, being too near cadet quarters . . . . It is apparent from a casual inspection that it could not well be put into habitable condition in the matter of decoration and furnishing under several months. The house, however, is unsuitable for its intended purpose, being on the one hand too large and costly to maintain, and on the other, improperly designed if intended for entertainment on any scale . . . . **Probably the best disposition which can be made of this building is to convert it at moderate expense into cadet sick quarters**.[135]

This impressive building stood for the next three years with plans of becoming sick quarters, being too grand for a superintendent's home. Sentiment fortunately changed, and in 1909, the Bowyer family moved into the quarters.

A house of vast proportions, there are 34 rooms and 16,000 square feet. To the Board of Visitors it must have seemed too large for intimate family living at the Naval Academy. In actuality, it is much more than a home. The first two floors are museum-like, harboring valuable naval antiques and portraits, and have been used for entertaining presidents, kings, queens, and hundreds of thousands of other guests from home and abroad. Always elegantly decorated and filled with fresh floral arrangements, today it is a magnificent example of Academy excellence. Only the third floor is restricted for personal use by the superintendent's family; the fourth floor is used to accommodate their many frequent overnight guests. The life of a superintendent's family is hardly a quiet or private one.

Holding Progress at Bay

New property was acquired to make way for the broad layout of the buildings, but on the corner of Hanover and Governor (now Buchanan) Streets, behind where the present-day Superintendent's quarters are located, the property purchasers met stubborn resistance from a local neighbor. From her perspective it was a case of David battling the giant Goliath. Old Mrs. Keeley did not embrace the Academy's new design, especially since it included her home and yard. For over a year she valiantly defied orders to move, and remained locked in her house so that civil authorities could not serve her with legal papers. She accepted food through her windows to keep from perishing, but she was eventually forced out of her home.[136]

Mary Taylor Alger Smith (Mrs. Roy C. Smith, Jr.) lived at Number 9 Blake Row at the Academy, next door to Professor Hendrickson in 1899, when she was seven years old. Her father, Captain P.R. Alger was a professor and long-time Academy resident. As Yard children do, she knew everything that was happening in her neighborhood. She recalled that Mrs. Keeley lived in a little wooden house near where the commandant's quarters are now, and would not sell her house to the Academy. The children would run around and scream at the desperately defiant old woman. Mrs. Keeley finally left, and the children all whispered that the house was haunted with evil spirits. Perhaps it was the children who actually persuaded Mrs. Keeley to "give up the ghost!"[137]

Sampson Row (Porter Road) Homes

Young Mary Taylor Alger Smith was one of the first children to live in the new "Sampson Row Homes" completed in 1905 during the reconstruction period. They were built to blend with the colors and elegance of the New Academy. Their placement on the Yard serves as a visual transition between the immensity of the new Flagg construction and the small proportions of eighteenth century buildings in Annapolis. These gray brick, double homes continue today as the quarters of the senior officers at the Academy and for the civilian academic dean. This street is known as "Captains' Row."

Lining the street are six double houses and one single house, Number 14, reserved for the Commandant of Midshipmen. Each unit has three floors of formal living areas plus a basement for informal use. The kitchen was originally in the basement, and prepared food was lifted to the main quarters above by a dumb waiter. Marble fireplaces with carved mantles, ceilings with plaster ornamentation, and graceful staircases still evoke turn-of-the-century charm.

In 1915, "Sampson Row" was renamed "Porter Row" in honor of the energetic Superintendent Porter and because of its proximity to the quarters on "Old Porter Row," which were razed to build Dahlgren Hall.

In 1923, all addresses at the Academy officially changed from "Row" to "Road," although one can still hear the term "Row" being used in present times.

John Paul Jones Finds a Home at Last

Another "home" was built at the Academy after the turn-of-the-century for the famous Revolutionary War hero, John Paul Jones. Jones, "Father of the American Navy," died and was buried in Paris, France in 1792. In 1899, a search was initiated to find his grave site, and to return his body to the United States. General Horace Porter, the United States Ambassador to France, headed this project; the casket was found in 1905 after six years of searching. The grave of the esteemed naval commander had been covered by buildings.

John Paul Jones' coffin was disinterred and identification was verified; his body had been well-preserved in a lead coffin filled with alcohol. After returning the coffin to the Naval Academy, a ceremony was held in Dahlgren Hall on April 24, 1906, highlighted by a commemorative speech by President Theodore Roosevelt. The coffin was shifted from a temporary brick vault to the ceremonial site, then to a niche underneath the stairs of Memorial Hall. In 1913, the grand crypt underneath the Chapel was completed and John Paul Jones was moved again. The design of the crypt is attributed to Ernest Flagg, the Academy's reconstruction architect, who took inspiration from Napoleon's tomb at *Les Invalides.*

John Paul Jones is, perhaps, the Academy's most celebrated resident, though a wanderer as much after his death as during his life. Professor Stevens commented about Jones' final resting place:

> Paul Jones. . . buried again. Proves that you can't keep a good man down, but 6 funerals for 1 corpse is tomb much. Usual number of Paul-bearers.[138]

Not only was Jones the "Father of the American Navy," he was also archetype of the refinement that is expected among residents at the Naval Academy. The ideals of honor and graciousness that have influenced social life for over a century and a half at the Academy were bequeathed by this posthumous resident of the Yard.

> It is by no means enough that an officer of the Navy should be a capable mariner. He must be that, of course, but also a great deal more. He should be as well a gentleman of liberal education, refined manners, punctilious courtesy, and the nicest sense of personal honor. – a definition based on the words of John Paul Jones.[139]

New Academy, New Century

It took a few years after the turn of the century to bring all the elements of Naval Academy newness together to be presented to the world. And, not all reactions to the grand scheme were favorable. Old memories, old attachments, and old patterns die hard. One reporter for *The Sun* from Baltimore wandered among the new structures in 1907, nostalgically musing about the old and the new.

> [I found the Academy an]. . . alien and entirely unfamiliar place . . . where little bits of the old have survived the ravages of reforming hands.
>
> It is hard to say just what are the visitor's first sensations on viewing the new academy. Chief of them all is probably one of magnitude and a sense that all change has been for the better. After this comes a feeling that much of the charm of the old academy has been lost in the formality and stiffness of the new.
>
> The old academy was built at different times. Its walks were laid out principally as coolness and beauty of view dictated; its buildings were put up chiefly for the convenience of the users. It had therefore a very human, sociable sort of atmosphere.[140]

If it were true, as the Board of Visitors declared in 1897, that the surroundings help to influence ones outlook and attitudes, then the dramatic changes in this environment were possibly a factor in altering the direction and scope of naval training. **The grand architecture of Flagg's design helped lift the vision of the new Academy out of the ordinary and provincial, to complement the pursuit of a more globally-focused ideal of excellence.** With its new look, the Academy presented to the world an image which suggested growth and expansion. Our country, too, had just adopted a posture of imperialism by acquiring Guam, the Philippines, and Puerto Rico, as well as by annexing Hawaii.

In step with these expansive attitudes, the Naval Academy enlarged its student body at a rate never before experienced. In 1888, there were only 35 graduates of the Academy. By 1905, there were 114, by 1908, there were 210, and by 1920, there were 461.

The portals swung open to admit an era of world-wide naval involvement.

CHAPTER TWO: FURTHER HOUSING DEVELOPMENTS

The Settlement Across the Creek: The Stable, the Stable Keeper's House, and the Gardener's Cottage

Concurrently with the Naval Academy's reconstruction of the main campus, across College Creek a smaller settlement was being developed. In 1901, the red brick Gardener's Cottage was built on County Road, the extension of King George Street. In nearby gardens, vegetables were grown for the Superintendent's family, tended by the gardener and his staff. On July 1, 1935, a memorandum was sent to ensure the supply:

> The gardener, Mr. Fox, will take the necessary steps to plant Alaska peas, sweet corn, and other vegetables so they will be available, fresh, upon the return of the Superintendent on 6 September, and these vegetables to last as far in the fall as possible.[141]

Vegetables were grown for the Superintendent until the mid twentieth century.

Greenhouses were later placed next to the cottage to grow the flowers needed for the beautification of the grounds. That practice continued through the twentieth century. Flowers for cutting were planted and nurtured year-round at the Academy to provide the Superintendent's House and the Commandant's House with floral arrangements.

In 1904, closer to the Creek on the same road, the red brick Stable Keeper's House with dormers, and the sturdy, unique stable were built. The previous stable for the Academy's horses was on the main campus by the old fort wall and the Annapolis Harbor, near Hell Point.

Through the 1990s, both the Stable Keeper's House and the doll-like Gardener's Cottage were used as officer housing. These houses along with the Stable are three buildings with the most unusual history still in use at the Academy, and probably the three most unnoticed historic structures on the Yard. Obscured by tall chain-link fences and surrounded by storage warehouses, these early twentieth century buildings sit modestly in their quiet setting by College Creek, no longer a significant part of the Academy's vast support system.

As an inadvertent memorial to a distant, genteel life-style, the old red-brick stable with its arched doorways was once used to dispatch elegant coaches and hacks for the superintendent and visiting dignitaries. The rows of small windows by the stalls once framed the heads of high-spirited stallions and mares. **Its vital importance to the early twentieth**

century culture became overshadowed when the heart-beat clop of horses' hooves was replaced by the whine and whir of motor cars. The old stable, which is now used only for storage, is fascinating not only because of its former use, but also because of its exceptional and well-maintained architecture. One can just imagine Superintendent Brownson's carriage or Mrs. Sand's stylish barouche being readied to take them on their social visits around town. In 1995, the Superintendent and the author discussed the possibility of restoring the stable for its historic value, and using it for midshipmen recreation.

The Marines Find a New Home, Again

One's first impression of the Naval Academy is not of a parade nor of the impressive "Noon Formation" by the midshipmen in front of Bancroft Hall. Instead, at each gate, a resident returning home or the day-visitor trailing behind costumed tour guides is greeted by the crisp salute from a Marine guard. These gatekeepers to the national monument known as the Naval Academy have been an on-going support system for the Yard since 1851. Their primary mission today on campus is to perform ceremonial duties.

First housed in sheds by the wharf, the Marines later lived more suitably in new barracks by the harbor, the quarters of the colorful Colonel Tilton. With the advent of the Academy's reconstruction, Marines once again found themselves without a home when their barracks proved to be on land needed for Dahlgren Hall. From 1898 to 1902, they were once again "homeless," and Marines were housed in tents across College Creek.

In 1902, construction was complete for a new barracks high on the rise of land formerly known as Strawberry Hill, across College Creek from the main campus. Designed by architect Henry Ives Cobb from New York, this graceful building with several twelve foot arcades or breezeways, was constructed with gold brick and a red-tiled roof to correspond with the Marines' colors. Worth the wait, the Marine Quarters was a fitting home for the official guardians of the Naval Academy.

Nearby on Bowyer Road beside Gate #8, three large officers' quarters were built in 1903 using gold and red colors to match the barracks. Finally having found a more remote and hopefully permanent home, this area became known as the "Marine Camp."

With the advent of the First World War, the enrollment of the midshipmen greatly increased. In 1917, the Marines were once again displaced, and instead, fourth class midshipmen were housed in the facility, a full mile from Bancroft Hall. These mids had a separate organization there, with their own "stripers," or leaders, and drum and bugle corps. It was also during this time that the larger Marine unit was sent to Quantico, Virginia, and only a small detachment was left at the Academy. In 1919, the former Marine Quarters were chosen to serve as the Navy's Post Graduate School. It was named "Halligan Hall," and the facility was never again used as housing.[142] In 1951, the Post Graduate School was moved to Monterey, California. The former Marine barracks became offices for Housing, Public Works, and the Supply Department. The graceful colonnades were enclosed to provide additional working space.

Dr. William N. Thomas, Jr., son of an esteemed Chaplain who was stationed at the Academy for twelve years in the 1930s, recalled when his family lived in 82 Bowyer Road, one of the homes previously built for Marine officers.

> I was fourteen years old when we first lived at Bowyer Road. Many midshipmen used to visit us (if Rodgers was "Oklahoma," Bowyer Road must have been "Oregon" for them.) Plebes, during the hot summer, seemed to enjoy the Hires root beer that I had bottled, many gallons at a time from extract. During the depression commercially prepared soft drinks were not so plentiful. A Navy Junior friend of mine from California lived with us while attending Cochran-Bryan Preparatory School for a year. (He later became the first Rear Admiral in his class of 1940.)[143]

A Hospital Community Arises

"Porter's Folly," that abandoned hospital, where the children hid from "evil spirits," was still standing in its sad state of disrepair near the Dorsey Creek Bridge. The old, broken building was a blight left in the fresh, new landscape developing on Strawberry Hill. Rear Admiral Brownson wanted to use the old hospital's foundation for a new hospital. Other officials recommended an undeveloped site nearby: the high bluff overlooking the Severn River next to the cemetery. Brownson thought that the hill beside the cemetery would be an unfortunate choice because it would be depressing to patients passing the graves on their way to the infirmary. His plan was defeated; the hospital was built on the bluff. Midshipmen dubbed the new hospital "the home beyond the grave."[144] This gray-brick structure was built to harmonize with the Academy's new gray-granite construction, and was completed in 1907.

A few years later, in 1911, three large single-family homes were built adjacent to the hospital, also with gray brick. These large, three story homes with porches and columns were originally built for officers and physicians assigned to the hospital. Facing north toward the Severn River and sitting high on a hill, these quarters commanded an unobstructed view of the river and the opposite shore.

The Academy's Housing Shortage

In 1919, there existed a housing shortage for officers on the Academy, and Annapolis tenants again raised their rents. In an impassioned letter to Superintendent Scales, Lieutenant Commander Schuyler F. Heim (later Commodore) explained the rental situation in town. He wrote:

May 3, 1919

I wish to report that the housing and living conditions in Annapolis are such as to make duty at the Academy for an officer living outside the Academy undesirable.

The rental prices in Annapolis are very high and all out of proportion to the accommodations provided . . . . At the present time conditions are such that Naval Officers are bidding against each other with Real Estate Agents to procure a place for their families to live while on shore duty even though they can not afford the cost of living on their salaries.

When the Post Graduate School opens the present bad conditions will become worse.

I am submitting this letter in hope that some official action may be taken to relieve the living conditions of officers . . . . forced to live in Annapolis.

S. F. Heim[145]

This plea was heard – all the way in Washington! One month later, Rear Admiral Scales, fearing that the housing situation in Annapolis would limit his ability to attract officers of excellence, penned a letter to the Honorable Josephus Daniels, Secretary of the Navy.

June 25, 1919

My dear Mr. Secretary,

I could get any number of officers who are suited from a professional moral and domestic standpoint, but for this one question of quarters. **Men of the type that we want here, whose personal and family influence we most desire, will not consent to willingly bring their families to Annapolis under the conditions that obtain.** On the contrary, they will do everything they can to avoid duty here.

. . . The best solution of the matter that I can see now, would be to take over the three blocks [Hanover Street] which would straighten the Naval Academy Wall and as a temporary measure, use all of the houses in that area for housing the Naval Academy faculty.

. . . Of course, the highest good of this Institution requires that the ablest and best officers in the service should desire duty here . . . rather than avoid it . . . . [T]he very source of the spirit and well-being of the Navy is not receiving the best that the Navy has to offer. [146]

Superintendent Scales' proposal to acquire townspeople's houses along Hanover Street seemed logical. Ernest Flagg had even drawn plans to include these blocks when he designed the new Academy. The existing structures were to be razed and replaced with officers' quarters reaching from Porter Road to Upshur Road. These three blocks on Hanover Street by Gate #3 are like a puzzle piece which fits nicely into the Academy grounds, linking the city with the institution.

The expansion of the Academy certainly created a stir. Tongue-in-cheek, an Annapolis mayor proposed that the entire city be torn down and the site be given to the Academy![147] Many residents did not approve of a plan to take three blocks of historic homes into the Academy's boundaries. Within these blocks on Hanover Street is the historic Peggy Stewart House, famous during Revolutionary War times, and built in 1761. A Signer of the Declaration of Independence, Thomas Stone, also lived in this house.

In 1925, a group called the "Company for the Preservation of Colonial Annapolis" was formed to keep an eye on the development of downtown. Because of close scrutiny by Annapolis preservationists through the years, this street with its historical significance maintains its civilian integrity even today. The three blocks of Hanover Street stand as a reminder that the Academy is in Annapolis, and not vice versa.

Those Cozy Bungalows

Without the acquisition of Annapolis property, officials at the Academy began looking for other relief for the housing shortage of 1919. A "quick fix" presented a temporary remedy. The Academy authorized the placing of war-time buildings or bungalows across Dorsey or College Creek near the Marine Camp. Two bungalows were built on County Road, or the King George extension, and thirteen more were constructed on Phythian Road near the hospital, where apartments now stand. Officially known on the Yard at that time as "Temporary Quarters," these houses were expected to be used for a year to a year-and-a- half.

In 1919, these fifteen wooden structures were shipped by train on the W.B. & A. rail line from the Naval Proving Grounds in Indian Head, Maryland. Called "ready-cut bungalows" or "knock-down" bungalows, they were complete with every detail, including all plumbing and the proverbial "kitchen sink." They cost the Academy $1.00 a piece, and could be fastened together with bolts. The only other cost was the labor and materials for installing them on the ground. The "Temporary Quarters" served as officers' quarters until 1937, for eighteen years.

From 1922 to 1924, twelve more bungalows were installed, known as "New Bungalows." These were constructed from salvaged lumber obtained without cost from East Camp, Naval Operating Base, Hampton Roads, Virginia, when the military base there was being dismantled. The material for these additional quarters arrived via barge up the Chesapeake and Severn River. They were perched atop a ridge near the Marine officers' homes and "Temporary Quarters." Because of the steep grade, the homes were built with many steps to the front door, so numerous that a memo from 1925 reported that even "a most active person has great difficulty in climbing it."[148] The back of one of the houses was set into the hill below street-level, which was not paved, and the windows and siding were constantly being splattered with mud. The "New Bungalows" had problems from the start.

In 1937, the Board of Visitors noted that these buildings were deteriorating and in need of upkeep. Most of the initial group of temporary bungalows was demolished to make room for apartments on Phythian Road. "New Bungalows," despite being World War I cast-offs, remained at the end of the twentieth century.

Mary Greenman Clark (Mrs. William Rae Clark) related that her parents, Commodore and Mrs. William Garret Greenman, lived on Bowyer Road in 1924 early in their marriage when he was a Lieutenant Commander. Because the residents were young officers and wives, there were lots of small children in the bungalows. She was told that the area was nicknamed "safety-pin alley." Safety pins were used to secure baby diapers. She added, "There were no pampers in those days."[149]

Naval Academy Professor Samuel A. Elder recounted another family story of life in the bungalows in 1924:

> On an earlier tour of duty at the Academy, before I was born, my two brothers (Dr. F. Kingsley Elder, Jr. and Dr. J. Tait Elder) lived on Bowyer Road. My mother used to tell about one of them, King, I think, who spilled a can of blue paint down the back steps. (Is there a trace still there almost 70 years later?)[150]

Betty Dudley (Mrs. John B. Dudley, Jr.) lived in the bungalows in the early 1950s. Captain Dudley was from the USNA Class of 1939. Like all residents, there can be difficult times mixed with the joy of Academy living. In the mid-century, polio was a dire threat to children in our country, and its devastation touched the Naval Academy community as well. She related:

> I enjoyed receiving at the fifth Battalion Brigade Hops, but thoroughly disliked serving at teas. . . . I became Head Interviewer for the Anne Arundel Welfare Board.

> My son and daughter attended West Annapolis School and both loved life at the Academy. My husband became Assistant to the Commandant, but we did not wish to move down to the parade ground as we enjoyed our quarters and especially our neighbors, Mickey and Strat Wentworth [Rear Admiral and Mrs. Ralph S. Wentworth, Jr.]

> In December, 1954, our 12 year old son had polio and that caused quite some consternation among the natives. We, of course, had to get our son away from the USNA hospital, hire someone to direct out way to Baltimore City Hospital as no ambulance would take us, burn all my son's possessions – even his school books, and everyone, including our maid, had to take some type of pill. Few people dared to call, but eventually our son recovered and the midshipmen helped in his therapy.[151]

In the late 1970s, Captain and Mrs. W. Gene Crooks lived on Bowyer Road with their two young sons, John and Mark. At that time the residents referred to the bungalow area, with its sloping green hill and grassy valley as "Skunk Hollow," a favorite place for youngsters to have fun, play ball, or sled down in the winter snows.

Although the quarters have been improved through the years, certain inconveniences still existed in the late twentieth century. Storage space was lacking, and one had to go outside in any weather down steep steps to the laundry room in the basement. In the 1990s, a resident skidded down the icy steps on her way to the washing machine, and broke her leg. Another resident laughingly told of furniture sliding sideways on downward sloping floors, and windows askew in buckled walls. But the proximity to Yard activities was desirable, and the residents were able to share their common experiences of life in the bungalows with each other.

Susan Forbes Snead, married to Commander James C. Snead, USNA Class of 1973, moved into her bungalow in 1991, and thought she had come to Paradise. The camaraderie among the neighbors was extraordinary. The day her family moved in, the neighbors were having a picnic for "bungalow dwellers," and these get-togethers were frequent. The children explored their own area on the hill, built hide-outs among the bushes and trees, and enjoyed numerous nearby friends.[152]

In the 1920s, twenty four bungalows dotted the hillside between the Marine Officers' Quarters and the hospital, and two more were on County Road. In the 1990s, nearly 75 years later, fourteen of these "temporary homes" were still in use: eleven on Bowyer Road, and three larger ones on Longshaw Road. The bungalows add to the unique variety of design in the "settlement across the creek." They were designated as quarters for commanders and lieutenant commanders.

Over the River and Through the Gate: Nonsense and Experiments

At the time Fort Severn was being built in the early 1800s, two more defending forts were erected on the north side of the Severn River: Fort Madison and Fort Nonsense. Fort Madison was close to the Chesapeake, and Fort Nonsense was built on a high hill further down the Severn River. Through the next century, the location of Fort Nonsense became as obscure as the origin of its intriguing name. A local citizen, Eric Smith, who was a columnist and political cartoonist for the Annapolis newspaper, *The Capital*, re-discovered Fort Nonsense when he was looking for Fort Madison in 1976. Mr. Smith's find inspired archeological investigations.

On May 17, 1985, a commemorative ceremony was held on the high hill, amidst a pouring rain, to celebrate the naming of the humble Fort Nonsense to the National Register of Historic Places. On that day, Naval officers, public officials, archaeologists, people from the media, and citizens dressed in colonial attire stood beneath a tent and umbrellas to recall the history that had been uncovered. Rodney Little from the Maryland Historical Trust spoke:

Legend has it that the fort was built for use during the War of 1812. After its construction, they discovered that the guns of that time would barely shoot to the water's edge from here – therefore, it was called Ft. Nonsense.[153]

It was thought that Fort Nonsense was a lookout point for Fort Madison. Later, this vantage point was used by troops assigned by General Butler, the Civil War general who commanded the Union camp at the Naval Academy. A plaque has been placed on the hill to honor its historic past.

A century after Fort Nonsense was built, the land was purchased by the U. S. government. Also acquired were twenty acres of waterfront property, an old farm house built around 1900, and an accompanying windmill. In 1908, on the site below Fort Nonsense, the Naval Engineering Experiment Station (EES) was developed to test naval equipment.

According to a 1925 report of the origins of the Experiment Station, "An old house located on the ground when purchased by the Government is occupied by the shop foreman. In 1912 there were completed and occupied six small cottages for the firemen, who are also night watchmen."[154]

In 1923, the old farm house became the Director's Quarters, or Quarters A. Captain Halford R. Greenlee, USNA Class of 1905, was the first Director of EES to live in this home. The foreman moved next door to Quarters E, a smaller stucco house built in 1912, which is still in use as officers' quarters in the 1990s. The other firemen's homes built in 1912 no longer remain.

Quarters A shed its "farmhouse" appearance in subsequent years. Mrs. Dorothy Cox Redue, daughter of Rear Admiral Ormond L. Cox, USNA Class of 1905, recalled that the first major renovation of Quarters A was made in 1939 after her father's tenure as Director of EES. Large extensions were added onto the house, and rooms were rearranged.[155] These quarters with over 5800 square feet of living space, are as graceful and commanding as "Tara" from the movie *Gone with the Wind*. The tall, white columns and surrounding verandahs make this house an imposing structure, reminiscent of plantation homes on the Mississippi Delta.

Quarters A has some unique features that add to its charm. In the basement is an old "reefer," or icebox which was taken from a German destroyer ship. The dining room is provided with a banquet-sized formal table for entertaining on a large scale. Enclosed porches flow off of many of the rooms, making the living areas seem even more spacious.

In the 1930s and 1940s, three other houses and one four-family apartment building were built at EES, creating a small community along Church, Kinkaid, and Greenlee Roads.[156] Alice Creighton and her parents, Rear Admiral (USNA Class of 1927) and Mrs. Liles W. Creighton, lived in one of these homes by the security gate in the late 1940s and early 1950s. Though living across the river, Creighton recalled that the children attended schools in Annapolis. She and other children from the North Severn area took a shuttle boat each day from the Station to

Dewey Basin at the Academy. Creighton then walked to the private St. Mary's School in town; a bus was provided for students going to the more distant public schools.[157]

Quarters B was built in 1941 atop the Fort Nonsense hill. Captain and Mrs. David James Knorr lived in Quarters B in the 1980s when the complex was known as the David Taylor Research Center. Quarters B commands a wide view of the Severn River and the Annapolis Harbor. According to Elizabeth Howell Knorr, their house was the "best location." They enjoyed entertaining in their backyard, especially on the Fourth of July when guests could watch the fireworks over the harbor, and during Commissioning week when the Blue Angels performed over the Severn. Quarters B by Fort Nonsense holds the finest water views of any of the quarters at the Academy.

When the Knorr family was quartered at the complex, all their neighbors were connected to the Research Center. Adding to its exclusive identity, the area was fenced and guarded to protect the sensitive research activities of the complex. Among the families living in the enclosure, there were pot-luck dinners and frequent parties, and the neighbors were well-acquainted. The officers merely had to walk down the hill each day to work. At one time, a nine hole golf course was installed near the main buildings for use by residents. The course in now covered with asphalt and is used as a parking lot.[158]

With the dismantling of the David Taylor complex, and with its becoming an adjunct of the Carderock facility in Washington, D.C., all of the quarters were acquired for use by Naval Academy Housing in 1990. Quarters A was designated as housing for the Commanding Officer of the North Severn Naval Station. In 1992, Captain Steven K. Laabs, USNA Class of 1964, was the first Naval Station Commanding Officer to be quartered here. Quarters B was held for the Commanding Officer of ECAC, the Electromagnetic Compatibility Analysis Center. The other houses and apartments had no specific billeting.

Today, Nonsense Hill still remains a great "lookout," as it was during the War of 1812. In this insular community, children can play on the grassy knoll in the summer, sled down the hill in the winter snow, and still pretend to guard the Annapolis waterways from the high vantage point. Residents who have lived beside the old fort say that their quarters are the "best kept secret" at the Academy.

The *Reine Mercedes*: The Fastest Ship in the Navy

The Spanish-American War introduced the Academy to the gallantry of the Spanish Prisoners, the orneriness of the parrot Cristobal Colon, and the most unique family residence in the Navy. In 1898, the Spanish cruiser *Reine Mercedes* was sunk by the United States at Santiago, Cuba. In 1912, the ship was overhauled and brought to the Academy to serve as the station ship. For a time, the *Reine* was the dreaded "brig" for disobedient midshipmen, replacing the *USS Santee* which was formerly used for this purpose. Also, assigned to live in these new quarters were single enlisted men, and the Commanding Officer of the Naval Station – and his family. **The *Reine Mercedes* became the only commissioned ship in the Navy to quarter dependents. She had a regulation ship routine, as any other commissioned ship.**

The *Reine* retained the charm of its Spanish origins. Each family living here had to quickly develop sea legs along the cambered decks tossed by rolling tides. The family's quarters of the *Reine Mercedes* consisted of three decks. The main deck had three bedrooms, two baths, a dining room, family room, and a galley or kitchen. Quaint Spanish balconies from the dining room and family room overlooked the Severn River. The second deck consisted of two master bedrooms and a bath. The third level was known as the "penthouse," and was perfect for entertaining in the lounge and on the sun deck.

Through the years there were many distinguished naval officers and families assigned to the *Reine*. Perhaps the most eminent resident was the well-liked and admired Fleet Admiral William F. Halsey, Jr., commander of the Third Fleet Pacific in World War II. In the late 1920s, then Captain Halsey had the third deck or "penthouse" installed, to the delight of later residents.

Mr. Robert S. Cooper, son of Philip Benson Cooper, and grandson of Superintendent Philip Henry Cooper, visited the Halsey family in December, 1929. The Halsey's daughter, Margaret was hosting a young lady from Cincinnati, and invited several friends over for a party. Providing an interesting picture of life on the ship, and a humorous story about the famous Halsey, Robert S. Cooper wrote:

> Mrs. Halsey spent a good deal of effort fixing up the living quarters. The stern of the ship was raised and was completely enclosed in glass. There were about five steps down to the living room which was about 15 feet by 20 feet and tastefully decorated . . . .

> She [Margaret] gave a tea dance on a Sunday before Christmas on the *Reine*. She invited about 15 midshipmen, seven or eight Navy junior girls and myself as the only civilian.

> Captain Halsey was seated in an easy chair in the stern where he could look down below. He was reading I suppose a Western novel and about every 20 minutes would pull a lanyard that was connected with a bell in the galley. The Filipino mess boy Saki would go running through the living room where we were dancing with a tall highball for Captain Halsey. We had nothing but fruit punch and cookies, and were enjoying the record player. We became noisier and noisier and every now and then I would look up and see Captain Halsey frown. . . . [W]hen the ship's clock struck six o'clock, Halsey pulled furiously on the lanyard. Saki came on the run, barely opened the glass door to the cabin, and Captain Halsey bellowed: "Saki, tell those G—D---- midshipmen and Robert Cooper to go home!" We hastily said good bye, and scurried over the side. As I was leaving, I looked back and I could see Halsey laughing. I was spared the epithet used on the midshipmen and I attribute this to the fact that Halsey's father had been a close friend

of my grandfather, and that my father and mother [Philip B. and Eleanor Cooper] knew the younger Halseys when they were a young married couple.[159]

Living on a ship can add an element of the unexpected to social gatherings. Another resident of the *Reine Mercedes* had the ship's wheel placed in a horizontal position, and covered with a glass top. The wheel made an attractive tea table for guests. Unfortunately, during a party, a submarine became entangled in the ship's rudder, and the wheel began to spin. Imagine guests having to dodge flying tea cups!

In the 1930s, the *Reine* was the site of a large tea and bridge party, held for the benefit of the Red Cross. Four hundred ladies mounted the gangplanks and joined each other at the bridge tables. The weather became rough, the ship began tossing, and one of the older ladies turned pale and abruptly left the party. She went to the deck for some fresh air. When she did not return, her partners went to look for her, and found her hat floating in the Severn River. The captain of the ship began plans for extensive search and rescue efforts, but amidst the turmoil the lady returned to resume her bridge game. Her hat had caught in the breeze, and she had gone home to get another![160]

One of the last families to live on the *Reine* was that of Captain, and later Rear Admiral C. Elliott Loughlin, USNA Class of 1933. Captain Loughlin, his wife Marjorie, and their three daughters lived aboard the ship. Around 1950, a newspaper article by Eugenia Mandelkorn featured the Loughlin family and their life on the *Reine Mercedes.* The article concluded:

The families who have spent tours of duty on her might well be known as the "saltiest families in the Navy" – for she has rocked them to sleep, splashed them with the Severn's spray, and forever doused their hearts with a special kind of navy brine.[161]

The *Reine Mercedes* never went to sea after coming to Annapolis, except to be overhauled in Norfolk. Always remaining tied fast to her dock, the midshipmen referred to her as "the fastest ship in the Navy." The *Reine Mercedes* was retired in 1957, after 45 years at the Naval Academy. The bell from the *Reine* remains on the Yard. Mounted beside Ricketts Hall, it serves as a memorial to the beloved station ship.

Perry Circle Apartments and the Kinkaid Road Quarters

By the 1930s, housing was still greatly needed, and the deteriorating, "temporary" bungalows were not intended as a final solution to the shortage. As early as 1931, the Board of Visitors expressed its concern, and offered a solution:

> Out of various building suggestions that have been advanced in the last 12 years to deal with this situation there has emerged one for the construction of 10 apartments houses, each to contain six 5-room apartments, of the type that is used successfully at the United States marine base at Quantico, VA.[162]

One proposal by the Board was that the new buildings be placed across the highway from the Post Graduate School, Halligan Hall, in the area known as "the Superintendent's Garden." The other suggestion was that they be built on the site of the nine-hole golf course which was to the north of the garden, and which overlooked the Severn River.

The wheels of progress turned slowly, but by the late 1930s, the plans were approved, and work was begun. The golf course by the Severn was spared. In 1939, ten new apartment buildings were completed atop the hill on the site of the old garden, and the area became known as "Perry Circle." Four additional apartment buildings were placed on Phythian Road closer to the Academy where the oldest bungalows once stood. The fourteen buildings together comprise 84 apartment units.

Unlike the scrap materials used to build the earliest bungalows, these apartments were constructed with quality materials. A design was selected that would be acceptable through the years to come, and that would be harmonious with the colonial architecture of Annapolis. The red-brick exterior and former windows echo the eighteenth century Georgian-style of the ancient city of Annapolis, and also blend with the homes on the Parade Field. To continue this theme, care was taken in furnishing each unit, as described in a memo from 1939:

> All apartments are furnished throughout in early-American colonial-type hardwood furniture; this is in keeping with the colonial architecture and construction of the apartment buildings. . . . [D]iversity has been secured by furnishing in three finishes; namely maple, walnut, and mahogany. . . .[163]

The apartments, as well as the other quarters on the Yard, are no longer provided with furniture.

The apartment buildings were originally identified by letters, beginning with "A" and ending with "N," but in the late 1900s, the buildings were numbered "1" to "14." The apartments all contain a living room, dining room, three bedrooms, and a kitchen. Five apartment buildings offer units with one bath; the remainder units have two baths. Each apartment has a basement garage located behind the buildings for aesthetic purposes. In addition to the apartment spaces, there is a maid's room for each unit located on the fourth floor, which is lined with dormer windows. In the 1940s, because of the severe housing shortage during that time, some of the "maids' quarters" were occupied by Post Graduate students. In later years, when domestic help was no longer customary, residents allowed guests and "drags," or dates for midshipmen, to stay in these rooms. In the 1990s, these rooms were no longer considered living space because of fire regulations, and they were assigned to each unit as extra storage areas.

Former residents have fond memories of living at Perry Circle. There was plenty of room for children to play. Michelle Foley McDaniel (Mrs. Tim McDaniel) wrote of her early experiences of living at the Academy, and of what she considered an idyllic setting for a youngster. She recalled:

> In 1946, just back from command of the USS Gainard in World War II, my father (Captain Francis J. Foley) received orders to report to the Ordnance Department at USNA. We arrived in June and stayed for a week or so at the "only" place to stay, Carvel Hall.. . . We soon moved into our apartment, Unit F-6 at Perry Circle. At that time our building overlooked the swimming pool and nothing else but rolling grassy areas to the river and some woods back near the creek. I was 12 years old when we arrived and was enrolled at St. Mary's School in the seventh grade.
>
> . . . In the afternoon I would [often stop to visit] my friend and classmate, Mary Glendon Newton, daughter of Commander Foy Newton, who lived with her parents on Rodgers Road.
>
> I loved Perry Circle for the then open spaces around it and would walk and run with my dog nearly every day up and down the rolling hills.[164]

Behind a fence laden with trailing red roses, up a steep, winding drive, through a hillside covered with forsythias which glow golden in the early spring, and past the anchor-shaped boxwood plantings stand the tall, spacious apartments many young Academy families call home. High above the city of Annapolis, these apartments command a lovely view of city lights by night and an overview of the Academy by day. In 1993, newly assigned resident Cynthia Godman Knapp (Mrs. Charles I. Knapp) was excited that she could see the Academy Chapel dome from her window. With a burst of nostalgia she told her children, "See, that's where Mommy and Daddy were married!"[165]

While the apartments were being built, in 1937, ten officers' homes at the North Severn Naval Station were also erected along Kinkaid Road to accommodate the growing need for military housing in this area. The single family, brick and wood two-story homes line the main road through the Naval Station. These three bedroom homes, also known as "S-Quarters," were billeted for commanders in the late 1900s.

CHAPTER THREE: SOCIAL LIFE AND CUSTOMS AFTER THE TURN OF THE TWENTIETH CENTURY

Carvel Hall

Annapolis began blossoming and growing into a more dynamic city while she endured the expansive building projects of the Naval Academy at the turn-of-the-twentieth century. In 1899, Winston Churchill, a Naval Academy graduate who was distantly related to the famous Englishman of the same name, wrote a best-selling novel about Annapolis, thereby increasing the town's esteem. The novel, set in colonial times, was called *Richard Carvel.* With renewed interest in colonial architecture, and with an eye on attracting tourism, an entrepreneur purchased the eighteenth century William Paca House, an historic five-part Georgian-style mansion on Prince George Street, and made plans to convert the old home into a "hostelry." Philip Benson Cooper, architectural assistant for the Academy's reconstruction project, was chosen to design a modern addition onto the back of the Paca House.

The nearly two acres of property behind the mansion had once been Mr. Paca's formal gardens in the eighteenth century; in the late nineteenth century it served as a working garden from which Mr. Richard Swann provided vegetables for Naval Academy families. With the early twentieth century additions, the former grand estate became the site of a large hotel with banquet halls and meeting rooms. The remainder of the garden area was paved to provide a parking lot and later a bus terminal near Academy Gate #2. Opening in 1903, this new 200 room "hostelry" became the center of cultural life in Annapolis, and was named after the famous romantic novel, "Carvel Hall."[166]

So great was the need at that time for living quarters among officers assigned to the Academy, many officers and wives took up residence in Carvel Hall. And, with its back entrance being on King George Street near the Academy's Gate #2, it was as convenient as officers' quarters on the Yard. In addition to being a home for Naval officers, it became a social center for the Academy as well, with hops, tea dances, receptions, and balls being held there through the years. An advertisement in Polk's Annapolis city directory hailed it as "Famous the world over as a Navy rendezvous." In the 1920s, the movie *The Midshipman*, starring the suave and romantic Ramon Novarro, included a scene of mids and "drags," or dates, on the porch of Carvel Hall.

Carvel Hall was a significant part of the social life for both the Academy and Annapolis for over sixty years. In its later years, the Naval Academy Athletic Association had a financial interest in the hotel. It was closed in 1965, being in bad repair, and plans were made to sell the property to another developer. Historic Annapolis Foundation, fearing the loss of the eighteenth century Paca House, bought the home, and convinced the State of Maryland to purchase the grounds. During twelve years of intensive historical and archeological investigation, the old 200-room annex was razed, the Paca House was restored to its original grandeur, and the cemented parking lot gave way once again to a beautiful eighteenth century-style garden. The home and gardens, the jewels of historic Annapolis, are now a highlight for visitors to the city.

A gentleman who worked at Carvel Hall was well-known by residents at the Academy, by the girls who came for hops, and by the midshipmen who counted on him as a friend. Marcellus Hall was a central figure in the social life of the Academy in the early 1900s. Hall was not an employee of the Academy, but he was always loyal to "his boys," as he called the mids. He was hired as a bell-hop at the hotel in 1912. Twenty-five years later, in 1937, he had received such fame in his position as Chief Porter he was interviewed for an article in the *Washington Post*.

Marcellus Hall was seen in several of the early movies made about the Naval Academy. He acted with Dick Powell in *Shipmates Forever* and also appeared on screen in *Annapolis Salute*. He held as his special friends some of the football heroes such as "Babe Brown," and "Buzz Borries." And, he was ready to help a midshipman in need.

Once, while on his way home late one night, he heard a whisper from the dark. Someone said, "Hey, Marcellus." Turning around he saw one of his friends, a First Class mid, or senior, and All-American football player who had been "frenching out" that night. "Frenching out" is the midshipman term for climbing over the Academy walls and sneaking out without permission. Mr. Hall admonished the celebrated football player for "frenching out" right before graduation, but the mid asked him for help, and he could not refuse. Marcellus hoisted the mid over the wall; the mid landed right into the arms of the security guards – known at the Academy as the "jimmylegs." The midshipman was reprimanded, but he was able to receive his commission, for which Mr. Hall was thankful. To protect his friend's identity, Marcellus Hall never revealed the name of the famous escapee.[167]

Carvel Hall was the premier place for girls to come, stay, visit midshipmen, and attend the famous hops. Mr. Hall worked at Carvel Hall so long, he had great insight into the changes in young women who came as "drags" to the Academy through the years. In the early years, he remembered that the young ladies wore "hobble skirts." If a girl used makeup, the midshipman would hesitate about taking her to the dance for fear that his friends would think she was not refined or too forward. By the late 1930s, the women had changed; they were no longer as "delicate" as before.

[I'm] not saying that there's been such a change in the Academy boys. Year in and year out they're pretty much the same, except now they seem a little younger, but the young ladies!

. . . These young ladies are easier to wait on. They've traveled more than the young ladies of 25 years ago. Why, back in those days they used to faint!

No, sir, these young ladies wouldn't faint, but that was just one of our problems with them years ago, when they came down to the hops.

[I] remember one young lady standing over there by the check room, saying over and over, "Marcellus, if you don't find my bag, I'm going to faint." [I] Told her that she shouldn't faint, because she might hurt herself fainting right on the floor of the lobby, but that didn't do any good. She just said, "Marcellus, my dress for the hop is in that bag, and if you don't find it, I'll faint.

I was pretty worried . . . so [I][looked high and low, until [I] found a bag which [I] thought might be hers. Is this your bag, Miss? [I] asked. It was her bag all right, but [I] wasn't looking for what happened.

"Oh, Marcellus," she said. [I] caught her as she fell.[168]

Annapolis Ties

Social life at the Naval Academy changed rapidly through the years from the early 1900s to the 1940s. The population on the Yard grew from a small, elite group of residents, to a large faculty, staff, and student body. Through the earth-shattering events of the next decades - World War I and the Great Depression- the Academy shifted from stiff and proscribed customs to more relaxed, less rigid ones. But until the World War II years, life at the Academy continued at its genteel pace.

Academy personnel helped to create a strong and lasting bond between the school and the city of Annapolis. In the early 1900s, one of the town's most recognized citizens was also a professor of English at the Academy, Professor William Oliver Stevens. Stevens began his career at the Academy in 1903. Shortly after his arrival in the fall, Professor Stevens met Miss Claudia Miles, the niece of Commander Hugo Osterhaus. It was Claudia who had befriended the poor captive parrot, Cristobal Colon, on Upshur Road during the Spanish-American War.

Unlike the Coopers, who were engaged for three years, Will and Claudia were married after only a few months, in February, 1904. They rented a small apartment in the historic Hammond-Harwood House on Maryland Avenue, down the street from Gate #3.

Stevens quickly gained notoriety in Annapolis from his several satirical works and cartoon sketches about both the city and the Academy. Annapolis took his sarcasm in stride, and learned to laugh at itself. A few years later, however, his social criticisms became more poignant. Naval Academy Professor Michael Parker, who has researched and written extensively about the life and literary works of Professor Stevens, provided an excerpt of an article written by Stevens in 1916.[169]

Stevens caustically remarked:

> This combination of naval influence with hoary tradition forms a kind of stopper that hermetically seals the mental life of Our Town. Music, drama, art, literature, science, social progress all put together do not weigh against an invitation to the Officers' Hops.[170]

In 1924, this man with sharp, biting observations was dismissed from the Academy by Superintendent Henry B. Willson. It was not because of his satirical essays, but from a difference in opinion with the Superintendent that led to his discharge. After leaving Annapolis, he cared enough about the Ancient City to write *Annapolis, Anne Arundel's Town* in 1937, which held a much more flattering perspective of the city and the school, and provided an excellent and entertaining look at lifestyles and personalities around the turn of the century.[171]

Many other Academy families provided a direct link with the city of Annapolis. Anne Howard Thomas (Mrs. Donald I. Thomas) was related to a long line of Naval officers, on both sides of her family. Her paternal grandmother and her father were Annapolitans. And, even though her father was in the Navy, somehow the family spent several tours and many years at the Academy. Her family lived here when she was two to twelve years old, from 1918 to 1928 on Rodgers Road, Upshur Road, and Porter Road, and she attended the Navy Juniors' School in Mahan Hall with Mrs. James Howard. She told of her early years:

> **Living in the Naval Academy in one's younger years had to be the best of all words – freedom and safety always. Plenty of harmless mischief, plenty of children and plenty of activity.** We played ball on Worden Field, fished from the old boat house (about in the middle of the street on Worden Field across from Upshur Road.) We had roped off seats for baseball games, football games and movies. We all went to Sunday School at the Chapel – a picnic in the spring (boat ride, then fun and games on the field in front of Porter Road – not there anymore). We played tennis and golf, had dancing class and many parties, rode bicycles everywhere. I was 12 when we moved out in town which wasn't too much of a change. The girls who lived in the Yard, and were a suitable age for midshipmen, had a great life and were very generous with their houses to the town girls and out-of-town girls. The hops were wonderful – stag lines forever![172]

Her parents returned to Annapolis after retirement from the Navy, and her father continued to contribute to life in town.

> My father's mother was an Annapolitan and he was, too. He returned and retired as soon as he could . . . . He became Dean of St. John's College, later President of Annapolis Banking and Trust, but died soon after that. So, I spent many years in the Annapolis area, including World War II. I hate not being there now, but my husband and children won out. P.S. Yes, I'll be buried in the Naval Academy Cemetery![173]

In addition to Naval Academy officers and families that spilled over into the local community, there were civilians who found their livelihood on the Yard. From 1923 to 1931, Fay Basil Baker (Mrs. F. Ernest Baker) was a familiar telephone voice for Academy residents. In the 1920s, she was one of five telephone operators on the Yard; in 1994, she was the only surviving operator of those five. The switchboard was in the Administration building, and she saw the superintendents frequently. She especially remembered Rear Admiral Henry B. Willson. She recalled, "'Henry B' talked so loud you couldn't hear him. He would go on trips and bring presents back to the operators."[174]

Although her husband was a CPA and Treasurer of the City of Annapolis, Mrs. Baker's family had a tradition of working at the Naval Academy. Her father, Arthur T. Basil, and her uncle, George C. Basil, were carpenters and bricklayers who helped to build the homes at the Academy around the turn of the twentieth century. Linking her family further with Naval traditions, she proudly attended the Commissioning in May, 1993, to see her grandson, Anthony Baker, graduate and become a Naval Officer.[175]

Social Activities at the Academy

"Paying calls" continued through the early 1900s. As late as the 1940s, "calling" was still a rigid convention. Rear Admiral and Mrs. Randolph King, who both lived in Parade Field Homes as children described the custom:

> In the 1930s and '40s, "calling" was formal, and expected. When someone was new, people would call and leave a card, and then the new person spent an afternoon returning those calls. Time was set asked, from 4:00 to 6:00 PM to accept visitors. If a family came, then a corner was turned down on the card. The children were expected to be polite. There were two man's cards, and one woman's card left. It sounds stiff, but it was fairly informal, a great bonding experience, and a good way to get to know people.[176]

This well-meaning, practical courtesy through the years developed into a weighty obligation as the number of officers and professors grew to a considerable size. Professor Stevens in a humorously exaggerated way, tells of the demise of this practice:

> . . . [W]hen the list of officers on duty had swollen to unheard-of numbers, all through the golden afternoons of October and November, the Yard would be filled with melancholy officers and professors being dragged by their wives, from one house to another, to pay official calls. Finally, one Superintendent, taking pity on those who wanted to watch football practice or play golf, abolished the whole business of compulsory calls. By that time, the Academy had become so enormous that no one could keep track of the newcomers anyway.[177]

Dress codes for social events reflected a more starched and ceremonious atmosphere on the Yard during the early 1900s. As recalled by Rear Admiral and Mrs. Randolph King:

Until World War II, many events at the Naval Academy were formal, including boxing meets, Masqueraders, and musical concerts. They were frequently preceded by formal dinners in quarters. Hats and gloves for the ladies were customary for parades, luncheons, cocktail parties, and Chapel. We recall that officers wore formal dress (frock coat) to Chapel, but I am not sure when that practice ended. Also, all the pews in Chapel were assigned.[178]

Naval Academy Women Fight the Depression

The 1930s were difficult economic times in our country, but the women of the Naval Academy found a way to support each other, and to use their considerable talents for community service. In 1930, the Naval Academy Women's Club was chartered under the inspiration and guidance of Mrs. Charles C. Slayton, and it initially met in her home on Duke of Gloucester Street. The tenor of the times reflected in the origins of the club. An NAWC history reported:

> These cultivated and active ladies felt the need, especially in those frugal times, to form a club of Navy wives to insure that the cultural aspects of their lives did not suffer because of their light pocketbooks.[179] (Naval Academy Women's Club Roster, 1992-1993)

The original group of women consisted of 25 members. Mrs. Slayton was an accomplished musician, and was hostess of a musical program on WBAL radio. Two other members had a background in opera, thus, the original interest of the club was music. Staving off the gloomy prospects of the times, the women met, organized, and rehearsed for musical productions in Mrs. Slayton's drawing room. Soon they performed Christmas concerts in Carvel Hall and on the Academy. The popularity of the musical group grew, and soon its professional performances were noted in the Baltimore and Washington newspapers.

Sara Corbin Robert (Mrs. Henry M. Robert) was also a charter member. Her husband was a professor at the Academy whose father had developed "Robert's Rules of Order." Mrs. Robert wrote the by-laws of the organization. In later years, Sara Robert chronicled the struggles and triumphs of the early, Depression born club. Her touching account also gave insight into the dire conditions of the town's economy, and the mutual support among the citizens.

> Then the meetings moved to Carvel Hall. A new host in friendly gesture toward town and town relations gave complimentary use of the ballroom and permitted hostesses to supply their own tea and cookies in return for a depression honorarium of $.10 per member for cream and sugar, hot water and service of the staff. Even with such concessions, disaster threatened in '33 and sudden closing of all the banks put what was left of the Club's meager funds beyond reach. Donations were out of the question but Navy spirit and bright ideas triumphed. Enough members paid their dues for a year in advance to keep the Club going for a regular season. By the tenth birthday, a drama group was formed and became the first women's group to give a performance on the Stage at Mahan Hall.[180]

The NAWC returned the kindness shown by the community. Among its many service projects, in 1936, the Club donated the proceeds of a musical production to the fledgling Anne Arundel Public Library.

Among the famous speakers to address the Club in the early years were Mrs. Franklin D. Roosevelt, who visited and spoke to the group four times, Mrs. Harry S. Truman, Mrs. Dwight D. Eisenhower, and Mrs. Lyndon B. Johnson. In 1937, Mrs. Roosevelt spoke to the NAWC about "Housing." "[T]ea was not served so that the normal refreshment payment could be donated to the Red Cross Flood Fund."[181]

The Naval Academy Women's Club was a child of the 1930s. The first successful and sustained women's organization on the Academy was born of dire times, but it served to elevate the spirits and status of these women. After carrying their husband's rank for nearly a hundred years, the Naval Academy women developed an aspect of daily life in which they could be "center stage."

Social Status of Officers in the Early 1900s

That presidents' wives would visit and speak at the Women's Club is not surprising. Naval Academy officers moved in those circles. In the earlier decades of the twentieth century, Naval officers had a relative affluence, especially during the Depression years. For example, a Captain, or "O-6" rank, had the same pay as a Congressman. And up to the mid-1930s, there were receptions for military officers at the White House, giving an indication of their social status at that time. Officers and wives were considered "ladies and gentlemen" in the most genteel sense.[182]

Honoring Tradition

Tradition and ceremony are the mainstays of Academy life. Our country's founding father, although belonging to the "other service," was commemorated at the Naval Academy in the 1930s. Seedlings were taken from an elm tree originally planted by George Washington and one was given to the Naval Academy. Academy Professor Samuel A. Elder's father, Captain Fred Kingsley Elder who also taught here, planted the "Washington Elm" near the old Isherwood Building in 1932. But, tradition and sentiment cannot always stand in the way of progress. The tree was about three feet in diameter when it was cut down in 1989 to make way for the new Alumni Hall.

In 1935, the Naval Academy honored not only its considerable past history, but sought to recognize its relationship with the cradle of its origins, the town of Annapolis. As recorded shortly after the event by Elmer M. Jackson, Jr., a local historian, the Academy and Annapolitans gathered to celebrate the ninetieth anniversary of their liaison. He wrote:

The Navy too appreciates the colonial setting in which its students reside. **Tradition is ever paramount in the service and on September 20, 1935, when the Naval Academy, through the interest of Rear Admiral David Foote Sellers, superintendent, observed its 90th anniversary, the ancient aspects of the Academy and city were not overlooked.** The front of a colonial mansion was constructed in the Academy Armory [Dahlgren Hall] which is large enough to hold a small row of houses. Towering white columns were erected fronting a colonial doorway, flanked by windows and green shutters. The guests were greeted on the brick porch of this portable house by the receiving committee dressed in colonial attire. The huge hall where thousands can dance at one time was an inspiring sight.[183]

Household Assistance and Support for Social Obligations

Festive galas, the tradition of "paying calls," formal dinner parties, the whirlwind of social requirements, and the genteel lifestyle of the early decades of the twentieth century would not have been possible if not for the additional assistance at home. Life during those years did not have all the pressures that were pervasive by the late 1900s and early 2000s. There were cooks and laundresses hired for the households. Maids polished silver, and scrubbed, swept and dusted the homes. At the dining room table, the father carved the meat, but the servants served the other dishes. The "colored gentry," as the domestic workers were known, supported the families and their activities at the Naval Academy. There was no daily sense of urgency and life was pleasant, gracious, and much more formal.[184]

Domestic help was available to officers at the Academy at rates that were well within their means at the time. Some larger households needed full-time assistance. Rear Admiral Randolph King recalled that, "In the 1930s, pay was $10 to $15 per week, and the help was in the house early and stayed until after dinner." According to Captain Philip Osborn who lived on Upshur Road in the mid-forties:

> The houses were furnished partially; with so many rooms it would have been difficult to properly furnish them with our then meager household effects. We had a maid twice or three times a week for only $3 plus taxi fare per visit!"[185]

Having someone help with household chores was a practice that declined with the better economic times after World War II. More employment opportunities and higher wages put household help out of reach for most Naval officers in the later 1900s. By the 1990s, household chores were either handled within the family, or, in a few cases, by licensed "cleaning services." Remnants of a buzzer system were still seen in a few of the quarters in the 1990s, and although no longer functional, they were a reminder of the former use of domestic help. In the early 1990s, Commander Fred Joseph Mallgrave III, USNA Class of 1971, his wife, Colleen, and the family moved into a bungalow in the Bowyer Road Homes. Their daughter asked, "Mom, what is this button for?" Mrs. Mallgrave quipped, "It's for the maid, dear, but she's not in."[186]

CHAPTER FOUR: EARLY TWENTIETH CENTURY RESIDENTS

Superintendent's Families

Finally furnished and equipped, the Superintendent's Quarters were readied for their first residents, the Bowyer family. In 1909, the *Army and Navy Journal* reported that:

> The family of the new superintendent, Captain John M. Bowyer, are[sic] now occupying the Superintendent's Quarters, Number 1 Blake Row. Besides the Superintendent, the family consists of Mrs. Bowyer and Miss Bowyer, his wife and daughter.[187]

Memories and anecdotes that span the centuries come easily for the Howards and Bowyers, two names in another multi-generational Naval Academy family. Anne Howard Thomas (Mrs. Donald I. Thomas) had a family story about her maternal grandparents, the Bowyers, who were the first residents in Buchanan House in 1909. She wrote:

> My father [Captain Douglas L. Howard, USNA Class of 1906] was Navy football coach in 1910 and my grandfather [Superintendent Bowyer] told him, yes, he could marry his daughter if they won the game. They won, and he and my mother were married two days later! My mother's brother had died while they were in the [Superintendent's] quarters and I don't think "Mr. Bowyer" (as my other grandfather referred to him) was very well in his last year there. He died not too long after they moved.[188]

Living in the Superintendent's Quarters and entertaining as frequently as is required lends itself to some dramatic moments. During the early years when transportation was still slow, an official from Washington made arrangements for a VIP party to visit the Academy on a particular day. Of course, a large reception was arranged at the Superintendent's Quarters to honor the dignitaries. Invitations were sent, and the usual elaborate preparations were begun. On the day before the event, the Superintendent received word that the esteemed party would be arriving that day – one day early! The visitors thought that they were arriving exactly as scheduled, and began making their way on the long day's journey to the Academy.

Panic gripped the Superintendent's household. The staff hustled to prepare the refreshments and libations while the Superintendent's wife frantically contacted all of the local guests about the sudden change. When the dignitaries drove into the carriage entrance, the refreshments were ready, the host and hostess were in place, local guests had arrived, and no one from Washington ever guessed that this was an impromptu party in their behalf.[189]

Children have also brought an element of spontaneity to the dignified world of the Superintendent's House. Through the years children have lived or visited here, and have amused guests at some of the formal functions. One youngster received great pleasure from pelting a head-of-state visitor with cereal from a window high up in the Superintendent's House. Another time, during a state luncheon, a Superintendent's grandchild ran out among the guests "naked as a jay bird" looking for a younger brother. This certainly broke the ice at the formal affair, and amid the laughter one of the foreign visitors in halting English declared that "Children are the same the world over."[190] Children can, when our pretenses are high, bring us back to the "bare" essentials.

Early Sampson Row (Porter Row) Residents

Looking through the eyes of a young Naval Academy resident at the turn of the twentieth century helps to experience life on the Yard as it used to be, and to imagine the grounds while it was being molded into the stately presence seen today. Mary Taylor Alger Smith (Mrs. Roy C. Smith, Jr.) was there to witness the transformation.

While plans for the grand reconstruction of the Academy were being made, Captain Philip R. Alger and his family were assigned to live at Number 9 Blake Row in 1899, when Mary was seven years old. Captain Alger was a member of the Professor Corps, which had military ranking in those days, and he served as Head of Mechanics and Mathematics. On the other side of the double house in Number 8 was the W. F. Halsey, Sr. family.

Over the next few years, the building of the Academy must have been fascinating to the children. Young Mary saw the slow, steady projects, gangs of workers, the constant hauling of supplies, the intrusive railways and train cars on the Yard, and heard the noises of hammering, sawing, grinding and shouting. These experiences shaped the sights and sounds of her daily life. The grounds were fertile for the cultivation of childhood curiosity and mischief.

Bancroft Hall was being built, and the children from the neighborhood played in it, as if it were a giant jungle gym. Chased by exasperated watchmen who were not as agile or as small as the children, Mary and her friends would wriggle through narrow openings and escape.

When the Chapel was being built, slabs of granite were hauled up in a large sling. Mary and other children would sneak into the construction site and sit on the sides of the sling, ride up, and then come down on the scaffolding like monkeys. "You know, I don't know why we didn't break our necks." [191]

At the age of twelve or thirteen, in 1905, Mary's family moved into Number 4 Sampson Row (Porter Row), the new senior officers' quarters. Mary had memories of a canal flowing in front of her house instead of a street, and a boardwalk for residents to reach their houses. This man-made canal was used by the construction crews to bring in materials on barges for the erection of the grand, new buildings. She recalled:

> . . . [W]e lived. . . in Sampson Row; we were the first people to move into the house. The first thing that happened was they came around and said, "The porch is cracking off from the house." It was all made ground, you know. I remember my mother having screaming fits and me thinking, "That would be fun, lovely, if the porch all fell off."[192]

For entertainment one evening, young Mary and her parents went to the old, round gymnasium to see a Japanese wrestling match. She recalled that the wrestlers were huge and fat, and were hitting each other, a sight quite shocking for the prim ladies of Victorian times. Several of the more delicate ladies fainted.[193]

Not all of the amusements for residents at the Academy were as exotic as Sumo wrestling. The Algers and other families entertained each other with tea parties and dinner parties. Mary related that at her parents' dinner parties there were cocktails, and the formal table was set with three wine glasses. "Afterward, in the old-fashioned way, the ladies went in the other room and had coffee, and the gents had brandy. . . or what-have-you, in the dining room. It was a very different life. And, you had 99 courses!"[194] Captain and Mrs. Alger had one of the first phonographs at the Academy, and they enjoyed inviting friends over for "music parties." Instead of making their own music like the Olivers on Upshur Row, they would listen to recordings of Enrico Caruso, the Italian tenor with the Metropolitan Opera, and Jean de Reszke, a famous Polish tenor. [195]

One of the highlights of the year in the early part of the twentieth century was, as it is today, attending the Army-Navy football game. In the early days of the 1900s, residents and families rode the trains to Philadelphia, taking a picnic lunch along. "Can you think of anything neater?"[196] Mary was present when Bandmaster Zimmerman performed the unknown, "*Anchors Aweigh*" for the first time after an exuberant win over that old arch-rival – Army.

As Mary got older her family moved into town. As a teenage girl, her activities were still focused at the Academy – though no longer climbing scaffolding or racing through unfinished buildings. Instead, she and her girlfriends slowly strolled around campus to meet the midshipmen, since the mids were restricted to the Yard most of the time. She attended hops in Dahlgren Hall where she danced waltzes and the "two-step," while her mother and other older ladies kept watch like ships' sentinels from seats along the side. And, occasionally there were barn dances held in Dahlgren for a change of pace, where "you merely pranced down more or less like a polka."[197]

In 1912, Mary Alger married Roy Campbell Smith, Jr., graduate of the Naval Academy Class of 1910, son of a career officer, and grandson of former Superintendent William T. Sampson. Sampson Row, where the Alger family had lived in the early 1900s, was named for her husband's grandfather. In fact, her husband, Roy Smith, Jr., had been born in the superintendent's quarters in 1888. Through their marriage, Mary and Roy helped perpetuate one of the longest lines of naval officers reaching back into early naval history, spilling into the present. The multi-generational Smith, Rodgers, Alger and Sampson families are noted for their contributions to naval excellence and their penchant for exciting and dramatic lives.

Mary Taylor Alger Smith grew up in a time when Naval Academy legends were being made. She lived next door to the W. F. Halsey, Sr. family, whose son emerged as a great Fleet Admiral of World War II fame. She saw the old Academy change into the new Academy in the course of her childhood. She was on the Yard in the early years of the exciting Army-Navy games, as that annual rite was being forged. She was present to hear Bandmaster Zimmerman perform the first "Anchors Aweigh," not knowing that the song was destined to become a pride-stirring link to the past not only for her children and grandchildren, but also for all future naval generations.

Another woman who lived at the Naval Academy as an adolescent early in the twentieth century, Mary Virginia Ramsay Sease (Mrs. Hugh St. Clare Sease), also provided sharp insight into the social life of the times. She lived at the Naval Academy from 1912 to 1915, as a 13 to 16 year old girl. Her grandfather, Captain Francis M. Ramsay, was Superintendent from 1881 to 1886. Her father, Martin Ramsay, lived as a teenager in the Superintendent's quarters, and harassed the midshipmen while they marched. Martin Ramsay did not attend the Academy, but joined the Navy after graduation from Fordham University. In 1912, Martin Ramsay was assigned as Paymaster of the Academy, and he and his family moved to Number 10 Sampson Row (Porter Row), one of the new houses built seven years earlier.

When the family arrived at the Naval Academy, they were greeted by an old friend, John "Tex" Ross, a big man with a white mustache. Ross had been a ship's cook in his younger years, and later served as cook for the Ramsay family in the superintendent's quarters when Martin was a young boy. "Mr. Martin," he said when he saw the new Paymaster, "I hear you will be on duty at the Naval Academy. I'm retired now; will you let me cook for you?"[198] He was hired, and Ross and his wife became familiar figures in the house on Sampson Row. The officers' families paid for any household help they had; only the Superintendent and Commandant had servants provided. The homes on Sampson Row had a kitchen with a big coal stove in the basement, and food was lifted upstairs by pulleys on a dumb-waiter which was attended by the cooks.

As in every decade, the children who lived on the Yard felt as if they "owned" the Academy. Children of officers felt "privileged." They could attend any of the sporting events at no charge. There was always a big gang of friends and never a lack of mischief and fun. In front of the Sampson Row quarters, now obscured by a large building, lay a large, green lawn where children could run and imitate marching midshipmen. And, when the ice wagon lumbered down their road three times a week with the tailgate down to deliver ice cakes to the residents, Mary and her friends hopped on board for a cool ride around the Yard.

According to Mrs. Sease, the Watchmen, known as "jimmylegs," always kept a grandfatherly eye out for the children who wandered out of the gates. The Captain of the Watch was named

"Graham," who was so old that he scared the children. Captain Graham had been hired by Mary's grandfather, the Superintendent, in the early 1880s.

Gate #2, adjacent to the Sampson Row houses, was open in those years, and Mary and her friends had to pass the gate guard, Watchman Gallagher, on their way into Annapolis. Gallagher always inquired if the children had permission from their parents to go out into town. Most of the time, she and her young friends went to Carvel Hall to talk to the Chief Porter there, Marcellus Hall. He was a fount of information in Annapolis, and the children relied on him for the latest gossip.

In the years Mary Ramsay Sease spent as a youngster living at the Academy, cars were not yet popular. One professor had an automobile, and this was considered quite extraordinary. Most people walked everywhere, or hired a hack from Caney's Livery Stable on West Street. The Superintendent kept his horse and carriage in the Academy's stable on the King George Street Extension, or County Road.

In Mrs. Sease's childhood, there were telephones in the homes, having become popular around 1908 on the Yard, but people still communicated by sending notes via servants. At age fifteen, a note was delivered to Mary's house from a midshipman inviting her to a hop. Her father did not share Mary's excitement about the invitation. He would not let her go, stating that she would become a "Naval Academy widow," and "worn out" if she began courting at that age. Her heart was broken. She had to write a formal note back to the midshipman with her regrets; she kept the memorable note from the mid among her treasures for most of her life.

The June Ball of 1918 was Mary Ramsay Sease's first date, a special evening with her escort Midshipman Forrest Sherman, Class of 1918. Midshipman Sherman later became an Admiral, Naval Chief of Operations, and for whom Sherman Field in Pensacola, Florida was named. The evening was magical. The band played as dancers swirled around Dahlgren Hall in formal attire. Mary, her long hair trailing down her back, wore a light organdy dress with scallops. A ribbon tied a dance card to her wrist. Her escort had filled in names of partners for each dance before the evening began. Girls did not wear corsages in those days. "They had to carry a bunch of flowers, "she said.[199]

The wife of a senior officer served as a chaperone for the evening, and parents came and watched from the balcony. As Mrs. Sease remembered, **"Everyone behaved! Social life was like that then. The social pattern was very carefully laid out for young people."**[200]

There was never any transportation used to go to the dances; everyone walked. If it rained before the dance, Mary pinned up her dance dress, put on her galoshes, and walked to the dance with her escort. The girls always carried a shoe bag for their dancing slippers, which they would put on in the powder room at the ball or hop.

On big occasions, such as New Year's Eve and Thanksgiving, all the midshipmen attended the hops. When Mary was a teenager, the 'gal' whose escort was chairman of the hop committee got to ring the huge brass bell at the Armory. "There was a big 'to-do' over ringing it at midnight. One year Kitty Knight got to ring the bell for Forrest Royal, USNA Class of 1915 and later the couple was married."[201] Mary, however, did not meet or date her future husband at one of these romantic affairs.

> I met my husband (Hugh St. Clare Sease, Class of 1917) at the Naval Academy, but he didn't pay any attention to me then. I met him at an "informal." "Informals" were held in the afternoons during Christmas and Easter holidays. I was too young then, and also a "Yard Engine," the daughter of a naval officer who lived at the Academy, which was a horrible crime to be – like the plague! Mids were afraid you'd tattle to your parents about them. I ran into him again seven years later in Norfolk, and was married in 1924.[202]

Schools for Naval Academy Children

Early in the twentieth century many Naval Academy children went to small, private schools as well as public schools in Annapolis. The public elementary school, Annapolis Elementary School, popularly known as "Green Street School," was considered "rough," but despite its reputation, Mary Alger Smith, Mary Ramsay Sease's brother, and other Naval academy children were enrolled. Academy children still attended this public elementary school at the end of the twentieth century.

The Green Street School, downtown near the City Dock, educated boys and girls separately in the early years. In fact, there was a tall board fence between the playgrounds so that the boys and girls could not see each other during recess. Discipline was strict, and a ruler brandished by the principal helped mold the behavior and served as an incentive for learning one's lessons.[203] In the early part of the twentieth century, Annapolis High School was located in the building next to the elementary school, and was attended by some Academy teenagers.

Having Naval Academy Children in the schools enriched the experiences of townspeople's children. Lester Trott, an Annapolitan, explained:

> The interesting part growing up in the area was that it was very sophisticated education-wise because you always had the influence of the Naval Academy through their children, navy juniors. And the navy juniors would come into the system, the educational system especially, and bring in new ideas, what had happened, where things were, what things were like in other parts of the world. . . . [T]he local people . . . were given a broader view of what was beyond the limits of Annapolis.[204]

Some boys from Academy families were educated in private local academies such as Werntz Preparatory School at 44 Maryland Avenue, Wilmer and Chew, or Cochran and Bryan. The girls also often attended small private schools, such as St. Mary's School. Mary Ramsay Sease recalled her early schooling:

> Many of the girls went to Misses Holliday's School off of Duke of Gloucester Street. That was where I went. It was run by two old maids. One day I came home and told my father that I knew as much as the teachers, so he hired a professor to tutor me. I went to Commodore [James L.,] Phythian's house, second house right out of Gate #3, to be tutored with the Pringle children.
>
> In those days the husbands went out to sea for a very long time, so families went to live with parents. Mrs. Pringle and her children were staying with her parents, the Phythians.[205]

In 1916, the Naval Academy began a school for Navy juniors who were between the ages of five and twelve years old. Multi-level classes were held in two rooms on the bottom floor of Mahan Hall. Phyllis Hammond Howard (Mrs. James Howard) attended the Navy Junior School as a child in the 1920s.

> In the twenties, Navy juniors from the Academy and Annapolis attended school in [Mahan] Hall, which was run by the Misses Mary and Eliza Magruder. Many of the boys went on to Severn School, and the majority later graduated from the Academy.
>
> We had a wonderful time during those years and our social life started with little dances. I remember several on Porter Road and a wonderful Halloween party. . . . Miss Eliza had the first three grades and Miss Mary – 4th, 5th, and 6th. There were two rooms and it was only for the elementary grades. I was about ten, and my sister Margaret, two years older. . . . I remember having to memorize and recite a poem the first day of school.[206]

Another former student, Captain William T. Dutton, USNA Class of 1934, lived with his family on Upshur, Rodgers, and Porter Rows as a child. He wrote of his time at the school:

> I did attend the school for Navy juniors – to one side but below the auditorium. Miss Magruder, I believe. [Other students] Captain Roy C. Smith is a classmate of 1934; Captain J. B. Rutter lived in the other half of our house on Rodgers Road, and Phyllis Hammond was the only girl that I ever waited for after school so that I could request to carry her books home.
>
> Very best regards, William, also, "Steel, Eel, Brooktrout" Gill [Dutton][207]

Captain Roy C. Smith, III also recalled his days at the Navy Juniors' School. Captain Smith was the son of Mary Alger Smith who lived on Sampson Row as a child. His classroom was to the left of the doorway in the back of Mahan Hall, across from the old Isherwood Building where the present-day Alumni Hall is located. He attended the school in 1919 at the ages of five and six; later he attended the Green Street School in town.

On the wall of the Navy Juniors' School was a lithograph of Washington crossing the Delaware River, Smith recalled. On the first day of school, Miss Magruder, the teacher, asked one of the other boys, "Who's that standing up in the boat?" The student answered, "He's a damn fool! My mother said that only damn fools stand up in boats."[208]

The school was discontinued about the time of World War II. Another school known as the Naval Academy Nursery School was started in 1946 in the old golf club house near Perry Circle. The old golf course was located between the Perry Circle Apartments and the Severn River, on the site of the present Arundel Estates Townhomes. The school outgrew this small building, and around 1951 was moved across the Severn River to the former Commissioned Officers' Club beside the current golf course, on Greenbury Point. In 1953, the school became known as the Naval Academy Primary School, or NAPS, and continued to offer programs for pre-school through fifth grades in the old wooden Officers' Club.

Fond Memories of the "Jimmylegs"

Navy juniors had special memories of the Naval Academy in the early part of the twentieth century because the fathers who spent much of their careers at sea were finally ashore with their families, according to Margaret Corn King (Mrs. Randolph W. King). Naval Academy duty was often sandwiched between sea duties. So, Dad was home, and there was security and fun.[209] As a child, Mrs. King lived with her family at the Academy, and also as an adult married to Rear Admiral Randolph W. King, USNA Class of 1943. Her father, Rear Admiral William Anderson Corn, USNA Class of 1914, was stationed at USNA several times.

Adding to the security and safety of the Yard were the "jimmylegs," the security guards, who were friends of the families, knew everyone's name, and watched out for the children. Often the jimmylegs were retired naval petty and warrant officers.

The term "jimmylegs" has uncertain origins, and was a slang term used affectionately by residents on the Yard. The words conjure the image of "jimmy crabs," and one can envision the scurrying that was needed to keep up with activities at the Academy.

According to an investigation by midshipmen from Professor Michael P. Parker's English class in 1982, the words were used to describe the security force at the Academy as early as 1898. In the *Good Gouge*, a publication of their research, the midshipmen reported that the words "jimmy guard" were used for guards at the St. James Palace in London in the seventeenth century, and could possibly refer to King James I.

A second source for the words could have come from eighteenth century merchant marine origins. A "jimmy" was then the first mate of a ship. Later the term was used to denote the master-at-arms, or police officer, on board. From their tongue-in-cheek investigation, the midshipmen concluded:

> The connection between jimmy and jimmylegs is logically clear. . . . [B]oth words denominate "a sort of cop" – but the addition of the suffix – legs is a puzzle. Patrolman H. A. Spies of the Academy Security Force offers the following explanation. In the old days of sailing ships, relates Mr. Spies, a certain first mate named Jimmy was charged with patrolling the deck of his merchantman. His shipmates below deck would keep close tabs on his comings and goings through the open hatches. From that vantage point, all they could see was the lower part of Jimmy's body; whenever he strolled by, they would say to each other, "There goes Jimmy's legs. . . ."[210]

The "jimmylegs" as police maintained a secure environment on the Yard. Their friendly vigilance enveloped this small community in a protective cocoon in which children could be raised in relative freedom. And, as seen with Marcellus Hall's friend who was caught "frenching out," "[T]hey [also] provide a 'welcoming committee' for those mids a bit tardy in returning to the Academy [on] Saturday nights."[211]

The use of the word "jimmylegs" faded, possibly because the security force felt it was a derogatory or disrespectful term. Also, as the size of the Academy grew, the interaction between the families and the security officers became less personal; instead of familiar faces, residents began to see more anonymous uniformed professionals patrolling streets in police cars. By the late 1990s, the term "jimmylegs" was officially obsolete at the Academy, but if an "old timer" used the word, everyone knew who was meant.

Halloween Tricks and Other Mischief

In their secure freedom at the Naval Academy, the children found plenty of opportunities for mischief in the early decades of the twentieth century. Halloween was when the children "let off steam," and enjoyed the benefits of their imaginations. That it was an evening of "nightmares" for the jimmylegs and other adult residents is an absolute certainty.

Captain Roy C. Smith, III grew up in Annapolis, and spent much of his early years playing on the Yard. Like his high-spirited mother, Mary Alger Smith, who climbed the Chapel scaffolding as a child, Roy was a familiar figure among the groups of youngsters there.

Of Captain Smith's early recollections of playing on the Yard was an incident with the jimmylegs. In the 1920s, he recalled throwing snowballs at the marching midshipmen, a similar misbehavior to that of the Ramsay boys in the 1880s. Superintendent Henry B. Willson walked up behind him, grabbed him by the neck of his jacket, carried him to the jimmylegs at Gate #3, and exploded in a huff, "Don't let him on the Academy for thirty days!" Smith and his parents lived just outside the gate at that time.

Creating their own adventures was easy for children on the Yard. Near the end house on Upshur Road, Number 44, was a large tree with a branch hanging over the water in College Creek. In the early 1920s, Roy Smith and his nine or ten year old friends tied a rope to this branch, from which they would swing, and then jump into the creek. An officer moved into Number 44 Upshur who complained about the noise the children were making. The Grounds Department had the limb cut off at the resident's request, and spoiled the boys' fun.

Young Roy and his gang of friends were angry. Halloween was near, and they secretly met to plan a way to retaliate. On the magic evening of Halloween, Roy and his accomplices sneaked to the side of 44 Upshur, raised a window, and smeared some Limburger cheese on a hot steam radiator just inside. Of course, the smell was offensive and the family upset, but the revenge was sweet. No one ever discovered the culprits![212]

According to the Randolph King family, Halloween tricks were also popular in the 1930s, not that THEY indulged in such pranks! On Worden Field one might find furniture run up the flagpole. Also, children made "ticktacks" which were spools with ridges on the sides, and string wound around the middle. The spools were put up against the windows, the string was pulled, and the ridges thumped against the glass causing a terrible sound. The noise was enough to frighten any resident on a spooky Halloween night.

Halloween cannot be the only time of mischief for young children; they must practice their craft on other days to hone their skills. Captain Smith told of another time that he and a young friend from the Navy Junior School, William Dutton, who lived on Upshur Road, set out innocently enough to go fishing in the Severn River from the old ship *America's* pier. To their dismay, all they caught were eels, and they were further disappointed when Roy's mother would not let the boys keep them. Not knowing what else to do with the slimy creatures, they stuffed them into a cannon at Dewey Basin, which is now Dewey Field. In those days, at nine o'clock each evening the gun was fired to mark the hour. As the cannon sounded, the eels blasted out of the gun, and were plastered all over the side of the old Power Plant across the basin. It took days to have the walls cleaned, but the jimmy legs never figured out how the mess was made, or who made it.[213] Young William, later Captain Dutton, USNA Class of 1934, became popularly known by the nickname "Eel."

Another friend of Dutton and Smith was Captain J. B. Rutter, Jr., USNA Class of 1936, who also lived on the Parade Field at 50 Rodgers Road from 1924 to 1926 as a child. His father was James Boyd Rutter, USNA Class of 1909. J. B. Rutter, Jr. recalled lots of playing and mischief among the youngsters in those days. One resident's daughter, he related, almost burned down the old stadium. He also remembers other activities and incidents. He wrote:

> Us Navy juniors used to play football on the then-vacant lot across from the Porter Road houses.
>
> . . . On one occasion my mother had to turn [a friend] into his mother when he fell into the creek and was drying out behind some wood piles behind Rodgers Road, naked in mid-January! She was sorry, but she thought his health was important.[214]

Childhood Beginnings on the Yard

Memories of life at the Naval Academy after the turn of the twentieth century bring back images of a long-lost existence, a world with unfamiliar trappings. Vice Admiral Ralph Earle, Jr., USNA Class of 1922, lived on the Yard as a six year old. Looking back nearly a century, he wrote of his experiences:

> My father was a duty officer at the Academy about 1906, and we lived in 44 Upshur Road. [There were] no automobiles in those days. . . . [I]n the nice backyard I raised chickens. It was a fine place.[215]

The Earle family also had Naval Academy roots. Vice Admiral Earle's father was Rear Admiral Ralph Earle, USNA Class of 1896.

For some people, the Naval Academy is linked with the most significant events in their lives. For Mary Greenman Rae (Mrs. William Clark Rae), life began in one of the quarters on Rodgers Road. She wrote:

> My mother never stopped telling how the navy doctor came to our home, with bed and all, to bring me safely into the world. That was July 14th, 1926. . . . Grandma was downstairs preparing lunch for Mother's doctor on that day in July – or overseeing Eva's preparation. The story goes that Grandma was distressed that the crab cakes Eva [the cook] was frying were from a can. A definite no-no![216]

Mrs. Rae also had strong Naval Academy ties throughout her life. Her father was Commodore William Garrett Greenman, USNA Class of 1912. Continuing the family tradition, Rae grew up and married an Academy graduate in the big Chapel. "Annapolis feels like coming home. . . . My Mother and Daddy are buried up there in the USNA Cemetery. . . . Those quarters [on the Parade Field] are a source of pride to me."[217]

Other former residents who spent their childhoods at the Academy have special memories of living in the quarters. Impressions of the close community, the feeling of security, and images of the unique, old houses stay with them throughout their lives. They enjoy recounting stories of "their" time on the Yard.

The family of Captain Thomas Starr King, USNA Class of 1911, lived at 50 Rodgers Road from 1932 to 1933. His son, nine year old Randy King, later Rear Admiral King, USNA Class of 1943, "cooked up" a way to earn money in the large family kitchen. He heated and boiled lead in a big pot on the old gas stove. Using about six different molds, he made toy soldiers from the lead – some infantry, and some on horseback. He then cut strips of cardboard that came from shirts from the laundry, and sewed about three soldiers to each strip. The young entrepreneur peddled his wares on Bowyer Road for five cents each. "Can you imagine how dangerous that was, boiling lead indoors like that? Of course, we didn't know it at that time."[218]

Robert G. Tobin, Jr., USNA Class of 1948, who became a Marine Corps Captain and later an Annapolis lawyer, lived on Upshur Road as an adolescent in the late 1930s. His father, Rear Admiral Robert G. Tobin was a USNA graduate of 1917. Young Robert's room was on the third floor, and when his parents thought he was safely inside and studying diligently, he would climb out of his window, scramble over the sleeping porches, and take off around the Academy. The fun seemed unlimited in those days; he enjoyed bicycling, crabbing and swimming in the creek, watching sports, shooting rifles, and playing lacrosse. The Annapolis winters were colder then, and he and his friends could skate on the solid sheet of ice covering College Creek.[219]

Next door in the big double house in the late 1930s was a younger girl who also had memories of her third floor room. Having the children so far away from the family areas had its advantages, but their distance also made for difficult communication. Caryl Sinton Carlson wrote:

> As the house was three stories in height and my room was on the third floor, my mother had an ingenious way of reaching me. The stairs were a straight shot from the first floor to the third floor, so my mother hung a bell at the top of the stairwell on the third floor with a pull hanging down to the first floor. Whenever she wanted me, she would ring the bell and I would go to the stairwell and we would call up and down from there.[220]

Caryl Sinton Carlson was the daughter of Rear Admiral and Mrs. William Sinton. RADM Sinton was a USNA graduate from the Class of 1920.

Children love the mysteries and legends that the old houses seem to conjure. Carlson's older sister recalled using an old fashioned bathtub with claw feet on the third floor. The tub was quite long, and rumor among the children was that it could be used to bathe a corpse. Carlson continued:

> The years we spent in Annapolis were the happiest years of my childhood. It was a wonderful and protected place for a nine year old. As my sister was 16 at the time, she thought it was pretty outstanding, also.[221]

Some of the children explored the homes inside and out. In the early 1920s, Commander Louis R. Hird, USNA Class of 1935, spent some time behind the scenes in his house on Upshur Road. Of his most unusual experiences he wrote:

> As a nine and ten year old I discovered hidden passageways behind the upper story walls. From one, by lying flat and inching my way between second floor ceiling rafters, [I] discovered a sizable secret room that I could drop down into, a room bounded on all sides by the backs of walls with no other way in or out. I also was intrigued by the intercom, a system of tubes to the kitchen area with whistles to get one's attention.[222]

Commander Hird's father was Captain Harry B. Hird, USNA Class of 1908.

The intercom tubes are no longer present in the Parade Field Homes, and residents relate that communication among family members in the tall homes is still difficult, but gives one an excuse for yelling.

Children living at the Academy have an early exposure to the appealing glamour of the parades and handsome midshipmen in uniforms. USNA Professor Samuel A. Elder wrote of his memories of living on Upshur Road as a very small child in the early 1930s.

> My earliest recollection in life is watching a parade on Worden Field. The earliest musical tune that I could identify was "Anchors Aweigh!" . . . .

> I remember a wicker baby carriage with a small triangular window from which I watched the parades sometimes, but also remember standing along the side of the field with someone holding my hand. The marching midshipmen looked enormous to me. I have never gotten over the excitement of hearing the Navy Marching Band![223]

Professor Elder began teaching at the Naval Academy in 1964. His father was Captain Fred Kingsley Elder, USNA Class of 1912, who also taught at the Academy from 1925 to 1931, and also 1940 to 1944.

Many of the young boys whose fathers were stationed at the Academy in the early decades of the twentieth century were inspired to become midshipmen, too. The Reverend Father Alister C. Anderson of Washington, D.C., who lived on Upshur Road in the mid 1930s wrote:

> As a boy of nine to twelve years of age, I watched many regimental parades and yearned to be one of those blue and white clad midshipmen marching past my front door. Later as a midshipman myself (USNA Class of 1946) I looked across Worden Field to those family quarters and said to myself: "Well, I made it, but now I want to get out of this place and into the fleet before the war is over.". . . . I also recall receiving my first kiss from a very cute twelve year old girl under the bandstand at the east end of Worden Field. The band played there quite frequently.[224]

Father Anderson's father was Rear Admiral Anton B. Anderson, USNA Class of 1912.

CHAPTER FIVE: MIDSHIPMEN, RESIDENTS AND ROMANCE

Midshipmen Social Activities

Holidays were infrequent for midshipmen in the early part of the twentieth century. Until the close of the 1930s, there was only one day of "leave" at Christmastime, but it was a day of revelry for residents on the Yard. The president of the First Class, or seniors, posed as Santa Claus, and led the midshipmen who were dressed in odd costumes around the Yard to the Superintendent's, Commandant's, and families' houses shouting Christmas greetings. Afterward, they met at the Armory, and the First Class mids changed uniforms with the plebes, or freshmen. The plebes then had their chance to order the "firsties" around. This custom died when a longer Christmas leave was granted.[225]

Since Porter's time as superintendent in the 1860s, midshipmen have had ample opportunity to engage in sports at the Academy. Beginning in the 1890s and continuing for many years, the Parade Grounds were the center of daily sports activity. Mary Gale Buchanan, Annapolis resident and active USNA supporter, reported that her father, Rear Admiral Charles A. Buchanan, USNA Class of 1926 and Commandant from 1952 to 1954, spoke about his life as a child living by the Parade Field in 1912. The mids played lacrosse and other games on Worden Field, and balls of all kinds were always dangerously flying here and there, often landing on his front porch. The Buchanans are another multi-generational Naval Academy family. Ms. Buchanan's grandfather was Captain Allen Buchanan, USNA Class of 1899.[226]

Another former resident, Commander Louis R. Hird, also lived on the Parade Field as a child in the early 1920s. He recalled not only the athletic games, but also the long-lost practice of "sham battles." He recounted:

> About Worden Field: two things stand out in my memory. The sham battles by the midshipmen shooting blanks were appealing because we would gather empty shells to sell in town. I remember also the baseball team practices in the southwest corner under Coach Chief Bender.[227]

An account of these "sham battles" is found in the 1903 *Lucky Bag*, the yearbook for midshipmen. Evidently, the field was not the green, park-like, manicured expanse seen today.

> We who received Prince Henry will always recollect what luscious mud can be furnished by this field on occasion, and all will remember the field for many and various drills and reviews. At infantry skirmish drill, we have died strictly according to rate; i.e., as plebes, we survived even the last charge; as Second classmen, we died early; but as First classmen, clean sleevers, we died at the first fire.[228]

That the Academy is somewhat of a separate culture is emphasized by the fact that midshipmen developed their own lingo from early years. In 1902, the *San Francisco Chronicle* describing some of the unusual terms used at the Naval Academy observed that a girl who cannot talk or dance, or is not pretty, was called a "gold brick." Also, midshipmen "drag," rather than escort ladies to events.[229] By the late 1930s, quite a collection of terms was in use, as reported by the 1940-1941 *Reef Points*. Some of the common "tongue salt," or slang words were:

Bone	To Study
Crab	A girl who lives in Annapolis
Crabtown	A fishing village on the banks of the Naval Academy (*Annapolis*)
Drag	1. To escort. 2. Young lady escorted
Hop	The knee-cracking Annapolis brand of dance
O.A.O.	The One and Only. Sometimes Off and On
Radiator Club	Those whose recreation is sedentary, the non-athletes
Red Mike	A dyed-in-the-wool misogynist
Savior	One who is academically brilliant
Savvy	Mental condition of a savior
Snake	Opposite of a Red Mike
Tea Fight	Annapolis tea dance, which must be seen to be appreciated
Yard Engine	A girl who lives in the Yard.[230]

With this translation in hand, one could understand this sentence provided by Rear Admiral Randolph King, who was a midshipman during the 1940s: "There was always a stag line at hops where the snakes kept roving eyes on the crabs, yard engines, and all other young women."[231] And, the people of "Crabtown," during those years, had their own slang for the Academy: "The Trade School," or "Canoe U."

"Courting" at the Academy

Midshipmen did not have ample free time to visit with their O.A.O.s, however, more than a few mids learned to stretch the limits to see the "fair sex." Eleanor Michelet Mulbry, married to Dr. Leonard William Mulbry, USNA Class of 1948, lived at 15 Porter Road with her parents in 1944. Her father was Captain William G. Michelet, USNA Class of 1924. Mrs. Mulbry recalled a story told about her grandfather, Captain Reed M. Fawell, Class of 1905, and his friend, Fleet Admiral William F. Halsey, when they were midshipmen. Both mids spent time in detention together on the old *USS Santee*, the station ship at the Academy, because they were caught going over the wall to see their girlfriends in Baltimore.

In 1904, Midshipman Fawell's "girl" came to the Academy as a drag to a hop, and the girl's mother came along as a chaperone, wearing black. The girlfriend wore an elegant formal dress, and arm's length white gloves. Attached with ribbons to her wrist was a "hop card," which had a list of the evening's dances and names of her partners. After descending the grand staircase in Dahlgren Hall, her escort presented her with a dozen long-stemmed red roses. Midshipman Fawell later married this lovely young lady, Eleanor's grandmother.[232]

Mary Ramsay Sease noted earlier how social patterns were strictly defined in the first decade of the twentieth century. In 1913, the Department of Discipline at the Academy set "dancing regulations" for the midshipmen, leaving no margin for impropriety:

1. None of the modern dances will be performed under any circumstances.
2. Midshipmen must keep their left arm straight during all dances.
3. A space of three inches must be kept between the dancing couple.
4. Midshipmen must not take their partner's arm under any circumstances.

5. Midshipmen will not leave the ballroom floor until the dance has been completed and all officers and their guests have left.[233]

Social life and interaction with resident families were important for the proper development of midshipmen, as noted by Professor Carroll S. Alden in a 1935 edition of the *United States Naval Institute Proceedings*. He wrote:

One diversion at the Naval Academy has continued during the ninety years without interruption, and it is not the field sports, football or baseball, nor the water sports, rowing or swimming. As will be readily guessed it is dancing. . . .

Since midshipmen. . . cannot journey about during term time to attend the parties other youths are enjoying, the girls accept the situation and come to them. **The hops are indeed a highly civilizing influence in the midshipmen's four years of monasticism. With the hops should be mentioned also the homes of the officers and of the people of Annapolis. Among naval educators, mothers and daughters have a place of no mean importance. They prevent midshipmen from becoming hard and boorish, and add cheerfulness to life.**

. . . [O]nly those who are determined anchorites cut themselves off from enjoying the hospitality of the officers' and professors' homes.[234]

Of dancing in the 1930s, Professor Stevens, who preferred the graceful styles of the nineteenth century, lamented, **"Nowadays, anyone who can shuffle and jiggle is as good as the best of them."**[235]

Mids and officers' daughters formed many lasting liaisons from the constant social opportunities on the Yard. Adelaide Fullinwider, married to Captain Simon Pendleton J. Fullinwider, USNA Class of 1917, lived on Porter Road in the early 1940s. She recalled that the mids were crazy about the beautiful daughter of Captain and Mrs. Edward E. Hazlett, Jr., of 44 Upshur Road. The daughter "caught," as they said in those days, the regimental commander and captain of the football team, a very handsome man. The couple were married in the Chapel. "I've never seen anything like it – two beautiful people like that getting married," Mrs. Fullinwider exclaimed. It was just like a fairy-tale wedding.[236] Captain Hazlett was from the USNA Class of 1915.

Teenage girls who lived at the Academy watched with rapt attention as the midshipmen marched across the Parade Field and to and from classes. The hops provided a chance to meet these mids while rigid schedules limited their free time. According to Robert S. Cooper, who was a young man in the late 1920s and early '30s:

It was generally understood that most of the Navy junior girls would wind up marrying naval officers; thus, some of them would dance with a civilian at a hop with an air of sufferance.[237]

Elizabeth Hill Drake (Mrs. J. B. Drake) remembered her teenage years living at the Academy in the early 1930s with her parents on Rodgers Road. Her father is Vice Admiral Harry W. Hill, USNA Class of 1911, and Superintendent from 1950 to 1952. Mrs. Drake explained the courting rituals of the day:

> Hops were grand. [We] didn't go with just one person, as they do today. There was a stag line of about 250 men in the center of Dahlgren Hall, and the women would be introduced down the line.[238]

In the early 1940s, Patty Wattles Robie lived with her parents on Rodgers Road as a teenager. Her father is Rear Admiral T. L. Wattles, USNA Class of 1921. She recalled:

> Imagine being a teenage girl with all those midshipmen who couldn't leave town! The hops were terrific, and there was always a huge stag line. At the hops I was cut in on so many times that I was never able to finish a conversation.[239]

As many of the Yard Engines, Patty continued the tradition, and married a graduate, Captain Edgar A. Robie, USNA Class of 1943.

"Tea fights" broke out frequently among the young folks at the Academy in the early to mid 1900s, and were a lot more civil than one would guess. "Tea fights" were a popular and rather circumscribed way of getting the mids and the young ladies on the Yard together for some fun. The Academy Social Director or "Hostess" helped arrange for the events on Sunday afternoons. The girls on Porter Road and the Parade Field homes would rotate having the fights at their houses. Residents filled a big bowl with grape juice and ginger ale punch, and made sandwiches for the "starving midshipmen." The young people would wind up the old gramophone and dance. At an early hour, everyone would go home.[240]

Frequently on Sunday afternoons there were tea dances at Carvel Hall. According to Elizabeth Hill Drake, in the 1930s the mids and drags danced to music provided by a three piece "colored" band,[241] which played such tunes as "Stardust" and "Dancing in the Dark." In 1932, the "Shag" was a popular dance. Bane McCormick (Mrs. James H. McCormick, Jr.), a Paca House docent in the 1990s, recalled coming from Baltimore in the 1950s with other private school girls to attend the tea dances at Carvel Hall, the historic Paca House annex. The girls wore white gloves, "Sunday" attire, and high heels.

Somehow, amid learning the "rates," "boning" for exams, and getting the "good gouge" from a "savvy savior," the "snakes" managed the time to "drag" "Crabs" and "Yard engines" to "Hops" and "tea fights" – even the "red mikes" – and "cut a rug" or dance the "shag" with their "O.A.O."

A 100-Year Family Tradition of Naval Academy Romances

Like a brightly colored thread winding through an antique tapestry, the tradition of Naval Academy romance is woven beautifully into the century-old fabric of the Randolph W. King family. The Kings serve as a rich source of social history and provide insight into the gracious life-style previously found on the Yard. The continuity in their lives over several generations is unusual for transient military families. The Naval Academy has been their steady point of reference.

In 1908, Rear Admiral King's parents met at the Academy in one of the red brick homes beside the Parade Field. Midshipman Thomas Starr King II, USNA Class of 1911, and Anne Gordon Winchester, of Wilmington, Delaware, were both visiting family friends at 44 Upshur Road. Despite Anne's distance from the Academy and the social constraints of that era, the two young people forged a lasting bond.

Both King and Winchester exemplified the Victorian ideals of social involvement. Midshipman King was an outstanding athlete and leader. In 1910 he was chosen the captain of the football team; he was also elected as president of the Class of 1911. Anne Winchester was a sporting young lady who raised horses, drove in trotting races, and competed in women's golf. Selected as the 1911 Color Girl by the midshipman company commander, Anne, along with Superintendent Gibbons, awarded the Color Company its special flag during the traditional Commissioning Week ceremony. The "Color Girl" tradition is long-standing, started by Superintendent Porter during his re-invention of Academy activities.

The couple wanted to marry immediately after graduation in 1911, but according to rules of the time, a "passed midshipman," or recent graduate, could not wed for two years unless special application was made. Undaunted by the restrictions of the day, Midshipman King wrote a letter to the Secretary of the Navy requesting permission to marry Anne. He assured the government official that his wife would not become a destitute ward of the state after their nuptials. The Secretary of the Navy returned a letter granting special permission. That letter remains today as a cherished memento of the King family's Naval Academy roots. Anne and Thomas, Color Girl and football captain, were married after graduation on June 14, 1911.

Later in his Navy career, Captain Thomas Starr King and his family were stationed at the Academy for three different tours of duty, and their children – Anne, Thomas, Jr., Elizabeth, and Randolph – spent much of their younger years under the magical influence of the Yard. Their daughter, Anne Gordon King, and her beau, Edgar Hadley Batcheller, USNA Class of 1934, and later Rear Admiral, wed in the Academy Chapel on June 14th, 1936, on her parents' twenty-fifth anniversary. The King family was living on Rodgers Road on the Parade Field at that time. One son, Thomas Starr King, Jr., later Rear Admiral, was graduated from the Academy in 1936, a few days before his sister's wedding. Another daughter, Elizabeth Winchester King, married John Porter Merrell Johnston, a graduate of the USNA Class of 1937. Both the Batcheller and Johnston families also have numerous Naval Academy graduates in their lineage.

The family of Rear Admiral William Anderson Corn, USNA Class of 1914, was stationed at the Academy for three tours, and in the late 1930s, lived on the Parade Field in 44 Upshur Road, only a few houses from the Kings. Among the Corn's children was their musically talented teenage daughter, Margaret B. Corn, or Margie.

In 1937, when Randolph W. King, youngest son of Captain King, was fourteen, he met the spunky Margie Corn on the bus to Annapolis High School, and their interest in each other was ignited. Flirtatious glances at social functions and romantic promenades around the Yard kept their young love ablaze. The two families subsequently moved away, the youthful romance fizzled, and Margie and Randy lost touch with each other.

Several years later Margie, who was studying music at the University of Rochester in New York, came to visit the family of Rear Admiral Oliver O. Kessing, USNA Class of 1915, on Rodgers Road. On a stroll around the Academy, she passed down Porter Road, saw the Kings' name listed on a house, and stopped in to renew acquaintances. Margie climbed the stairs to the senior officer's quarters and rang the bell. The door was opened by her lanky, handsome, teen-years sweetheart. Randy, then a midshipman, was at home that day visiting his parents. Their romance sparked once again, and this time the flame was sustained.

Randolph W. King and Margaret B. Corn were married in the Chapel by Chaplain William Thomas the day after graduation, on June 10, 1943. Fortunately for the Kings, the Academy had just rescinded the regulation requiring mids to wait for two years following their commissioning to get married. World War II separated the newlyweds, and while Randy served at sea, Margie applied her considerable talents and vibrant energies to the war effort in Annapolis, and to singing and dancing in Navy Relief shows.

The King family romantic saga continues. Randy and Margie King came to live at the Academy again in the late 1960s, and were assigned to 6 Porter Road. Randy's parents had lived in 7 Porter Road when he was a midshipman, and when he and Margie renewed their friendship. One of their sons, William Anderson King, Class of 1970, and who was a midshipman at the time, met the "girl next door," Carol Lee Doty. Carol's parents were in Quarters 7 Porter Road, and her father is William Kahlen Doty, USNA Class of 1946. As generations before, Carol and Bill strolled along "Lovers' Lane" in the central park, and were married in the Chapel after Bill's graduation.

The close community on the Yard, though comprised of constantly changing names and faces, provides focus and familiarity to the uprooted families of the Navy. After over 100 years of King-family involvement, the twenty first century found the Randolph Kings supporting and nurturing the honorable values and social traditions of the Naval Academy. They made Annapolis "home."[242]

A Fictional, Fairy Tale Setting for the Early Twentieth Century

Handsome college men in uniforms, and daughters of officers who lived at the Academy helped set the stage for excitement and romance. Academy life in this picture-perfect locale even made a great theme for fiction!

Young readers could glimpse into the appealing life behind the walls of Bancroft Hall by purchasing the popular "Dave Darrin" series by H. Irving Hancock, published in 1911. With one book for each year at the Naval Academy, the daily trials and ethical challenges of a fictional mid are chronicled for young, aspiring Naval officers. "Dave Darrin" helped intensify the dream of many boys to attain an appointment to the Academy. In *Dave Darrin's Third Year of Annapolis*, Dave was not only a loyal citizen and an exemplary midshipman, he was also quick to defend the honor of a damsel in distress.

"I? Good times with you?" cried Belle, her cheeks flaming. "I've never even spoken to you when I could avoid it."

"That's false!" cried young Ardmore hotly.

"Stop right there!" warned Dave Darrin in a quieter voice than ever, though his face paled swiftly. "Did I understand you to remark that Miss Meade had made a false statement?"

"You did!"

Whack! Darrin's clenched right fist caught the fop on the temple, felling him to the ground.[243]

The silver screen made its debut as a major form of entertainment in the twentieth century, and the genteel and glamorous life at the Naval Academy was a fitting stage for early black-and-white romantic films. In 1925, a silent movie, *The Midshipman*, starring the handsome Latin "lady's man" Ramon Novarro and the lovely Harriett Hammond, wooed audiences with the story of an upper classman who fell in love with the sister of a plebe. Scenes were shown of Carvel Hall, and of Hops at the Academy where the girls wore "dance cards" on their wrists.

Annapolis, a silent film from 1928, starring John Mack Brown, portrayed two clashing classmates. *Salute*, a year later starring George O'Brien and Helen Chandler, depicted the service rivalry between the Naval Academy and West Point. Of course, there was romance and an Army-Navy Game.

In 1933, *Midshipman Jack*, a black and white "talkie," was a humorous but stylized film in which Bruce Cabot, playing a midshipman, fell in love with the Commandant's daughter, played by actress Betty Furness. Draper L. Kauffman, who became Superintendent 32 years later, was a midshipman when this movie was being filmed. He recalled seeing Superintendent Thomas C. Hart bolt out of his quarters while the cameras were rolling, halt the costly production, and insist that the incorrectly designed "Hollywood" uniforms be changed. Romance blossomed in front of the camera, as well as behind the scenes. Midshipman Kauffman, USNA Class of 1933, "courted" the charming heroine of the movie, Betty Furness. Rear Admiral Kauffman later related:

> [Betty Furness] was the heroine and she was then, I think, about eighteen or nineteen. Her mother came down with her as chaperone and they stayed at the old Peggy Stewart Inn, right outside the main gate, where my mother was living. The two mothers met and got to know each other and, as a result, I was the only one allowed to date Betty. Well, dating a movie star! I thought that was the height of something and, believe it or not, I gave Betty my miniature [class ring]. I've never seen it since. I've been tempted to write her a note or call her since I started seeing her in Westinghouse ads! But it was a very amusing climax to my Naval Academy career.[244]

Shipmates Forever, from 1935, also involved mids and romance. This movie, as with most of the films made on the Yard, fascinated the residents and disrupted life at the Academy during its production. The Reverend Father Alister C. Anderson, USNA Class of 1946 (son of Rear Admiral Anton B. Anderson, Class of 1912) recalled his involvement in the movie:

> I suppose the most exciting event that occurred when I lived as a boy on Upshur Road was the making of a Hollywood movie . . . starring Dick Powell and Ruby Keeler. All of the residents of those quarters were

invited to sit in the reviewing stands in order to simulate the crowd that would be attending the June Week Ceremonies when the USNA Superintendent would present the colors to the winning company commander's "Color Girl." All of the older children who sat in the stands for many hours in the hot summer sun received the huge sum of $5.00. I recall those years with great happiness and joy.[245]

Another movie in 1935, *Annapolis Farewell*, featured Sir Guy Standish. Three more in 1937 – *Navy Blue and Gold* with the all-star cast of James Stewart, Lionel Barrymore, and Robert Young; *Annapolis Salute*, about a romance and June Hops; and *Hold 'Em Navy*, rounded out the spate of Hollywood offerings of Academy life during those first few decades of the twentieth century. The glitter and glamour of the silver screen reinforced the sentiment that this was indeed an extraordinary, enchanted place to live.

CHAPTER SIX: THE WORLD WAR II YEARS

A Chaplain for All Seasons

On the Yard where families come and go on a frequent basis, one of the most constant and welcome figures for two decades was that of Chaplain (Rear Admiral) William Nathaniel Thomas. From 1924 to 1928, he served as Assistant Chaplain, and from 1933 to 1945, he was Head or Chief Chaplain. For many years, Chaplain Thomas's presence helped to bolster Academy residents during the turbulent, heart-breaking years prior to and during World War II.

Chaplain Thomas's son, Dr. William N. Thomas, Jr., shared his memories of being a child on Bowyer Road and later Porter Road while his father was stationed on the Yard.

> Our family entertained many people there, including midshipmen and their "drags," some of whom from out of town stayed with us, as did many distinguished men who came to address the midshipmen in the Chapel and at Bancroft Hall.
>
> The Reverend Peter Marshall, on December 7, 1941, had prepared a sermon, but told my father that he had an impulse to speak on an entirely different subject, and my dad agreed. Dr. Marshall preached on the subject of death; that afternoon he heard on the radio of the Japanese attack on Pearl Harbor.[246]

Chaplain Thomas's wife, Martha Ellen Fondren Thomas, also recounted this story. She noted that the famous theologian, Peter Marshall, had dinner at their house on 12 Porter Road following the sermon. He stated that he felt like something momentous was about to happen. Within a few minutes they heard that Pearl Harbor had been attached. The Academy gates were locked immediately; the United States was at war. Years later, in 1955, the biographical movie, *A Man Called Peter*, featured Reverend Marshall's stirring sermon given that fateful day in 1941 at the Naval Academy Chapel.

Among the many notable projects that Chaplain Thomas accomplished in his years here was arranging for the extension of the Chapel nave in 1940, giving the church the shape of a Roman cross. He considered this expansion as his greatest contribution to the Academy. The enlarged Chapel could accommodate 2500 people rather than 1500. Chaplain Thomas's spirit continues to touch the lives of midshipmen in a more intangible way; he composed the beautiful *Midshipmen's Prayer* that serves to inspire his beloved students today.

Chaplain Thomas was a man of many accomplishments, but he also focused his warm attentions on the midshipmen and residents who needed his support. His kindly manner was held in esteem by the Randolph King family. Rear Admiral King and his wife, Margie, were married by Chaplain Thomas during the war years. Later, they came back to Annapolis for the christening of their children by him. Dressed in his white robe for christenings, Chaplain Thomas was an imposing and radiant figure, with prominent white teeth and white hair. After christening their second child, Bill, in the late 1940s, the Chaplain came down from the dais to embrace the family. The King's oldest son Randy, Jr., looked up at the man in white and exclaimed, "Is that God?!"

Chaplain Thomas left the Naval Academy to become Chief of Chaplains of the Navy in Washington, D. C., and attained the rank of Read Admiral. Both he and his family left a legacy to the Academy and Annapolis. His son, Dr. William Thomas, Jr., wrote:

> Incidentally, Thomas Walk is named after my father; it extends from the Administration Building via the front of the Chapel, to the Superintendent's quarters.
>
> After my early retirement from the Navy as a result of being disabled in action while serving as a Battalion Surgeon with the Marine Corps in Okinawa, I spent most of my professional life in the Annapolis area.[247]

Dr. William N. Thomas, Jr. related that he was the first radiologist in Annapolis and Anne Arundel County, Maryland.

War-Time Activities in Annapolis

Annapolis was home to many Navy families during the war years. There was a support system here for wives and children, and many homes on Duke of Gloucester and King George Streets became apartments for small families. Volunteering as well as bridge, poker, and mahjong games kept the young women busy. They needed an abundance of diversions; every night another widow was made somewhere in Annapolis.

Margie Corn King volunteered as a Mariner Scout troop leader, the girl's counterpart of Sea Scouts. Her troop participated in JANGO, the Junior Army-Navy Guild Organization, to help with the war effort. JANGO girls wore red and white pinstripe blouses and blue jumpers. Her other volunteer efforts included sending letters daily, rolling bandages, and making "Bundles for Britain" before our country's involvement in the war.

Rosemary Rutt lived as a young girl with her parents, Captain and Mrs. Burnice L. Rutt, at 47 Rodgers Road during the war years from 1942 to 1943. Captain Rutt was from the USNA Class of 1924. As a twelve and thirteen year old, she assisted with King's JANGO project by rolling bandages in the library, collecting money for the Red Cross, and ushering at the old Circle Theatre in town for the benefit of the Navy Relief.

Rutt had vivid memories of the volunteering spirit at the Academy during her young years here. She recalled that on top of the Maryland Inn, teenagers and adults worked as "Air Spotters." They searched the sky with binoculars for airplanes, consulted charts for each plane's profile, and called a central office to report their findings.

Naval Academy families also assisted with the war efforts in personal ways. The residents were asked to place a three minute time limit on all phone calls. Rutt's family had an egg timer beside the telephone as a reminder. "Victory Gardens" also sprung up around the Academy. Vegetables were raised in backyards, and a large garden was provided on the Naval Station near the rifle range where the "big stuff" such as corn and potatoes were grown. There were no coupons for gas, so residents stayed close to the Yard.[248]

An Annapolis resident, Jane Wilson McWilliams, also recalled Red Cross efforts during the war:

> During the Second World War my mother belonged to the Red Cross and the Red Cross ladies ran a cafeteria in the golf course building – the Naval Academy Golf Course which was where the swimming pool and the townhouses are now.
>
> It was used during the war by the Red Cross to serve meals to service personnel attached to the academy. My mother would take me there sometimes with her to work. I was kept back in the kitchen or allowed to run around outside while they were serving. Sometimes other women brought their children and we would be allowed to go out on the golf course and run. I don't remember it being a real golf course with greens. I didn't know what they were at the time. They were just places where there was sand that was fun to jump in. I didn't ever see anybody playing on it, but I remember that it was beautiful and green.[249]

In addition to the tremendous amount of volunteering on the Yard during the war years, there was also top-notch entertainment. Nationally known "talent" bolstered the Navy Reserves at the Academy. Art Lund, who sang with Benny Goodman and appeared in *A Most Happy Fellow* was at the Academy, and performed in his spare time. The Navy Relief shows were extravaganzas, composed and directed by a Reserve dentist, Commander Clay Boland. Margaret Corn King also volunteered her talents by singing and dancing with the traveling Navy Relief shows, among them the popular and professional *Sea Legs*.[250]

As during the Spanish-American war, prisoners were brought to Annapolis, but this time the residents were not as cordial. From 1943 to 1946, German prisoners of war could be seen around the grounds of the Yard with an armed Marine guard. Working in neat fatigues, they served as grounds keepers, and were billeted at the Naval Station. Margie King remembered them as handsome young men. She felt sorry for them, and would always give them a smile.[251]

Children's Stories

The children were affected by the war years, and spent time volunteering, but they also had their daily dose of normal activities and mischief. Sally Marable Camm lived as a child in a Perry Circle Apartment in 1943, and also at 35 Upshur Road from 1944 to 1945. Her father is Captain Herbert H. Marable, USNA Class of 1930. She recalled what an exciting time it was for a 12 year old girl. The mids were "gorgeous" and she could watch them out of her window on the center line of Worden Field. Her third floor room was like a sanctuary, too far upstairs for her parents to bother her.

Camm attended school at Miss Woodward's Private School on Southgate Avenue, which had first through eighth grades for both boys and girls. Because it was "war time," Sally found Annapolis to be a quiet town. She remembered it as being "tiny" and "run down" in those days.

Her most vivid memory of the war years on Upshur Road was of a private battle in her own kitchen. Her mother called on the phone for her to start cooking dinner. The quarters had a big old gas stove with two ovens. She turned the oven on, lit a match for it, and nothing happened. Realizing that she was trying to light the wrong oven, she quickly put the match into the other one. It exploded and blew the door off. Luckily, she was not injured, except for her pride.[252]

Simon Pendleton Fullinwider, Jr., as a child at 11 Porter Road during the war, received a heavenly gift delivered to his front door. His mother, Adelaide Fullinwider (Mrs. Simon P.J. Fullinwider) was walking toward Gate #3 down Maryland Avenue one day with Mrs. Thomas O. Cullins, Jr., a resident of Rodgers Road Homes.[253] A big police dog began sniffing around her feet, and she motioned for it to leave. Further down the street, it approached her again. When she reached the gate, the jimmylegs asked, "Is this dog yours?" She replied, "No," and they shooed it away. When she arrived at home, the same dog was on her porch waiting for her. Her son, a ten year old, saw the dog and exclaimed excitedly, "Mother, look what God has sent me!" Of course she had to keep the pooch. They named the dog 'Totsin," which means "ring the bell" in navy terms, and for the next eight years, Totsin loyally guarded their door and alerted the Fullinwider family of any visitors.[254]

Rosemary Rutt was frequently awakened late at night by the train that ran behind her house on Rodgers Road, beside College Creek, and into the Academy. The train cars coupled-up and changed tracks outside of her sister's bedroom, making an awful racket.

A more pleasant childhood memory for Rutt was of sleep-over parties. She and her friends camped out on the screened sleeping porch that jutted from the side of the house on the second floor. Both the train and the old sleeping porches are now gone. The train is no longer needed to transport building supplies and coal to the campus. The sleeping porches were difficult to maintain, and were removed in 1981.

Homoja Village

In the early 1940s, the population of the Naval Academy swelled to greater numbers because of war-time training and an enlarged military. To meet this immediate need for housing, the Academy prescribed a rapid remedy. Dome shaped Quonset Huts quickly mushroomed over the wooded landscape south of the Academy. The tract of land which is now identified as Rowe Boulevard was once filled with corrugated metal semi-circular "homes" which lined streets known as "Walnut," "Mimosa," "Elm," "Cypress," "Birch," "Grape," "Hickory," "Ivy," "Fir," and "Pine." Similar to the bungalows, these homes were installed on a temporary basis. The huts were assigned to transient officers and enlisted personnel assigned to ships in port.

The first development of Quonset quarters consisted of 100 huts. Ninety of the smaller huts supplied 180 apartments. The additional ten larger, or "elephant huts," were used for laundry, administration, and shop buildings. The area developed its own identity, and became known as "Homoja Village."

The word "Homoja" was made from a composite of letters from the last names of famous naval officers. "Ho" was taken from Admiral Frederick Joseph Horne, USNA Class of 1899, who had lived in 32 Upshur Road as a Lieutenant Commander in 1911. In 1942, he was appointed Vice Chief of Naval Operations. "Mo" was from Admiral Ben Moreell, who was Chief of the Bureau of Yards and Docks in the early 1940s. Admiral Moreell began the Seabees, and there is a memorial for him located behind Bancroft Hall. "Ja" was from Vice Admiral Randal Jacobs, USNA Class of 1907, who was Chief, Bureau of Navigation in 1941.

After the war, the huts remained. The need for housing in Annapolis was so great, that officers from the area made special requests to be assigned to Homoja Village. In 1945, Lieutenant John P. Henner wrote the Housing Officer:

> We have been searching for suitable quarters in Annapolis for the past two months with no success. At present we are living in an isolated area on South River. My wife is employed as a case worker by the Anne Arundel County Welfare Board in Annapolis. We have no automobile. Transportation for both my wife and myself from home to work or to a shopping district is a serious problem....[T]he Naval bus running from Homoja Village would solve my wife's [problem.][255]

Quarters for Lieutenant Henner and his wife were approved. They rented an apartment in one of the huts for $1.00 per day.

Post Graduate students and their families also filled the metal apartments after the war. Because of the growing demand for quarters, in 1946, more family units were installed. By 1947, there were three Quonset hut developments: Village #1 consisting of 180 units, Village #2 with 120 units, and Village #3 with 160 units. Some huts had been placed on the North Severn side of the Naval complex near the Naval Station. "Temporary" Homoja Village had grown into a sizable town.

After the war, Naval Academy volunteerism was still high, and war tragedies continued to touch residents' hearts. Under the leadership of Mrs. Robert Trudel and Mrs. J.L. Poritz, the women of Homoja Village collaborated in 1946 to assist the war-torn population in Europe. They collected clothing for the American Relief for France. A notice was sent to residents from the wives and approved by Superintendent T.R. Wirth, which read:

> The destitution and suffering of the peoples of reclaimed Europe stand in bleak relief to the way of life we know. Spanish refugees are wrapping their babies in newspapers - French children are using burlap bags for shoes – Not one person in Yugoslavia has a complete suit of clothing – In Warsaw the living have dug their own graves.
>
> This is an appeal for you to help alleviate this suffering. . . . We are asking you to give as much as you can – trousers, shirts, underwear, sleeping garments, blankets, sheets, and towels. Children's clothing and shoes are high on the list.
>
> . . . .All hands possessing clothing for contribution are requested to leave the clothing at Laundry Building No.2, Dogwood and Spruce Streets, In Homoja Village. . . .[256]

In May 1951, the Quonset huts began to be vacated for two reasons: the Post Graduate School was being moved to Monterey, California, and the State of Maryland wanted to build Rowe Boulevard, the grand entrance to Annapolis through that tract of land. In the late 1990s, a few of the larger rusting Quonset huts were still used as storage sheds and shops. Behind the fence across County Road, near the old stables and the Gardener's House, they are sad reminders of the "war to end all wars."

1945: Celebrating One Hundred Years

Street celebrations and giant dancing Conga lines, bands playing among fluttering flags and drifting confetti – with much fanfare towns across America honored soldiers and sailors returning from World War II in 1945. Amidst the national jubilee, the Naval Academy staged a week-long celebration of its 100th Anniversary in October of that year.

Of this 100 year old institution and its Annapolis home, Hanson W. Baldwin of the *New York Times Magazine*, October 7, 1945 edition wrote:

> The old town of Annapolis, cramped, crowded and colonial, still shoulders the Naval Academy's walls. The old brick sidewalks are as uneven now as they were twenty years ago, though worn and trampled by the hurrying feet of countless thousands of midshipmen, many of whom as commissioned officers of the United States Navy have made history or have sacrificed their lives in this war. . . .
>
> The homes of Annapolis . . . still look down upon the future admirals. There are still the afternoon "tea fights" in the shabby elegance of Carvel Hall. On Maryland Avenue, a street trod by many of the country's greatest seamen, jewelers, tailors and haberdashers. . .welcome today, as they did when Nimitz and Halsey were midshipmen, a new generation of future officers. The environment and the setting of the Academy seem unchanging and unchangeable.
>
> **There is, too, within the Academy's walls a strange sense of timelessness, which is, one realizes, an inherent part of the tradition – the tradition of sea and of ships, the tradition of valor and of service – which forms so large a part of any naval training worth its salt.**[257]

With the memory of the war still fresh at the Academy, the anniversary was begun on October 7, 1945, with a memorial service for alumni who had died in the line of duty in the past 100 years. Rear Admiral Thomas, United States Navy Chief of Chaplains, declared for those attending in the Chapel, that:

> **. . .[T]he sacrifices of academy alumni who died in the line of duty make every inch of these grounds, on which they once walked, hallowed earth.**[258]

Following the service, informal receptions were held.

On October 10th, a parade on Worden Field honored graduates, and included color guards in costumed replicas of the 1845, 1870, and 1900 uniforms. The early uniforms, much more flamboyant than today's, sported white trousers, blue Eton jackets with gold buttons, and jaunty straw sailor hats set with waving blue ribbons.

On the evening of the parade, residents and other Academy guests gathered at Memorial Hall for a banquet to continue the celebrations. Rear Admiral Wat Cluverius from the USNA Class of 1896, a former Upshur and Blake Row resident, was the guest speaker.

The midshipmen and their drags celebrated in the usual fashion:

Topping off the events on a social note, the midshipmen had their fling at a ceremonial hop where the girls wore hoopskirts and bustles.

The lowly, unprivileged plebes sat watching enviously.[259]

PART III: MID TWENTIETH CENTURY TO EARLY TWENTY-FIRST CENTURY: Dancing to a Different Tune

CHAPTER ONE: THE MIDDLE YEARS OF THE TWENTIETH CENTURY

The Final Housing Development: Arundel Estates

After the war, Congress wanted affordable housing for people returning from overseas military posts. Developers were encouraged to build new apartments and homes, known as the Senator Wherry Projects. On the site of the old golf course by the Severn River, modern townhomes were built to accommodate the burgeoning Academy population in 1950, and were known as the "Wherry Project Homes" or Arundel Estates. Across the river at the Naval Station, the "Severn River Homes" were built for enlisted personnel and families. First priority for assignment to the townhomes was given to families displaced by the removal of Homoja Village.

Managed by a private company, Arundeland, Inc., the townhouses on the South Severn side were offered as rentals, especially for Post Graduate students and families. As noted in a memo from that time, "The Navy's responsibility in a Wherry Project. . . is limited primarily to one of referring eligible tenant applicants to the project management." Much to the dismay of the property management company, the PG School was moved the next year to California, and this "god-send" of additional housing became difficult to fill. For the first time in Academy history, housing was overly abundant.

Commander Robert O. Clark, USNA Class of 1946, wrote of his short time spent in Arundel Estates:

> My wife Barbara and I were the first paying residents of 12 Sellers Road, Arundel Estates. This happened in early July, 1951. I was a first-year student at the Naval Post Graduate School. Most unpleasantly for us, this school was soon relocated to Monterey, California, and we had to move out in December, 1951.
>
> The reason it was 'most unpleasant' for us to leave was because living there was very enjoyable. . . . Our neighbors were generally in our age group and very friendly. Also, there was the camaraderie of first-time "settlers." The one bedroom "house" was pleasantly large enough for the two of us and still cozy. Other amenities such as the PG School, pool, hospital, Naval Academy, commissary, etc. were quite convenient. . . .
>
> There were some minor downside factors. One was the clothes-drying situation. Outside clothes poles/racks were verboten. Supposedly it was because of "décor." There was an inadequate number of dryers in the adjacent building's basement. Someone promulgated a "watch list," which listed the assigned times for each dwelling, which was often inconvenient.[260]

Indeed, the property managers were concerned with the appearance of the grounds around Arundel Estates and were sensitive about their reflection on the local community. The "clothes-drying issue" was addressed in a memo to residents:

It is regret that we cannot permit any outside drying. . . Arundel Estates is located at the entrance to historic Annapolis, and consideration must be given to the general public as to the outward appearance of the apartment buildings.[261]

The Wherry experiment of independent management was not a success at the Academy. In 1963, Arundel Estates became the sole responsibility of Navy Housing. In the late twentieth century, these 98 townhomes, some overlooking the Severn River, were billeted for junior officers and senior enlisted families. After over 100 years of continual expansion and building at the Naval Academy, Arundel Estates was the last officers' quarters to be built.

Time has not altered the picturesque setting of these homes. A resident in 1993, (Mrs. Craig M. Diffie) depicted the idyllic experience of living at Arundel Estates. She wrote:

We had the good fortune of being assigned a house on the end of a fourplex unit facing the Severn River and the Old Severn River Bridge. We had a "House with a View." Our front yard consisted of a huge field that ran along the river bank to the Old Annapolis Road. We knew our sons would relive many of the adventures of Huckleberry Finn and Tom Sawyer all over again, and they surely did.

. . . Sitting out front in our Adirondack chairs looking over the Severn River is one of our fondest memories of life at USNA. We enjoyed so much watching the sailboats go by, or the crew team glide by in their shells with the faint sound of the coach's voice echoing off the water. Sometimes we could hear the yells and cheers of midshipmen coming from Hospital Point where they were competing in one of the many sporting events.

When we first moved to Sellers Road, we read in the newspaper the controversy surrounding the construction of the 80 foot high bridge to replace the Old Severn River Bridge. Surely, we thought, this would not happen while we were living in Annapolis. Within six months the earth was being redesigned and we were able to witness firsthand the building of a high bridge!

After becoming settled, it's the neighbors that really help to make a USNA tour memorable. We had some wonderful neighbors. . .It was a safe environment and everyone basically looked after one another. We miss the ability to let the children run out the door and into a field of fun. . . . We miss the BBQs and wonderful crab feasts. We miss the camaraderie of knowing we were all one family working for the same great school. I miss standing outside watching my children enjoy themselves playing with their friends while I talked with my good friends. . . .

Undeniably, it was an Ozzie and Harriet existence, but it was an experience I would relive in a heartbeat.[262]

Annapolis – Academy Relations

Annapolis and the Naval Academy enjoyed a relatively happy century-old marriage by the mid 1940s. They grew and developed together through the decades. In the latter part of the twentieth century, however, several policies and directions taken by the Naval Academy affected the delicate relationship with the town and the integration of the military into the local community. At one point, the grande dame, Annapolis, was no longer willing to be gracious about property acquisitions, and considered her marriage to the Academy as being on shaky ground.

During war-time, Annapolis was especially supportive of the military families, but once the war was over, the two great entities engaged in their own skirmishes. And the battle lines were drawn along an issue of the heart for the city: the historic preservation of Annapolis.

Following World War II, with patriotic exuberance, the Naval Academy again wished to continue the tradition of expansion. But land mass was limited on one side by the river and harbor, and on the other by the city of Annapolis. A proposal was made to purchase and raze the nearly 200 year old St. John's College, which was conveniently adjacent to the Academy. Agitated businessmen were afraid that unless the city complied with the wishes of the Naval Academy, the entire school would be lured to broader spaces on the west coast, thus ruining the dependent economy of Annapolis. Therefore, the Chamber of Commerce was willing to sacrifice the age-old traditional liberal arts college, a backbone of Annapolitan culture, to the Navy.

But the ire of the townspeople was raised, and a formidable battle ensued. Evangeline Kaiser White, an Annapolitan embroiled in the combat, wrote of her first-hand experiences:

> . . . [T]he defenders of our heritage. . . was a group of women of Annapolis of which I was privileged to be one. We joined forces with the St. John's group and waged a fight so fierce and far-reaching that the attention of people in almost every state in the union was attracted to it and in sympathy with it by way of the press or through personal letters written by our people.[263]

St. Clair Wright, a nationally known Annapolis historic preservationist who also had strong Naval Academy roots, recalled the fervently fought battle pitched by the townspeople of that time. She wrote:

Private individuals without assistance from the state, county or city formed a militant group and successfully opposed the Naval Academy's plans, thus emphasizing the role of the private sector in Annapolis preservation.[264]

Annapolis won. She kept her heritage, her dignity, St. John's College – and the Naval Academy. This fight added strength and legitimacy to the preservation struggles the city met during the following decades. And the Academy has been "kept in its place" ever since.

Another Annapolis resident, Missy Weems Dodds, also recalled this mighty struggle between the Academy and the townspeople, and other factors which created a chasm between the military and the local people. She observed:

> Until the forties, most Navy families lived in the residential neighborhoods of Annapolis. The. . . post graduate students, and retired officers and families were a large and influential part of the community and

there was a lively exchange with the "old families" and St. John's. In fact I would be hard put to name an "old family" that didn't have a Navy connection through marriage.

With the war came expansion and a terrible housing shortage. The Navy built a large apartment complex for quarters. The impact was irreversible. The Academy became sort of an isolated compound, and when further expansion plans of the USNA included taking St. John's or the two blocks from King George to Hanover, a lot of strong feelings were generated from Navy-connected locals and historic preservationists.

The loss of the Post Graduate School, the moving of USNA's Main Gate from Maryland Avenue, the decline of Carvel Hall (Paca House) as the social center. . . these things and many more had an impact on the city. . . .[265]

Other factors led to the growing distance between the people of Annapolis and the Academy. Prior to the 1970s, midshipmen were required to attend worship services on the weekends. Streams of mids flowed from the gates on Sundays to participate in local church-related activities. One Annapolitan remarked that the midshipmen in their handsome uniforms were an integral part of her church's life, often volunteering and also serving as ushers in the church services. Getting to know the townspeople at church, the midshipmen were involved in the lives of the Annapolitans on a personal level. But in 1973, following a legal suit brought about by six midshipmen and an Army cadet, the requirement for service academy students to attend church was rescinded. Many mids subsequently chose to stay in their dormitories on Sunday mornings. This significant opportunity to interact with the community was lost.

Mid Twentieth Century Life and Traditions

The war was over, and life at the Academy fell into a steady peace-time rhythm. For many residents, the years after the war were a time to become acquainted with normalcy. Vice Admiral Eli T. Reich, USNA Class of 1935, was assigned to teach at the Academy in 1946. Of his time here he remarked:

Of course, we got quarters and really this was my first shore duty and I don't have to tell you what duty at the Naval Academy is like – but it was pleasant – in terms of amenities and it was really the first time that I'd lived a normal life with my wife. . . .[266]

Vice Admiral Reich was a famous submariner, and became Deputy Assistant Secretary of Defense.

Phyllis Hammond Howard (Mrs. James H. Howard), who attended the Navy Junior School as a child, returned to the Academy with her husband in 1947, and lived on Upshur Road. She remembered the houses, then nearly 60 years old. She said:

It is an added pleasure to have had that opportunity for the houses are so beautiful, spacious, and comfortable, and I'll never have the luxury of back stairs, porches, an enormous kitchen, a butler's pantry and a walk-in closet, in addition to a large third floor.

Our three years are nice to look back on and it is interesting that eight members of 1930 [Class] were all living on the row while we were there. Parade days were always special and the sound of the band in the distance meant the midshipmen on parade would soon be on the field. In summer we even crabbed from the seawall and one afternoon we fished young George Seay out with the crab net after he fell in.[267]

Dorothea Caldwell (Mrs. H. Howard Caldwell), who lived in Number 9 Porter Road from 1948 to 1951 remarked about the one distinguishing feature of Navy housing: that the quarters all looked alike. She wrote:

The Walter Prices moved in. Like some of the occupants, their little Scottie had trouble finding his home and in the beginning would come to our front door. . . .

Needless to say the whole family loved Annapolis, but I wonder how I survived – four floors with just a cleaning woman once a week, no dishwasher, and lots of company. The answer is I was younger![268]

Lucille Pauli (Mrs. Robert H. Pauli) visited the Academy as a Navy "drag" from 1936 to 1940. She married a midshipman, Robert Pauli, USNA Class of 1940, and later, in 1956, her family moved into a Rodgers Road home. She remembered:

My husband and three daughters moved us into 47 Rodgers while I was in the Naval Academy Hospital with my new born son for a week.

It was a wonderful three years at the Academy. As a Navy drag from 1936 to 1940. . . .I never dreamed I'd be living in this wonderful old house. . . . [O]ur quarters were redecorated and carpeted. The garden was maintained by the Academy gardeners. If we needed new light bulbs they were replaced for us. At Christmas huge trees were delivered to us. Wood was piled in the garden for our fireplaces by the Navy. Shadow boxes were placed in the front hall windows. . .the midshipmen would judge the shadowbox Christmas decorations. I won with two papier mache angels!

There were six Class of 1940 graduates in quarters, so we had many parties.

Captain [Eugene B.] Fluckey [later Rear Admiral] was chairman of the building fund for the Navy Stadium and my husband was his assistant.

The King of Saudi Arabia was visiting the Academy. He was very generous giving watches to everyone he met, so we hoped he would give a donation to the Stadium fund. We made boxes with Arabic lettering and placed them in various places he might visit, hoping for a donation. (We never received one).

The hops at the Academy were all formal – full dress for officers. The Masqueraders' musicals and plays and the boxing matches required formal tailcoat uniforms. It was always a problem for my husband to know "what to do with the tails" when sitting down in Mahan Hall and at the boxing matches.[269]

Guests and Christmas traditions were also remembered by Edith Neese (Mrs. William Gordon Neese). In 1956, on the second day after moving into quarters at 31 Upshur Road, they had official house guests. They continued to have guests for 14 more weekends in a row.

The Christmas tradition mentioned by Mrs. Pauli was also recalled by Mrs. Neese. The Naval Academy Garden Club sponsored a popular Christmas competition for the residents in the 1950s. Public Works delivered large boxes to fit the front hall windows of each house. The residents then decorated the box with a Christmas theme. They were judged by midshipmen, and the winners received red and blue ribbons.[270]

As a member of the Naval Academy Garden Club, Mrs. Neese initiated a Junior Garden Club for boys and girls in 1954. The Junior Club remained active for several years at the Academy.

Naval Academy Garden Club

The aesthetic beauty of the grounds gives the Naval Academy the perfect setting for its genteel lifestyle and its air of romance. Supporting this tradition of elegance, Edith Neese as well as many other residents of the Naval Academy channeled their artistic and creative talents into the Naval Academy Garden Club, which was organized in 1934, and federated in 1953. At one time, the Garden Club was restricted to wives of active duty military officers, and hosted highly competitive flower shows. Later in the twentieth century, membership was opened to any woman with Service or Naval Academy connections.

The Garden Club, in addition to being an educational resource for women interested in horticulture and environmental issues, has offered the energy and expertise of its members to assist in the beautification of the Naval Academy grounds. Many of the ornamental plantings and landscape groupings around monuments, along walls, and at gate entrances around the Academy and at the Naval Station have been designed and donated by these dedicated women. As recalled by Ann Snell (Mrs. William H. Snell), NAGC president in 1972:

> Every November the Naval Academy Garden Club would plant tulips in the beds down in front of the Chapel. The gardeners would prepare the soil, the Academy paid for the bulbs, and we ladies did the planting. Invariably, the chosen planting day was always cold, and on several occasions, I can remember it sleeting. No wonder I now have very creaky knees![271]

The Snell family lived at 4-C (formerly D-3) Perry Circle from 1969 to 1974.

For decades, the Garden Club has decorated for Christmas around the Yard, with members gathering in the basements of Porter Road, Upshur Road or Rodgers Road Homes around Thanksgiving, snipping, wiring, and skillfully arranging branches, leaves, and red berries to prepare for the extensive "hanging of the greens." In springtime, the Club has provided colorful May baskets for the gates, in conjunction with the long-standing Annapolis May Day Celebration.

The Academy Chapel also benefited from the efforts of these ladies. Snell remembered:

> The Sunday flower arrangements for the altar in the main chapel and the small chapel downstairs were done by ladies from the Garden Club and Chapel Guild. We would choose a design from books [with] photos of past displays or create a new design. [We would] order the flowers, then on Saturday morning or afternoon do the arrangements. As chairman one year, it was my duty to return to the Chapel at "0" dark-hundred on Sunday mornings to ensure that all flowers and arrangements were still in excellent condition – not easy if one had been out late the night before.[272]

To support their considerable projects around the Yard, cheerful, bright yellow mum corsages with blue ribbons were made on the screen porches of Parade Field homes, and sold at the football games to raise money. From the greenhouse near the hospital, the Club offered potted chrysanthemums to residents in the fall, poinsettias at Christmas-time, and annual flowers for planting in the spring. Creating a new tradition in 1988, the Garden Club began sponsoring an Easter Parade for children. The youngsters wore flower-adorned bonnets or rode their brightly decorated bicycles around the walkways of the park in front of the Chapel. With giggles and sly glances, they would chase a lively seven-foot tall Easter bunny along the paths. The women of the Naval Academy Garden Club support a long-standing tradition of colorful, creative service to the Academy.

Other Residents Remember the Old Homes

Jean Grkovic, a resident of Number 50 Rodgers Road from 1957 to 1959, was the busy president of the Garden Club during her stay at the Academy. She had many fond memories of life on the Parade Field. Mrs. Grkovic was married to Captain George Grkovic, USNA Class of 1943.

When the Grkovic family moved into their quarters, the previous residents sold them a large, carved piano for $25 because it was too heavy to move. In turn, when they left, they sold it to the next family. Mrs. Grkovic visited her former home ten years later, and the piano was still being passed down by residents. The piano disappeared from the quarters sometime before the 1990s.[273]

The family of Captain Asbury Coward, III, USNA Class of 1938, lived in three homes at the Naval Academy. Their first tour was on Perry Circle and Upshur Road. Captain Coward's wife, now Jean Coward Mason, recounted her unique experiences as the wife of the Superintendent's Aide in the late 1940s, and of their return to the Academy years later. She wrote:

Red [Asbury] became Aide to [Vice] Admiral Hill and [Rear] Admiral Holloway. Our boys were about three and seven. They loved sleeping on the sleeping porch with their friends and rushing to the parade grounds every time a parade started.

Our days were busy and exciting and I remember a friend telling me that you could always tell an Aides's wife by the white gloves over the bathtub. I also remember the guilt and horror I felt one Sunday morning as we drove in comfort to the Chapel with the Holloways and looked out the car window to see Sandy with his new trousers pinned up – walking through the rain to Sunday school.

In 1959 we returned to the Naval Academy and lived at 16 Porter Road. What a wonderful time that was! We had brought a miniature grey poodle named Beau home from duty in London. Beau loved grabbing young ladies' stockings when they were visiting and running merrily down the stairs from the third floor with the girls in hot pursuit. He also led the Easter procession up the main aisle of the Chapel one Easter Sunday morning as we watched in shock.

Our bedrooms were seldom empty. Curt would bring his friends from St. Andrews, and midshipmen, parents, dates and friends kept the house filled. It was a delight.

Now Sandy [Asbury Coward IV, USNA Class of 1964] is in 6 Porter Road [in the 1990s] and we are enjoying the happiness he and Croom feel with their constantly filled quarters. **Memories flood my mind every time I return to that treasured road. And so it will continue for all of those who were and will be privileged to be a part of the legacy.**[274]

Residents of Academy homes have been all over the world, and their décor is always varied, reflecting the different overseas duty stations. Anne C. Madden (Mrs. John C. Madden) recalled decorating their house in Number 43 Upshur Road in the early 1960s. "At that time the house was partially furnished and we completed it with our furnishings. Having come from a tour of duty in Ankara, Turkey, we had a variety of brass and Turkish rugs."[275]

In the early days of the Academy, up to the mid-twentieth century, the residents on the Yard were provided with furniture, firewood, and gardeners. The Public Works department even employed skilled cabinetmakers and carpenters to make and maintain the furniture. By the late 1900s, occupants moved into empty, uncarpeted homes, and filled them however they could. Residents of today, unlike the families of earlier years, maintain their backyards, purchase their firewood and Christmas trees, change their light bulbs, and clean their own homes.

Living on the "50 Yard Line"

Residing in the middle of a long row of houses, all of them the same, does not seem to offer much distinction. The exception is when an officer's family lives in the center of Upshur Road, and has a proximity to the focal point of the midshipmen's regimental parades. The jubilant, colorful, and well-attended parades, which are the pride of the Academy and a gift to tourists and parents, have been reviewed by world-renown notables since the 1800s. Presidents, Congressmen, Kings, Queens, and military leaders have visited Worden Field to be honored by the passing brigade. And "50 Yard Line" residents experience the benefits and drawbacks of this special location.

Shirley H. Childs Pritchard (Mrs. C.A. Pritchard) and her former husband, Captain Donald Childs, having no previous Academy connections, quickly became enchanted and enmeshed in Academy life. She offered her experiences from the late 1960s:

> It wasn't long before our home was filled with drags and mids every week-end, holidays and any time they could come over. We "sponsored" mids before there was an official sponsor program. Among our mids were many athletes, since my husband got to know many of them at the dispensary and hospital. Among them were Roger Staubach, Skipp Orr, Pat Donnelly, Tom Lynch and many more.[276]

> Our quarters were open to any and all mids, and since Dr. Childs was Officer Rep [representative] for the Protestant Choir, we "adopted" a great many mids from the choir and glee club, and had many a song fest in our living room.

> Since our quarters were directly behind the canopy section on Worden Field, our porch was used as a temporary first aid station on Parade day, and a corpsman, with a litter and first aid kit, was stationed there.

> We seldom missed football practice and attended most away games. Coach Forzano once introduced me as an "assistant coach" at a Monday Morning Quarterback Breakfast.

> I'll never forget the blizzard of '66 which occurred on the day the mids were due back from spring leave. The Academy was closed – and some of our mids walked several miles from their stranded cars or buses. They arrived at our quarters and we dried them out and warmed them up in front of two fireplaces. Since I wasn't prepared to feed 12 or 13 mids on that day, I started calling grocery stores, but found only a 7-11 open. I made out a grocery list and several of the mids took a sled and walked to the 7-11, so I could make a huge pot of spaghetti for dinner. . . We were rewarded by having our sidewalks shoveled and cars dug out of the snow banks. It was great fun and I will always remember that day.

> Dr. Childs retired from the Navy in 1967, and became Assistant Medical Officer for Anne Arundel County. We bought an historic house near the Academy, [on Charles Street] so we wouldn't be far from the Yard and our mids, who, in true form, named our house "The Bancroft Annex."[277]

Dr. and Mrs. Donald R. Childs were examples of families who have served the Naval Academy enthusiastically with their caring involvement in the lives of midshipmen. Shirley Childs Pritchard was president of the Naval Academy Women's Club from 1966 to 1968. She helped organize the Naval Academy Tour Guide Service, and served as the Tour Guide Director for 15 years.

Marjorie Becker, wife of Rear Admiral Charles Becker, recalled living in 37 Upshur Road from 1966 to 1968. She wrote:

We always numbered those delightful days among our finest hours. The hours seemed ever filled – to bulging – with friends, midshipmen, and "drags." I _almost_ didn't mind dragging the vacuum up all those flights of stairs. The "50 yard line" location on Worden Field added a very special touch of joy.[278]

Captain and Mrs. John W. Renard also have special memories of life on the "50 yard line," at 35 Upshur Road. Captain Renard is from the USNA Class of 1955. Because of the location of their home, they were asked to provide a rest room, if needed, and communication lines for Vice President Gerald Ford when he was reviewing a parade in 1974. Donna Renard recalled the panic she felt when her closets and drawers had to be searched. The house was specially "wired" for that day, and it was filled with Secret Servicemen. The rest rooms, however, were not used by the Vice President.[279]

Children – The Bane of the Jimmylegs!

Emmie Spalding Hamilton (Mrs. Thomas J. Hamilton) lived with her family at Number 44 Upshur Road from 1946 to 1947. Rear Admiral Hamilton was from the USNA Class of 1927. She recalled many of the shenanigans of her children during their stay at the Academy. In her entertaining and detailed memoirs, _My Story: Second Fiddle to a Pigskin_, she wrote:

> That summer [1947] Tommy and Bill invited Buck Buchanan to spend a weekend with us. Kack and Charley [Buchanan] were stationed in Washington, where he was aide to the Secretary of Defense, Mr. James Forrestal.[280]

> Buck was a cute freckle-faced redhead and our boys had always liked him. So did we. . . He and Bill together could dream up plenty of mischief – that we knew.

> On Friday night we took the boys to a movie at the Academy. They rode their bicycles, and we walked over and met them at the theater. After the show we walked back to our quarters, and the boys rode their bicycles ahead of us.

> Before we reached home we heard the fire engine, and saw it drive up in front of our quarters. The alarm had been set, but there was no fire to be seen. Tom sent the firemen back to the station, and went upstairs to check out his suspicions. Bill and Buck were in bed on the sleeping porch, snoring. Tom said, "Did you do it?"

> Silence.

> "_Did you do it?_"

> Both boys jumped out of bed fully clothed. "Yes sir."[281]

The Hamiltons moved to Number 7 Porter Road in 1948, and the mischief continued. Emmie Hamilton recalled:

> Tommy and Bill went out after supper with the "gang." Tom and I were reading in the living room when we heard heavy steps running down Porter Road. They ran up on our porch. There were five or six boys. . . breathing heavily. Bill, who was the spokesman said, "They used storm troop tactics!. . .All we did was climb up on the marine engineering building. We weren't doing anything wrong. Then 'they' came. They yelled at us, 'Who goes there?' We were scared and didn't answer. Then they took search lights and ladders and used storm trooper tactics."
>
> Tom calmed them down, knowing that the "jimmylegs" would soon arrive to make their report. He agreed with them that the boys were wrong, and told the police to take the necessary steps to punish them.
>
> Through all the years, Navy juniors have been the bane of the "jimmylegs" existence. I am told that Bill had an outstanding record in that department. He admitted to me that he felt a compulsive urge to outwit them.
>
> Several years later, when Bill entered the Naval Academy as a plebe, the jimmyleg at the main gate looked at him, covered his eyes, and said, "Oh, no!"[282]

Reminiscent of the time that Superintendent Porter became annoyed with Robert Means Thompson's fish horn, Jean Grkovic told of her son's short-lived accompaniment to the famous Navy Band in the late 1950s. Commander (later Captain) and Mrs. George Grkovic were under the canopy watching a parade and sitting behind Superintendent William R. Smedberg III. As the band began playing, everyone heard a loud squawking noise coming from the Grkovic house on Rodgers Road. Her son, who had been learning to play the bugle in Boy Scouts, was enthusiastically tooting along with the band from his third floor window, and it sounded terrible. Rear Admiral Smedberg turned to the horrified parents and said, "Skip hasn't gotten much better." Embarrassed, Mrs. Grkovic rose from her seat to leave, hoping to stop her son's musical attempts, when she saw the jimmylegs go up to her front porch. They quickly took care of the situation. According to Grkovic, **"The jimmylegs were like grandfathers, always looking out for the children here."**[283]

Captain Jack Renard related that while living in Upshur Road Homes in the early 1970s, their son John held the record for having his name on the jimmylegs' "list." In one incident, the security police caught him swimming in College Creek. John vehemently denied the charge and claimed his innocence, he was merely lying on a raft, propelling himself around. With only his arms in the water, how could they call that swimming?

Children on the Yard are connected through the generations. One special connection was with the Randolph King and Leon Escude families, both living in Number 50 Rodgers Road, but decades apart. Rear Admiral Randy King, who lived in the Parade Field home in the 1930s, told the Escude family about burying some money in the backyard when he was a young boy. He forgot to dig it up when the family moved. Chandler Escude and next-door neighbor Jimmy Dodge, both around age 13 in 1993, were found digging holes in the back of Number 50 Rodgers, hoping that the treasure could still be found – 60 years later!

Marylee Klunder, (Mrs. Matthew Klunder), wrote that her children added to the high pitch excitement of Army-Navy games in 2008, playing tricks on Vice Admiral Jeffrey and Mrs. Katie Fowler, the Superintendent and his wife.

> The Wednesday before the Army Navy Game of 2008, Merrick and Madeleine and I sneaked over to the carriage entrance of the Superintendent's Quarters armed with a bucket of chalk and lots of ideas! In the biting cold we worked quietly and quickly decorated the sidewalk entrance with sayings and pictures, "GO NAVY! BEAT ARMY!" The kids then "Ding Dong Ditched the Supe!" grabbing their bucket of chalk and darting off into the bushes while eyeing the door! Fortunately since it was only 6:30 and no one answered that door![284]

Countless hours and endless days are marked by children who romp around the Academy, a literal field of dreams. Beside the Parade Grounds, a marble water fountain stands to replenish and buoy the spirits of these children past and present. A memorial to the vibrant four-year-old son of Commander and Mrs. George Donald Florence, the fountain serves as recognition of the vitality shared by all youngsters who enrich Academy life. The Florence family lived in Number 34 Upshur Road.

Commander Florence recounted the inspiration behind the fountain dedication:

> One of [David's] main interests was the Navy Band on the Parade Field. He really enjoyed the music and the marching and David and his friends would march with their toy horns and drums on the side of the Parade Field. I believe that the band members enjoyed the children as much as they were enjoyed by the children.
>
> David was playing just across the street from where the fountain was placed. His heart stopped following a blow from one of his friends with whom he was wrestling. Services were held in the small Chapel and David was carried to the Cemetery with members of the USNA Band playing en route and at his burial in the Cemetery – up the hill from Hospital Point. The music I remember most is "When the Saints Come Marching Home."
>
> One or two days later – or it could have been the same day – during a June Week Parade, a lady was. . . brought to our door after having fainted at the Parade. She wanted and needed water and there was no drinking fountain.
>
> At that moment I knew I wanted to dedicate a drinking fountain there in memory of our son. The then Superintendent – Admiral Calvert – gave approval. I designed the fountain. . . drove to Vermont to have the stone cut, and brought it back in my car. Public Works installed the fountain the following spring of '70 in time for Spring Parades and June Week.

The drinking fountain on the USNA Parade Field was dedicated to all the little children who give joy but in particular to the little children who march and play as David and his friends marched and played with their toy horns and drums during practices.[285]

The memorial, which displays the figure of an engraved toy bugle and drum, eternally poised for a parade, reads:

In Memory of

The Love and Joy

Little Children Give

David Donald Florence

7 June 1963 – 30 May 1969

Top Dog – Famous Academy Resident

When Captain and Mrs. Philip J. Ryan moved into Number 35 Upshur Road in 1969, they frequently spotted a small mongrel dog prancing around the Yard, receiving privileged treatment from the residents and midshipmen. "Midshipman Dog" or "Dodo" certainly had the run of the campus.[286]

Dodo wandered into a second class midshipman's room, wet and shivering from the cold, sometime in the fall of 1966. He was toweled and fed. From that time he maintained a constant presence around Bancroft and at the daily mess in King Hall, the midshipmen's dining room.

Dodo was held in such esteem that he soon earned upper class ranking; plebes stood at attention as "Midshipman Dog" passed by. It became an honor to have him in academic classes, and professors allowed him to keep whatever timetable he chose. He attended Chapel from time-to-time, but did not express a preference for a particular religion or denomination.

Dodo did not play favorites among the midshipmen, either. He visited many different mids in their rooms. He did, however, prefer the company of mids, and would go out of his way to avoid officers, professors, and children. And even though the officers were ignored, they did not restrict his "unleashed" spirit. He enjoyed the freedom every midshipman dreamed of.

After Dodo's full acceptance around the Yard, he became a more endearing unofficial "mascot" than the regally aloof Bill-the-Goat. The Brigade had a blue and gold blanket made for Dodo, who wore it with pride to the Navy football games. Emblazoned on the blanket were the words, "Bite Army!"

When Dodo died in 1971, he was mourned by the Brigade, and received an obituary notice in the Annapolis newspaper, *The Evening Capital*. The article from March 26, 1971, stated:

> Dodo dies – A legend in his own time, Dodo, the official Naval Academy dog, died last week. The black and gold mongrel was found ill in the Yard last Friday and died later at the veterinarians' office. No one is quite sure when Dodo arrived on the Academy scene, but rumor has it that he was a turnback from the Class of '69. In classrooms where Dodo slept through countless lectures, on the parade ground where he marched with the Drum and Bugle Corps, in the midshipman mess where he took every meal and in Bancroft Hall where he slept each night, Dodo will be missed.[287]

CHAPTER TWO: SPECIAL HOUSES AND SPECIAL RESIDENTS

Athletic Directors

With Naval Academy sports being of prime importance on the Yard, Athletic Directors are always in the limelight and lead fast-paced, exciting lives. Rear Admiral Thomas J. Hamilton, USNA Class of 1927, was an All-American halfback at the Academy. He returned to coach football in 1934 and again in 1946. Hamilton became Athletic Director at the Academy in 1948. After retiring from the Navy, among many national honors, he was chosen as the Executive Director of the "Big Five" Football Conference, and received a Football Hall of Fame gold medal.

The Hamilton household, as most of those at the Naval Academy, was constantly poised for entertaining. Accepting a position and home at the Academy implies a willingness to harbor guests and host frequent parties. In an article by columnist Vince Johnson, the active, mid-century lifestyle of the Hamilton family is captured. Johnson reported:

> **Annapolis, Md., Dec.22 [1948] – A Navy wife at the Academy must have four essential attributes: charm, poise, a cupboard full of cocktail glasses and a good cook.**
>
> Mrs. Emmie Hamilton has all of them.
>
> At the Academy, the Hamiltons either are giving a dinner or just going to one. Usually it's the former. About 5:30 pm guests begin dropping in for a casual cocktail and just as casually Mrs. Hamilton tells Beatrice Hollis, her cook, to put another plate or two at the dinner table.[288]

Emmie Spalding Hamilton (Mrs. Thomas J. Hamilton) recalled some of her family's experiences on the Yard. She wrote:

> Almost every Sunday we would invite midshipmen, 4 or 6, for noon dinner. Most of ours were members of the Navy football squad because Tom was head coach, and later Athletic Director.
>
> My outstanding memory of Number 44 Upshur Road was the day of the Army-Navy baseball game in either '46 or '47. [Fleet] Admiral Halsey attended the game as guest of the Superintendent. We had known him personally for many years (his daughter Margaret and I had been schoolmates). So we invited him after the game. He accepted, and all our friends were so excited to meet him. He arrived in a

limousine with his 5-star flag flying, and stayed at our party for quite a while, mingled informally with our friends, and gave us all "something to write home about."[289]

The Hamilton family lived on Upshur Road on the Parade Field, and later on Porter Road when Tom Hamilton was Athletic Director.

Timing is an essential skill for a winning athlete. Another Athletic Director, Captain William S. Busik, USNA Class of 1943, used his finely honed sense of timing to choose the perfect years to be stationed on the Yard. Describing his active time and some of the demands of his position while residing at Number 4 Porter Road, he wrote:

> I was assigned the quarters because my duty assignments were Director of Athletics and Head of the Physical Education Department. I and my family (wife and three children) lived in the quarters from 1962 to 1965.
>
> With a daughter and two sons in high school, there was much activity at 4 Porter Road, not to mention the many entertainment requirements because of my job. Post football game receptions at the quarters called for advanced planning and "prepositioning" of food and drink.
>
> Visitors to the Academy, seeing my name on the doorsteps, did not hesitate to ring the doorbell or come in to visit and/or have a cool drink. This was great when they were old friends or shipmates, but rather awkward when they were not, thinking the government was paying the bill.
>
> The top deck was "boys town" and my two sons had a great time with their friends. They also knew the Academy well and made many midshipmen friends. What a great way for teenage boys to grow up in those surroundings! My daughter had the best of both worlds – at high school and in the Yard. She was to marry a 1964 graduate while we were stationed at the Academy. [The] wedding at the Chapel [was] followed by a reception at Carvel Hall, which at that time was owned by the Naval Academy Athletic Association.
>
> Although "boys town" was on the top deck, the basement was the scene of much activity – the pool table saw many competitive scenes, as did the ping pong table.
>
> Outdoor sleeping was available topside where a screened porch and awning gave the boys a bunk room for their guests. I note the outdoor bunk room has since been removed.
>
> It was a memorable three years – the formable years for the children and three very successful athletic years for the Academy - #2 in the nation in football and a bid to the Cotton Bowl, National Championship in lacrosse, soccer, rifle, pistol, and a Heisman trophy winner in Roger Staubach.[290]

In 1988, Athletic Director Jack Lengyel, the first civilian to hold this position at the Academy, moved into Number 4 Porter Road. Because of their children, the Lengyels already were familiar with life on the Yard. Sandy Lengyel (Mrs. Jack Lengyel) wrote:

> It was an honor and a privilege for the first civilian Director of Athletics and his wife to live at 4 Porter Road. We spent eight years visiting the Naval Academy while our sons attended. David (Lengyel) graduated in 1980, and Peter (Lengyel) in 1984.

We occupied the house from 1988 to 1993. During this time of sponsoring mids and entertaining guests, like everyone else on the street, our family had many memorable times. David became engaged in Memorial Hall at Bancroft and was married in the Chapel with many of his classmates and fellow Marines in attendance.

Peter, a P-3 aviator, also came home as often as possible with his wife and children. Daughter Julie (Lengyel) visited every year from St. Croix with her husband and son. Her youngest son was born in Annapolis bringing the total to six grandchildren. Hopefully some of them will attend USNA.

The neighbors on Porter Road are a close and caring group, and when my arthritis made knee replacement necessary, they all rallied round and kept us plied with food and company. Father Hines moved into the home when my doctor said it would be better not to climb so many stairs. By all accounts, he loved it there also. The drawing by Jack is of Father Hines and the Porter Road Girls, called, "A View from the Alley."[291] (See drawing in pictures.)

The Commandant of Midshipmen's House and Captain's Row

Assistants preparing for parties and receptions, distinguished guests visiting and staying overnight, and old friends dropping by to glimpse the historic, well-appointed Commandant's quarters at Number 14 Porter Road keep the occupants in whirlwind of activity. Add to this excitement the exuberance of a college-aged girl living in the quarters. Mary Gale Buchanan was the young daughter of the Commandant, Rear Admiral Charles Allen Buchanan, USNA Class of 1926, and lived at Number 14 Porter Road from 1952 to 1955. She has fond memories of her years there, and her recollections give some insight into the lifestyle of a busy Commandant's family. She recalled:

> Our quarters were often be-decked with SPIRIT and BEAT ARMY banners and sheets. There was a sense of excitement and history in the quarters. I can just remember the preparations and bustle before the receptions.

> I remember that it was not as much fun for my brother Buck (Class of 1956) whose father was Commandant (Rear Admiral) Charles Allen Buchanan. Buck and I have many mutual friends due to our closeness in age. His love of life caused him a fair amount of restriction-time, but he managed to have fun, none-the-less. However when Buck and classmates took off the garage door late at night, they put him back on restriction.

> I especially remember all the graciousness and love my mother expressed to all the mids. They truly loved her, and called her "Mom B" (when Dad wasn't around)!

> I respected my father and his job as Commandant and was and am very proud of all he accomplished here and throughout his Naval career, but it wasn't until later years that I learned and fully realized that with the Commandant's job goes many long days and nights agonizing over honor, academic, and conduct cases.

In the 1950s there was just as much pride and motivation within the Brigade as there exists in the 1990s. Much has changed, yet just as much has remained the same, and that to me says "all the right stuff" with our Naval Academy today. The administration, the faculty, and the coaches imbue the tenets of our mission here to the mids, who, upon graduation, do the same to those in their charge. A beautiful, lasting legacy.[292]

Mary Gale Buchanan has carried with her the pride of the Naval Academy and its mission through the years. As an Annapolis resident in the 1990s, she continued to assist the Academy through her ever-present support of the leaders, the athletics, and the midshipmen.

Another college-aged resident recalled her experiences on Porter Road in the early 1950s. Michelle Foley McDaniel (Mrs. Tim McDaniel), who lived with her parents, Captain and Mrs. Francis J. Foley on Perry Circle in her earlier years, was excited to know they would return to the Academy to live. Captain Foley was in the USNA Class of 1931. Michelle McDaniel wrote:

> We arrived in June of '52 and promptly moved into the wonderful "mansion" at Number 7 Porter Road. For a family of three, a home on Porter Road was beyond our wildest dreams.
>
> . . . My mother was hard pressed to adequately furnish this huge place. I remember that we could "borrow" art and books from the USNA Library, which we did gratefully. The library wanted to know which authors she was interested in. She replied, "I don't care, I just need six feet of red books."
>
> I was 18 when we moved there and just enrolled as a freshman at Mary Washington College. . . . To this day, I count it as one of the most incredible blessings of my life that I was privileged to live for three years on "Captains Row" at a time in my life when dating midshipmen and having friends home to stay over for dragging was the most exciting thing in the world. I was the envy of my friends. . .[293]

Another Commandant's family on the Yard from 2008 to 2010 was "The Klunder Krew!!!" – the family of Rear Admiral and Mrs. Matthew L. Klunder (Marylee). RADM Klunder, USNA Class of 1982, was the 83rd Commandant of Midshipmen.

Mrs. Klunder wrote about her experiences living at the Academy on Porter Road, and the joyful and continuing connections to USNA. It seems the whole family has collected stories to tell and savor through the coming years.

> Just as a background, my husband, Matthew and I are blessed with four enthusiastic, energetic, adventuresome and fun loving children. Michael, USNA Class 2014, Martin, Merrick, and Madeleine.
>
> On 12 May 2008, Vice Admiral Jeffrey Fowler [Superintendent and USNA Class of 1978] called Matthew and offered him the position of the 83rd Commandant of Midshipman at the United States Naval Academy! We were thrilled! Matthew took over the Commandant position on 6 June 2008! Thus began our new family adventure, a new chapter in the Klunder Krew Kronicles!

We lived at the Commandant's Quarters on 14 Porter Road from August, 2008, to August, 2009. During the summer of 2008, all the homes at the USNA were in the long process of major renovations. Due to the needed renovation of the Commandant's Quarters we moved 50 (FIFTY FEET !!!!) to 12 Porter Road. We moved from there in July 2010!

Matthew and I met on a blind date 17 August 1980. He was a Midshipmen 2nd Class at USNA, Class 1982, Company 5! We have so many memories of walking The Yard, dating back in those days.......strolling down Porter Road...... then to bring our 4 children and LIVE at USNA on PORTER ROAD was thrilling!! We have been married 23 years in 2011 – since April, 1988!!

Merrick and Madeleine (the only ones home at this moment!!) are telling stories so fast, too. . . . "Mom what about this one!?? Can we include this story?"[294]

One of the residents on Wood Road recalls the Klunder family with great affection. Mrs. John Paul Rue (Elizabeth) wrote the following story, adding to the priceless legacy of children on the Yard.

Marylee Klunder's fourth grader used to come out of their Porter Road home (Commandant's Quarters) for morning colors, toot his USNA football horn on the porch and stand at attention for colors. Then he would shout, "Go Navy - Beat Army" after colors was over! We all loved them! [295]

Mrs. Rue also recalled the Klunders feeling the brunt of mischief during the blizzards of 2009-2010. She wrote:

The midshipmen seemed to find a way to put all that snow to good use. Apparently they saw it as an opportunity to play a prank on their very good-natured, and well-liked Commandant, CAPT Matt Klunder and his wonderful wife, Marylee. They packed their front door portico with snow, so that when they opened the door, or window, all they would see was snow. It wasn't until later when Marylee noticed it was "kind of dark" in the house that they discovered the mischief.[296]

The Commandant's family has entertaining duties beyond the normal social requirements of the Yard. Marylee Klunder describes formally entertaining the midshipmen leadership and other Naval Academy leaders in Number 14 Porter Road as well as in Number 12 Porter Road, with a twenty-first century flair. Her recounting of these events held from 2008 to 2010 gives insight into how families bring their special touch to Naval Academy traditions.

I was happily surprised to learn that I was not required to set up, prepare, cook and serve the food, and clean up from these formal events! Although, along with Matthew's Secretary, Anna Ward, and the Naval Academy Club Staff, I was involved in planning the meals for these events! The members of the Superintendent's Staff, Bill and Ricky were assigned to the Commandant's Quarters to weekly clean the first floor of the house! I was forever grateful for their wonderful help! They did a fantastic job, right down to shining the brass doorknobs!

On the day of the assigned Party, a Party Rental Truck would arrive at Noon and deliver crates of dishes and glasses as well as hangers of tablecloths and napkins to the downstairs kitchen of 14 Porter or 12 Porter Road. At 4 pm five gracious members of Naval Academy Staff of would arrive to start setting up the bar on the porch, staging the upstairs and downstairs kitchen, and setting the table with linens, dishes, utensils and wooden trays. I always provided my same "Navy Blue and Gold" handmade centerpiece consisting of a simple tall copper vase overflowing with silk flowers of Navy Blue Mums, golden sunflowers and greenery. This was then highlighted with seven miniature Commandant of Midshipmen Flags that I had purchased at the Midshipmen store. Seven represented the Seven Seas of the World.

By 5:30 pm the food started arriving to the basement kitchen. Most of it was transported to the upstairs kitchen using the dumbwaiter! Anna Ward arrived to oversee all the activity! At 5:30 pm, the Commandant Combo of Musicians also arrived to set up! Tom played guitar, Blake played the piano and Nick was on Drums! It was exciting to have so many people preparing for these Parties! The Klunder Kids were thrilled at all the commotion and were constantly watching and chattering! Matthew usually arrived home from work at 6:00 pm. We were then given protocol instructions on how to greet the guests. The Mids started lining up outside the house by 6:15 pm for the 6:30 to 8:30 Party! Merrick, age 8, and Madeleine age 5, were excited to be an integral part of welcoming the Midshipmen and civilians to their home! After Matthew and I would personally welcome each guest, Madeleine would direct them to the porch and nametags. Merrick would take their coats and usher them to the appetizers and drinks on the porch! All 50 guests had arrived by 6:35 pm!

In an effort to truly be a part of the Party, and maintain our Motto of "Bloom Where You are Planted", in the weeks of preparations prior to the Parties, Martin, Merrick and Madeleine decided they wanted to perform some sort of Entertainment for these Gatherings! Inspired by the many-viewed Midshipmen Parades at Worden Field and the Drum and Bugle Corps practicing daily in front of our house on the lawn of Ward Hall, they decided that an "Informal Dress Parade" would do the honors!

The three of them worked for hours to create and perfect their Marching Musical presentation. Parade Uniforms were a must! NAVY Spirit Wear was the selected Uniform of the Day! It consisted of the following: Navy Shorts and Gray Sports related t-Shirt; fuzzy blue Spirit hats recovered from a Football Game; beaded spirit football necklaces; blue and yellow floral Leis; a belt holding several NAVY Pompoms as well as yellow and white terrible towels; navy blue and gold face paint from the Mid Store; bare feet; and each child carefully carrying their Japanese Mt. Fuji Walking Stick/Sword.

The "Guests of Honor" had been previously secretly selected by Matthew! At 1850 sharp, the Klunder Kids would identify and escort these three stunned, but honored Midshipmen to their pre-labeled seats on the couch. I had gently pulled back the blanket resting on the back of the couch to reveal their names printed on an index card! All other guests were encouraged to move to the perimeter for the room in preparation for the Entertainment!

I had written and typed a "skit" modeled after the Narrator's words read at the Midshipmen Formal Dress Parades, but with a respectful twist. At the assigned time, Madeleine marched onto the "Parade Field" in the living room, holding a small American Flag on a stick. As Madeleine proudly raised the Flag high, I announced for all guests to rise and say, "GOD BLESS AMERICA!" Other highlights woven into our Narration included interesting historical facts about the Commandant's Quarters at 14 Porter, and then later at 12 Porter Road; the impressive large painting adoring the walls of Thomas Jefferson, Admiral Farragut, and David Dixon Porter; the working dumbwaiter; the 7 non-working fireplaces; the Dining Room Sideboard from the USS Constitution; the 10 foot dining room table that is one of three library tables used by Midshipman in 1889. You can still see where a Midshipman spilled a bottle of ink! The Midshipmen lined up to sit in Admiral Farragut's Gold covered Victorian Gentleman's chair because due to legend, those Mids who sat in his chair would have "good Luck" on upcoming exams!

As I introduced the Guests of Honor, we were able to previously learn of funny things about these guests. For example, one Midshipman had a real fondness for Bagel Bites! I introduced him as being from a certain city and state and being the CEO of the Largest Bagel Bite Factory in the US!

I had given the Commandant's Combo a copy of my script so they could provide marching music at the assigned time! As my Narration continued, I introduced the "Brigade of Midshipmen." Each child decided what city and state they wanted to be from. They changed it for each "Parade" of the many parties we had! Madeleine was always the Midshipman Captain and led the March On and Pass and Review! Martin and Merrick were each Regimental Commanders! With live Marching music played by the Commandant's Combo, the Kids dressed in their Spirit Wear Uniforms, marched from the hallway, around the dining room, and into the living room, stopping before the Guests of Honor. They preformed a 7 minute well rehearsed "Midshipmen Informal Dress Parade Routine"! Madeleine gave all the appropriate orders prepared for "their Parade": "Forward March; Halt; Eyes Right; Swords; Stop; Toss" She didn't even flinch as her brothers tossed their Mt. Fuji Walking Stick "Swords" high above her head like the Silent Drill team, as she slowly and methodically walked back and forth beneath. They even completed a Pass and Review, marching in perfect unison, around the room in front of the guests and proceeding from the parade field as the music continued until they were well out of sight.

After thanking everyone for joining us "tonight for the Informal Dress Parade", I introduced the Commandant of Midshipmen, Captain Matthew Klunder. Matthew then welcomed everyone again and offered a blessing, and invited all to eat. It was only 1910. After all guests were served, the Klunder Kids got in line, and plopped themselves down next to Midshipmen and chatted away!

These parties flew by, and at 2030 sharp, the Midshipmen stood up, graciously offered their appreciation for the great evening and departed. They were serenaded out the door by Merrick playing on a large purple Spirit horn he collected at a Football Game! The Commandants Combo quietly packed up, said goodbye and left. By 2115, the Staff had cleaned up the dining room, sun porch and upstairs kitchen, transporting everything to the basement kitchen. At 2130, the Party Rental truck returned to collect the dishes and linens. The wonderful staff left at 2145. Everything was back to what it was before the party. An eerie silence fell over the first floor. Except for the lasting memories of that evening, one would never have guessed that just an hour prior those same rooms were bursting with music and boisterous conversations of over 60 people and the smells of mouth watering food! As Merrick reflectively noted, "Mom, it is like, "POOF, there is a Party, and then POOF it is GONE!" It happened that fast.[297]

Following the Klunder family in 2010, Captain Robert E. Clark II, USNA Class of 1984, continued the Commandant's tradition of leading and inspiring the midshipmen. An internet newspaper recounted Captain Clark's rally of the students on the momentous death of Osama Bin Laden. *The Huff Post College – Internet*, August 20, 2011 stated:

Commandant Captain Robert E. Clark II gave a rousing speech about the death of Osama Bin Laden to an enthusiastic crowd of students Sunday night at the U.S. Naval Academy.

"They woke a sleeping giant in 2001," Clark yelled at the crowd, "You can hit us, you can knock us down, but we are going to get up, and when we do we are going to find you and kick your a**."

The crowd then erupted in cheers and Clark lead the students in a deafening version of the U.S. Naval Academy's "I Believe" cheer.

Perhaps the Navy had cause to be extra rowdy last night. It was a team of Navy SEALS that executed the mission to kill Osama Bin Laden.

Superintendents' Stories

A candle-lit buffet in the formal dining room among the highly polished silver serving pieces, butlers and maids gliding about offering cocktails from lace-draped trays, distinguished visitors smiling and clasping the many outstretched hands of greeting, men and women in crisp military uniforms, other guests in elegant and fashionable civilian attire, and music from the professional jazz ensemble of the Academy Band are elements of a typical reception at what is now known as "Buchanan House**." The Superintendent's Quarters, built in 1906 and named for Commander Franklin Buchanan in 1976, is a monument to the continuing tradition of social responsibility initiated by the first superintendent in 1845. As in the early days of the old Dulany mansion, the superintendent's quarters are the showcase of the Academy.**

The superintendent's family models military etiquette and sets the standard for social activity on the Yard. Buchanan House and its residents uphold the finest of Naval traditions and graces, following the example set by John Paul Jones in the eighteenth century. The Buchanan House is a perfect backdrop and anchor for the continuity of this tradition of refinement.

Vast amounts of preparation, skill in planning, and a flair for elegance are needed for entertaining at the Superintendent's house. Superintendent and Mrs. Harry W. Hill, who served as "first family" at the Academy from 1950 to 1952, combined all the above qualities for successful hosting, including juggling with a meager budget.

Elizabeth Hill Drake (Mrs. J.B. Drake) was married and living out of town when her parents were in the Superintendent's Quarters, bur she and her family visited often on holidays. Her mother, who was an Annapolitan, redecorated the quarters for the first time in many years. Mrs. Hill was a good hostess, enjoyed having guests, and entertained many international friends.

According to Drake, her parents only received $1200 a year for entertaining, so they had to stretch the budget with their imagination and ingenuity. At that time there was a vegetable garden for the superintendent, which was located across College Creek in Government Farm. Superintendent Hill had a "cool room" installed in the basement of his quarters where temperatures could be maintained around 55 degrees, and fresh vegetables could be stored. Her mother taught the stewards how to preserve and freeze items from the garden. One of the stewards at the Superintendent's Quarters, Chief Reddick, had been stationed with her father when he was in the Pacific.

The Hills made good use of the supplies at hand, and consequently developed a marvelous knack for entertaining. Many years later, Mrs. Draper Kauffman, wife of the Superintendent in

1965, asked Mrs. Drake if she still had her mother's old recipes and menus. Unfortunately, they could not be found.[298]

Rear Admiral and Mrs. Draper L. Kauffman continued the tradition of elegant entertaining and interaction with midshipmen at the Superintendent's Quarters. The quarters were constantly filled with guests, and large groups of noisy "drags" who often stayed overnight swished up and down the curved staircases in their slim skirts or voluminous formals.

Mrs. Kauffman especially seemed to enjoy her social leadership role at the Naval Academy. Attempting to train the young Aide's wives in social skills, she had them attend to details. For example, at dinner parties they were told to check their glasses for "lipstick marks," something that a nervous young lady would overlook. Commander Wertz, who worked with the Superintendent, heard her tell the wives: "Circulate. Don't talk amongst yourselves. Circulate with the guests."[299] With Mrs. Kauffman, the junior officers' wives began to appreciate the mechanics of hosting a social event.

As a reprieve from all the activities at the Superintendent's Quarters, the Kauffmans liked to relax and entertain in a more casual manner on the Superintendent's barge, the *Claudia Stewart*. The *Claudia Stewart* had been named for Mrs. William R. Smedberg III, wife of the Superintendent from 1956 to 1958. Rear Admiral Kauffman had a favorite stuffed chair and ottoman which he would take to the barge. The stewards could be seen wearily carrying the items back and forth. According to Commander Wertz, the stewards would grumble, "Got to go to the Supe's quarters again and pick up that darn chair and that ottoman, and take it down to the boat."[300]

Vice Admiral and Mrs. James F. Calvert, who lived in the Superintendent's Quarters from 1968 to 1972, had just married and began their new life together at the Academy. The old house also withstood the escapades of very young occupants – two boys with boundless energy and curiosity. Life at the Superintendent's house had a different quality during these years. Of his time spent in these historic quarters, Vice Admiral Calvert wrote:

> We have many pleasant memories of our four years as Superintendent of the Academy. For one thing, Buchanan House (not called that in our time) was our honeymoon cottage. We had been married in Athens, Greece in April of '68 when I was with the Sixth Fleet. We reported to USNA about June 2 or 3, 1968.
>
> We had two sons, one each from previous marriages – Kemp and Charley – both aged 11 at the time. In addition to endless lacrosse and touch football games in the garden, these two learned how to use the tunnels (utility tunnels, I believe) between Bancroft Hall and other buildings for secret trips. Needless to say, they had many run-ins with the Jimmy Legs.
>
> During our time, we started the Forrestal Lecture Series and always had a dinner at Buchanan House for the Speaker (and spouse, if along) after the lecture. I always made a thank-you toast and, usually, the lecturer responded with an informal talk for us.

> Some of the memorable ones were Herman Wouk, Art Buchwald, F. Lee Bennet, Alex Haley, Stan Waterman the underwater photographer, and Gloria Steinem (no response from her).
>
> Most of the responses were 5 or 10 minutes in length, but Alex Haley went on for half an hour, and then all through dinner until 1:00 in the morning. We were all fascinated – he was a great raconteur.[301]

The Forrestal Lecture Series begun during Superintendent Calvert's tenure has become an enduring and much anticipated tradition at the Naval Academy.

Rear Admiral and Mrs. Thomas C. Lynch, who resided at the Superintendent's Quarters from 1991 to 1994, were energetic and gracious representatives of the Naval Academy. Involved in the life of the Academy with midshipmen and residents, with the Annapolis community, and with a larger circle of national and international leaders, they successfully fulfilled all of their social duties with aplomb.

Kathleen Quinn Lynch (Mrs. Thomas C. Lynch) had a busy daily schedule at Buchanan House, and shared some of her experiences of life as the wife of a Superintendent. She stated:

> There are at least two social events every day. As you know, we entertain over 16,000 people per year at Buchanan House [second only in number to the White House]. Each day I talk to the staff about hosting or planning events, about seating arrangements, who's staying in which bedroom and what special gift is to be placed there, and likes and dislikes of food.
>
> I do research on a country and customs if there is a special foreign visitor. This week we are hosting a delegation from Tunisia, and I try to find a mid or someone familiar with the language or country to sit with the delegates. If there are any special requests, I try to meet them. For example, the Tunisian wife liked the wicker chairs here on the porch, so I tried to get information about similar chairs to send to her.
>
> I also spend time each day with communication – making phone calls or writing notes, and making connections with people.
>
> I always had a career, but I wanted to make the most of being here, and to enjoy what there is to enjoy. So, in addition to my daily activities as hostess, I also think it is important to connect with the community. A main focus of mine is to reach out in the community – with volunteer work, with Hospice fund raising, volunteering in the schools as a tutor, and the fund raising committee for the renovation of the Maryland Hall for the Performing Arts. I feel a responsibility to the Academy, the Brigade, and the Annapolis community. It is a big challenge to keep it balanced.
>
> ## As far as helpful advice when we came to Buchanan House, someone told me, "When you have so much pomp and circumstance, it is the perfect stage for high comedy."[302]

Although tradition is the binding glue from generation to generation at the Naval Academy, social life and customs have evolved to a greater complexity. Events on the Yard are no longer shared by small groups; they now are of national import. Rear Admiral Lynch, USNA Class of 1964, described some of these differences:

In recent years it seems to be a whole new world. For example, former Superintendent Calvert noted a big difference in how we conduct the Board of Visitors. During his tenure, he met with Ross Perot [USNA Class of 1953] and two or three people for the meetings. They were quiet and not open to the press. Now, these events are much more visible. We might have eight senators and congressmen, six distinguished civilians, thirty faculty and administrators, The New York Times, the Associated Press, The Washington Post, and several others from the media present.[303]

The social activities surrounding the Superintendent's position remain as varied as ever. However, with the addition of Alumni Hall in 1991, entertaining was able to take on larger dimensions. Rear Admiral Lynch discussed social events that are hosted by the Superintendent:

I am not sure if these things are new, but we get all the first class midshipmen here to Buchanan House. We also have mids over in informal ways, such as different teams and clubs for pizza and Cokes.

The use of Alumni Hall is new to my administration, so we can do a lot more than before. Here [at Buchanan House] we are limited to 40 for a comfortable dinner. At Alumni Hall we can host larger groups.

We like to get the policy makers from DC onto campus to see what life is like and to meet the mids. We have also been able to bring such notables to campus such as President Clinton, Margaret Thatcher, General Colin Powell, Bob Hope, Tom Peters, Richard Cheney, and many others.[304]

The twenty-first century saw great changes in our country, and in the activity of the military after "9-11," September 11, 2001. Traditions at Buchanan House marched forward, with a slight shift in focus to serve midshipmen's needs. Vice Admiral Jeffrey Fowler, USNA Class of 1978, served at Buchanan House as Superintendent from 2007 to 2010. Mrs. Katie Fowler gave her perspective of this unique opportunity. She wrote:

Buchanan House Memories

I had the greatest honor and privilege to serve as the Superintendent's wife of the United States Naval Academy. I cannot imagine a better tour of duty (although my husband considers his command of a nuclear powered submarine a close tie). In this role one is an ambassador, hostess, mentor and representative of the United States Navy and the United States of America. We attended everything from Forrestal Lectures, ceremonies, performances, sporting events, graduations and sadly to say even funerals. Most rewarding was seeing young midshipmen come as scared teenagers and leave as confident leaders.

The number of VIP's who walked through the Buchanan House doors was endless. President George W. Bush was in our home for the Annapolis Peace conference along with Condoleezza Rice and other world leaders. Secretary of Defense, Robert Gates, ate dinner with us. Tom Brokaw spent the night. We hosted visiting dignitaries and foreign government officials nearly every week.

We had a wonderful team of culinary specialists who tirelessly prepared exquisite meals. We had a professional staff, including our protocol team, who were very engaged and extremely helpful with the entertaining aspects. We had Navy musicians who performed at our functions which added such a touch of elegance. We opened our home to thousands of people a year. My husband and I wanted to make sure each individual's experience in the Buchanan House was a memory of a lifetime.

Most of the above was probably similar to my predecessors.

However, all of the midshipmen during our time at the Naval Academy knew they were going to serve during wartime, which has not always been the case. That is why we ensured we maintained the proper environment for such an important future responsibility. Additionally, we started one new initiative to focus our midshipmen on that serious future upon commissioning. We gathered our senior midshipmen by the communities where they were going to be assigned after commissioning rather than by company. They had an enjoyable meal and discussion with their future shipmates as well as active duty and retired leaders within that community.

Upon reflection I walk away with the greatest satisfaction that my husband and I SERVED our midshipmen and the Navy enthusiastically and professionally. We were and always will be . . . "Team Fowler!"[305]

The residents of the Superintendent's House, since Franklin Buchanan's time, have held a visible position of social leadership at the Academy. As the Academy has grown and as society has become more complex, information more readily available, communication more swift and responsive, the job has increased in its demands. As the twenty-first century rounded the bend, events formerly of interest within these walls became items of national interest. In addition to administrative expertise, the Superintendent must have finely honed skills of diplomacy. And yet, because of the nature of the small community at the Academy, that person, like the current superintendent and all predecessors, must also be able to blend with the residents and local citizens.

CHAPTER THREE: LIFE IN THE LATE 1900s AND EARLY 2000s

Residents of Recent Years: the Sum of the Past, and Less

The steady, timeless rhythm of life at the Naval Academy continued for residents into the twentieth-first century. The stories are familiar by now. Amidst the traditions, changes are evident.

Sara Friesz (Mrs. Raymond H. Friesz) recalled a bustling four years at the Academy, when she and her family lived in Number 50 Rodgers Road in the early 1970s. The quarters were often filled with house guests; during one June Week, or Commissioning Week, she hosted 13 overnight guests at one time.

Of fascination to the Friesz family was the series of buzzers in the house. From a central panel in the kitchen, other rooms in the house could be rung. This handy communication system is no longer in use in the quarters, although mysterious buttons remained on the walls in some rooms of the houses.

A special treat enjoyed by the residents was the use of the Commandant's yacht. Department Heads at the Academy could borrow the yacht on a rotating basis. Captain and Mrs. Friesz spent several memorable evenings entertaining the officers from the Dental Department among the waterways of Annapolis. Three people operated the yacht, and King Hall provided refreshments. This activity is no longer available to the residents.[306]

The home of Captain and Mrs. James A. Kenney, like that of the Friesz family and officers' quarters throughout the years, was filled with guests and commotion. Captain Kenney, USNA Class of 1958, remembers the bustle of activity on Upshur Road in the late 1970s. He wrote:

> We sponsored many Mids (we had to leave or we wouldn't have been able to afford another year there), including several of the foreign students. We put up Hood College girls for the Messiah, the foreign students who came in early for language training and the females from '81 who came in the night before and the Academy did not want them in town.[307]

Having students from Hood College to combine with the Naval Academy Glee Club for the annual Christmas *Messiah* concert in the Chapel was a long-standing tradition during the holiday season on the Yard. The Chapel filled yearly with expectant residents and citizens of Annapolis to hear Handel's majestic piece, accompanied by the Annapolis Symphony Orchestra. In 1996, the two choirs celebrated their fiftieth year of performing the *Messiah* together. Academy residents offered to keep the students from Hood College in their homes. The chorus from the Western Maryland campus visited for a weekend, practiced with the Mids for the performance, toured the grounds, and reveled at the restrictive lifestyle of a military academy. Yet, many a young lady from Hood College returned to date and marry a handsome Navy man in the Academy Chapel.

The choral music program was conducted from 1971 until 2006 by Dr. John Barry Talley, who then retired after 35 years of service to the Naval Academy.[308] Dr. Aaron Smith replaced Dr. Talley as director of choral activities.

Attending the Naval Academy remains a strong tradition in families throughout the years, as it was in the 1800s. Families like that of Captain Roland Brandquist perpetuated this connection. When Janet and Ron Brandquist, Class of 1960, lived in Number 39 Upshur Road in the late 1970s, their two sons, Geoffrey (Brandquist), Class of 1983, and Kurt (Brandquist), Class of 1984, entered the Academy. Their daughter, Kristen (Brandquist), married an Academy graduate in the Chapel in 1991, also passing the family's affiliation to the Yard onto the next generation.[309]

That romances are spawned at the Academy is evident, but midshipmen and their "drags" are not the only young people to meet at the old houses on campus. Rebecca Caldwell (Mrs. Robert K. Caldwell) recalled the "Mystique and romance at the 'little house' in the middle of the Parade Field – Numbers 33 and 34 Upshur Road." These quarters were occupied by the families of Captain John T. Kennard, USNA Class of 1958, and Commander Robert Caldwell, also Class of 1958. Mrs. Caldwell wrote:

> It was during the 1984 Olympic Soccer Venue at the Navy-Marine Corps Memorial Stadium that Bob's son Dave (Caldwell), a recent graduate of George Mason University, was looking for helping hands for painting and construction, and first met the girl next door. She was John Kennard's daughter, Kristina (Kennard), a three-time All American swimmer and recent graduate of Kenyon College. The Olympics were, of course, a resounding success, thanks in no small part the Caldwell-Kennard construction team. But somewhat to the surprise of Bob and Becky, John and Donna, the C-K team was turning into more than a working relationship. In November, 1985, wedding bells were heard in the Naval Academy Chapel.[310]

Mrs. Caldwell added that now the Class of '58, and the 33-34 Upshur Road duplex have several "pure-bred" grandbabies!

Halloween has been a time for Academy festivities into the twenty-first century. Ann Snell (Mrs. William H. Snell), who lived at Perry Circle in the mid-1970s, remembered elaborate preparations for the ancient tradition:

> Halloween was quite an affair! Members of each building in Perry Circle would decorate their respective lower (ground floor) entrance halls. And I don't mean with just black and orange crepe paper. One year we dropped the stairwell ceiling with a parachute, hung spiders and webs, bats, etc. from it. [We] had a coffin in which we all took turns. [There were] black lights and dry ice and a super eerie tape for special

effects. As I remember, we were so good, that some of the little tykes refused to enter. I think we parents had as much fun as the kids.[311]

Weather conditions in Annapolis sometimes provide interesting diversions from the many planned social events at the Academy. In 1993, a late spring blizzard cancelled some activities, but provided a new agenda for the children. The Captain Leon R. Escude, Jr. family living at Number 50 Rodgers Road with children Laura and Chandler recalled:

> The promise of a gentle spring was in the air at the Naval Academy this year in early March, with budding trees and bulbs pushing their way up into the warmth of the sun. But in keeping with the high drama available with living at the Academy, residents experienced a mid-March snow and ice show hailed by the media as the "Storm of the Century." Under clear skies on Friday, March 12, 1993, we watched weather reports as the storm inched its way up the eastern seaboard toward Annapolis. We awakened Sunday morning to see the ground covered with white powder. All that day as we relaxed in our Worden Field home, we heard the wind howling around the corners of the old house, rattling the glass in the windows, and whistling and blowing with high and low pitches reminiscent of a freight train. It was like a Yukon blizzard. Later in the afternoon as the evening light turned the snow on Worden Field to a pale blue, we saw lightning and heard thundering in the distance.

> The next day, Sunday, the snow became icy, and travelling was so treacherous that we had to cancel a Chesapeake Youth Symphony Orchestra Reception for a hundred people at our house. Snowbound as we were, we still had plenty of entertainment. Chad Hegna and Bobby McCabe, eight year olds from up the street, offered to scrape our walkway for only ten cents! (We gave them more).

> Later that day when I glanced out the front window, I couldn't believe my eyes. The Stroop and Wilson boys were playing hockey on a thoroughly frozen Worden Field, gliding around easily on ice skates![312]

Weather can be a show-stopper at the Academy, and struggling with snow storms can produce some of the most memorable times. But, the Academy as a ski resort? Commander John Paul Rue, 1993 USNA graduate, and his wife, Elizabeth Rue, lived with their children Milo, Madeline, Meredith, and Max in Number 2 Wood Road on Hospital Point. Commander Rue served as the Head Team Orthopedic Surgeon at the Academy. Elizabeth (Beth) Rue writes of the "Blizzards of 2009-2010."

> Our best and most lasting memories of life here on the Academy came in the winter of 2009-2010. Our first big snowfall hit in December with a total around 23 inches. The play value was short lived as the day after Christmas it rained heavily and all melted away. Towards the end of the month of January we got hit with two back-to-back giant snowfalls that exceeded 25 inches each. Needless to say the Academy was beautiful with multiple feet of snow on all the roads and paths for several days. Here on Hospital Point, we have our own little microcosm weather system. The wind whipped our snow into huge drifts in front of the house that were seven-plus feet high.

> During the worst of the blizzard in late January, my husband, an orthopedic surgeon, had to cover a wrestling tournament in Lejeune Hall. He was unable to get the car out of the driveway so he scrounged up our old cross country skis which hadn't been used in 15 years and skied to work! The rest of the week he skied to the office on the roads...since with so much snow, plowing didn't happen immediately.

Our oldest, Milo, 11, thought this was great fun and decided to get out his downhill skis for a run down the hill and across the parking lot towards the athletic fields on Hospital Point. It was too much work for a 30-second mediocre run across the parking lot with the huge trudge up the hill in clunky ski boots. In his can-do spirit, he begged Dad to help him figure out a tow rope of some sort so that he wouldn't have to work so hard!

Some of our fondest memories were formed that winter, even with all the wet gloves, hats, coats, boots that we dried and re-dried. Every afternoon during the many days off from school, the children on Porter Road organized a massive snowball battle where the kids from all over the yard joined in, all the way up to the oldest high-schoolers!

These snowfalls were among the only ones to ever cause the cancellation of classes at USNA for more than a day. The mids had nearly a week off of classes since there was so much snow and nowhere to put it. (There was) nowhere for professors to park, and many were still snowed in days after the snowfall only to have another blizzard hit before the digging out was completed from the first blizzard![313]

Fun, family-oriented social events on the Parade Field continue through the ages, and new traditions have begun. Elizabeth (Beth) Rue, Number 2 Woods Road resident in 2011 wrote:

We created yet another lasting memory on June 27, 2011. We hosted what we think was the first ever movie night in the gazebo on Worden Field. We had all the neighborhood kids out playing Kingpin on the field and then repaired to the gazebo on a beautiful night to watch the 25th anniversary showing of *Ferris Bueller's Day Off*. It was spectacular and we hope to make it an annual summer event! [314]

Army-Navy Football Games still offer opportunities for emotional release and campus antics into the twenty-first century, and involve everyone in the family. Marylee Klunder, Mrs. Matthew L. Klunder, wrote about the game in 2008.

NAVY Football Season 2008 was in full swing! We were thrilled when the Athletic Director invited Michael, Martin and Merrick to work on the fields during Home NAVY Football Games! Michael was a Ball Boy for NAVY. Martin was a Ball Boy for the Visiting Team. Merrick was the Water Boy or "Hydration Specialist" for NAVY! The boys were issued official NAVY Team shirts, sweatshirts and ball caps! They wore Khaki pants or shorts, and took their jobs very seriously! Madeleine proudly wore a Cheerleading outfit we purchased at the Midshipmen Store! We cheered wildly from the stands!

Many times before the Football games, we would be awakened at 0200 by about 60 Midshipmen singing "The Goat Is Old and Gnarly"! The Mids would then burst into "We want the Commandant! We want the Commandant!" Of course, Matthew was happy to greet them at the door, standing there in his Navy Jammies! The kids begged us to wake them up whenever the Midshipmen made their late night/ early morning visits! Sometimes the Mids even came twice in one night! For the Army Navy Game a 10 piece band from the NAVY drum and bugle corps played rousing hymns at 0500! The whole neighborhood was awake now! We would awake delighted to find colorful spirit banners suspended from the trees and draped over bushes! At times, they even attached the banners to the porch pillars so we would have to crawl underneath! The Mids clearly had become an endearing part of our family! Madeleine, at the tender age of 5, once exclaimed, "Mom these Midshipmen are so CUTE, I just CANNOT decide which one I am going to marry!"[315]

Revitalization!

The senior officers' quarters along Porter, Rodgers, and Upshur, Roads, have sheltered families and witnessed many social changes throughout the past 100 years. With every family that leaves the quarters, another layer of paint is added to cover the marks and memories left behind. Through the years, the paint also obscured some of the Victorian details of the homes such as the delicate ornamentation around mantelpieces, the finely-hewn staircase railings, the ornate molding defining the tall ceilings, and even the marble fireplace surrounds. In addition, by the late twentieth century, the clanging steam radiators were like ghosts from a much earlier era. These beautiful old homes that seem stately and timeless from a distance, had become worn and ragged up close, but still dearly loved. And, those "temporary bungalows" from the early 1900s, were still in use at the end of the twentieth century!

The mid-1990s offered a brighter outlook for these monuments to Naval Academy family life. Funds were appropriated for a "Revitalization Project" to modernize the heating and cooling systems, shore up the sagging structures, and restore the interiors to some of their former luster. Again, in 2008-2009, more renovations were made with officers' quarters. Future generations of Naval Academy families will be as proud of their homes as those of the past. Hopefully, these homes listed on the National Historic Register will remain a visible reminder of fine Naval traditions.

Ghost Stories!

The history of Naval Academy quarters is replete with tradition, mystique, romance, excitement, mischief, and, of course, ghost stories. In 1993, Jennifer John (Mrs. Michael John) uncovered a secret from the distant past about some Upshur Road quarters.

While being given a tour of their Parade Field home before moving in, Commander Mike John was told that in the early history of the house an officer living there had slipped down the steep back stairs and had died. Jennifer and Mike were not concerned about this disclosure, but a year later their interest was piqued when they met a couple at a party in Norfolk, Virginia, who told them of a spooky experience in a Worden Field home.

The officer at the party told the Johns that a former resident of a house in Number 32 Upshur Road graciously let him and his bride spend their honeymoon there alone, after their formal wedding in the Chapel. But he and his new wife did not have a peaceful evening. Alas, putting nuptial prerogatives aside, they searched the dark closets and cabinets with flashlights all night long, urgently looking for the source of strange noises and restless spirits. It was a horrifying experience, more fitting for a gothic romance novel.

After discussing the location of the house, and the names of the former residents, the Johns concluded that the "haunted house" was theirs![316]

Social Life and Hops: Mere Ghosts of the Early Years

The walls and guarded gates surrounding the Yard and the restrictions placed on these well-groomed, mannered, and almost inaccessible midshipmen created a Naval Academy mystique that proved an irresistible lure for young women in the 1800s and 1900s. Their aloofness and separation from mainstream college life made midshipmen seem very special, indeed.

Mid-twentieth century was a heady time for young ladies to visit or live on the Yard. Mary Gale Buchanan described the social scene during her college years as the "Commandant's daughter:"

> We had a group of friends on Porter Road in the '50s who had many fun and festive times sailing, playing tennis, and having parties and picnics. And, of course, we made fast friends with the jimmylegs on the gates.
>
> Gate #2 by the Commandant's quarters, Number 14 Porter Road, was open in those days, and the bus station (a small one!) was where the Paca House and Garden walls are today. Can you imagine a bus-load of "drags" disembarking there every weekend? And for me and my friends, all we had to do was tote ourselves and our luggage across the street, through Gate #2, and we would be home from college.
>
> We had room on the third floor to bring friends home on weekends from college. We took over the third floor with our long dresses and crinolines and hoops!
>
> Some of my friends in "Drag Houses" would bring their mids over after the hops, and we would put on the "record player" and dance some more – or play pool and ping pong in the basement – in our long dresses! And then it was just a short block to Bancroft so the mids could eek out every last second of liberty.[317]

Mary Gale's friend down the street, Michelle Foley McDaniel, had similar experiences. She wrote:

> I came home from college several weekends a month for dates. . . On Sunday evenings just before the mids had to be back at Bancroft Hall at 7:00 pm, there would be a traffic jam of girls leaving the Greyhound terminal on King George Street near Gate 2.
>
> My best friend in those days was Mary Gale Buchanan who was a classmate at Mary Washington. . . .Her house on Porter Road was even more grand than ours. Mary Gale was extremely popular and I enjoyed the "luster" that rubbed off on me as a result of our friendship and close association. Porter Road was very lively in those days.
>
> After three memory-filled years, countless football games, hops, sailing dates and crewing on yawls, movies on the *Reine Mercedes* and afternoons strolling the Yard, our tour of duty ended. We moved away after June Week of 1955.[318]

One teenage resident reported an extraordinary encounter with her silver screen idol, casting a romantic aura onto her life at the Academy. Popular actor and singer Pat Boone visited the campus for a show in the late 1950s. The parents of Carol Gebert Bowis, Captain and Mrs. Wesley Robert Gebert, offered to host Boone at Number 47 Rodgers Road for an overnight stay. Carol was thrilled to give up her room. She was later able to boast to her envious friends that the suave and handsome crooner slept in her very own bed.[319]

Though the social life of midshipmen and Navy juniors lucky enough to live on the Academy remained lively, the later years of the twentieth century brought definite changes in the long-established customs. As early as mid-century, Emmie Hamilton (Mrs. Thomas Hamilton) noticed the differences associated with "dating" that had developed at the Academy since her early "courtship" days. No longer did mids and young ladies go to the hops in large groups and mix to become acquainted with many people. She tried to alter this new trend, and like her husband, became a "coach" herself.

> After WWII, the midshipmen were inclined to "go steady," and dance only with his date at the hops. This bothered me, having been accustomed in the late '20s and '30s to long stag lines and having several partners during each number via "cutting in." I felt that the girls were missing a lot, and the boys, too. I talked about this to several of the football players, and they said, "Come to the hop with us and show us what to do."
>
> I stood on the sidelines with about six boys who did not have dates that night. I told each one to pick out a girl he might like to meet, preferably dancing with one of his friends. I said, "Go up to them, tap the shoulder of the friend and say, 'may I cut?'" Well, I started the ball rolling. That night, at that hop, the boys were cutting in, dancing with several different girls, amid lots of fun and laughter.[320]

Even with Mrs. Hamilton's enthusiasm, the old social traditions did not hold.

Academy hops have become very different affairs from earlier years. Emmie Marshall (Mrs. James A. Marshall) became the first official Social Director for the Academy in 1959. An abundance of hops, tea dances, and balls were arranged for midshipmen to serve as training for the social demands of being an officer.

At the tea dances and hops, midshipmen and girls were "matched" in an effort to assist midshipmen to meet young ladies, and to retain the tradition of stag lines. These affairs, known surreptitiously as "pig pushers," had a unique format. The Social Director invited women from different colleges to hops. A large sheet was hung in the middle of Dahlgren Hall with male mids in a line on one side, and the women guests on the other. As the male mid came to the front of the line, he met a young lady, and became her escort. Resisting such "required" and circumscribed affairs, some mids secretly placed bets on who got to dance with the least attractive female, or "pig." That mid "won" the accumulated loot for the evening.

Through the middle of the 1900s, the social life of the midshipmen at the Academy revolved around these frequent "socials." Until the 1970s, hops were arranged every Saturday night and Sunday afternoon, and college and prep-school girls came to Annapolis for the entire weekend, staying with an officer's family or at "drag houses" in town. After the 1970s, it was more difficult to attract women each weekend. Both the midshipmen and the women expressed a dislike for "matching" and formal receiving lines. Along with the breakdown of the monastic way of life with more "leave" time and the introduction of women into the student body in 1976, the intrigue and allure of the mysterious midshipmen diminished.

In 1976, Carol Baysinger (Mrs. Reaves Baysinger) who was assisting Mrs. Marshall, suggested that the tea dances be discontinued, and more casual "mixers" be introduced. Mrs. Marshall retired in 1980 after twenty-one years of nurturing the development of social graces among midshipmen. Mrs. Baysinger followed as the new Social Director. Arranged events for midshipmen continue to adapt and evolve with changing times.

Ring dances have retained their special, romantic appeal, however. Marylee Klunder, (Mrs. Matthew Klunder), describes her experience in the 1980s:

> Second Class Ring Dance was indeed a Highlight! I wore that floor length pale blue spaghetti strap dress to the Ring Dance on 23 May 1981 in Dahlgren Hall!
>
> The evening of the Ring Dance, we all went to the Chart House for dinner. Most of the dates had received a small imitation USNA Miniature ring on a blue ribbon from their Mid. We wore it around our necks proudly. It was a night full of happiness!
>
> I remember walking into Dahlgren Hall and marveling at two massive gold rings positioned at the Bay Side end of the Hall. They were replicas of the Naval Academy Ring! There was a long line of Mids and dates awaiting their turn to step INSIDE those rings. Then as you stood inside the Ring, you dipped your Miniature and the Midshipman's Ring in a font containing waters from the Seven Seas!

In the late twentieth century, the plebes had one "Mixer," and three formal balls. Upper class midshipmen had about six "Mixers," and four balls. The "Mixers," still held in Dahlgren Hall, were mainly attended by second and third class midshipmen who wore uniforms to the affairs. Music was provided by a combo from the Naval Academy Band, or from a "DJ," or disc-jockey, who brought popular records, tapes or CDs. "Mixers" were no longer by invitation to just the women from other schools; now that the Naval Academy included women midshipmen, both male and female students from nearby colleges were invited. The students who attended usually left Annapolis after the dances; many had their own cars or traveled by chartered bus. Yard residents became less involved in midshipmen's social events after the 1990s. Wives of Naval Academy senior officers no longer served as chaperones for the dances; "matrons" from town were hired to sit, watch personal belongings, and be available to assist guests.

Ballroom dancing instruction, once required, is today an extracurricular activity enjoyed by a few mids as a novelty. In the 1990s, midshipmen would don cowboy hats, boots, and blue jeans, and head out to a country dance hall to learn the complex steps of the "Boot Scootin' Boogie." Dancing, as always at the Academy, was still popular. But at the end of the twentieth century, to the beginning of the twenty-first century, mids and drags "danced to a different tune."

The hops, mixers, and balls were arranged to help midshipmen practice proper etiquette and to provide opportunities for dating. However, the Academy seems to intervene less and less in the social life of the mids. The old social conventions of the Academy that were so well known have dwindled. In 1993, the formerly prominent position of Social Director was reduced to "part time," and in 1994, it was abolished altogether.[321]

More Movies and Television

The Naval Academy continues through the decades to be a focus for fiction: life is still magical on the Yard, and makes a great subject for the grand illusion of the silver screen. Even residents can hardly believe their life on the Yard is the "real world." Though not with the frequency of the early part of the twentieth century, the Academy has still been the subject of many stories and shows.

In 1955, *An Annapolis Story*, a movie about the "Rover Boys" was filmed in color. With John Derek and Kevin McCarthy, this movie gave a close up of living quarters, lecture rooms, and parades. In 1957, television viewers watched a series known as *The Men from Annapolis* starring Darryl Hickman and Jack Diamond.

In the 1980s, the Academy received frequent attention from television. Two TV miniseries were made with scenes from the Yard: *Space*, in 1984, with James Garner and Beau Bridges, and *War and Remembrance*, in 1987, in which Robert Mitchum and Victoria Tennant, acting as a graduate and his fiancé, are shown getting married in the Chapel. In 1988, the acclaimed *Magnum P.I.* detective series filmed a show at the Academy with heartthrob Tom Selleck. In 1982, comedian Bob Hope hosted an *All-Star Birthday Party* at the Navy-Marine Corps Stadium with Brooke Shields, Christie Brinkley, James Coburn, and Bernadette Peters. In this raucous celebration, the irreverent **Bob Hope joked, "I can't tell you how glad I am to be here at the only federally funded yacht club."**[322]

The filming of the movie *Patriot Games*, based on the best-selling novel by Annapolis resident Tom Clancy, added to the excitement of Academy life in 1991 and 1992. Worden Field residents looked out their windows to see mess tents, make-up trailers, and equipment trucks parked on the east side of the parade grounds. During the cold, inclement weather for two weeks after the Christmas of 1991, Yard dwellers shared stories of "Harrison Ford spottings." Townspeople gathered, bundled from the elements, around Gate #3 to watch a Marine guard race down Maryland Avenue with a pistol, time after time, hour after hour, only to see this action flash by in a few seconds in the finished production. The Academy residents and midshipmen were given a special preview of *Patriot Games* months later on a giant screen in Alumni Hall, and everyone was eager to see if he or she had been immortalized on camera in one of the Academy scenes.

Tourists

The same glamorous Naval Academy life that provides fodder for films also lures sightseers. Residents of the Academy at first recoil from always being "on show," or "living in a fishbowl," but eventually the droves of visitors become a part of daily life. That tourists have had a perennial presence on campus is evident from comments about town visitors from the earliest days of the Naval School. That hoards of sightseers have become sometimes laughable and problematic was noted as early as 1906 by the acerbic pen of the sharp witted Professor Stevens. Devoting an entire letter of the alphabet to Academy tourists in his book, *An Annapolis Alphabet*, he provided a poke at the manners of some of these "welcome" intruders. He captures them in a cartoon as they stand gaping in front of Herndon Monument, sporting their nametags and strewing their snacks. He wrote:

X is Xcursionists rude,

A wild-eyed, inquisitive brood;

The badges they wear

Would make Sousa despair,

And they're not at all bashful with Food.[323]

Children at the Academy have been vexed by tourists through the years. One woman confessed that when she was a child living on Porter Road early in the twentieth century, she and her friends delighted in throwing grapes from third floor windows at the waves of tourists passing down the street. Elizabeth Hill Drake, who lived on Rodgers Road in the early 1930s, recalled how she and her friends "put up with" the sightseers who walked around as if they were looking at monkeys in a zoo!

During one fall afternoon in the late 1950s at the Academy, Jean Grkovic's husband (George Grkovic, USNA Class of 1943) and their three children were at a sporting event. Enjoying some time alone in her home at Number 50 Rodgers Road, she answered her door and found two ladies wearing proper pearl necklaces and gloves. They stated that being taxpayers, they wanted to see a house supported by money from the government. Though stunned by their request, Mrs. Grkovic politely invited them into the house. After seeing the furnishings, they exclaimed that the Navy provided generously for the families here. Mrs. Grkovic explained that the furnishings were hers, not the Navy's. As the meddlesome ladies were ready to ascend the stairs to the other floors, the hostess' patience broke, and she told them to leave. Many residents through the years have been asked for impromptu tours from inquisitive and insensitive tourists.

Shirley H. Childs Pritchard (Mrs. C.A. Pritchard) and her former husband, Captain Donald Childs, lived on the "50-Yard Line" on the Parade Field, Upshur Road. She offered her experiences with tourists from the late 1960s:

> We noticed very early that some visitors assumed that our homes and yards were public domain, and we actually had some come early for the parade and picnic in our front yard. We solved that problem by turning the sprinkler on the lawn before the parade. More than once we had people walk in to use the bathroom or ask for a drink of water or if they could sit on the screened porch.[324]

In the early 1990s, teenager Laura Escude was amused when, standing on Blake Road with her friends from the Yard, a couple came over to her and inquired where the Chapel was. She turned and pointed to the large, domed edifice a few feet away. "Couldn't they see it?" she exclaimed later, rolling her eyes.

In 2008, Marylee Klunder and her family experienced having tourists gawking from the very first day in her family's quarters. She wrote:

> I have vivid memories of our move into the Commandant's Quarters on that hot Friday of Plebe Parent Weekend! A huge orange truck was parked in front. As I was instructing movers where to place the boxes, tourist and Plebe parents were taking our photos! The kids asked how to respond to all this attention! I said, "Just smile and wave!"[325]

In the twenty-first century, tourism seems as popular at the Naval Academy as ever, and combined with the "Museum without Walls" concept of Historic Annapolis, the area draws crowds nearly every day of the year. Thousands of visitors, from active school children swinging lunch bags and sticks to the slower moving gray-haired centenarians wearing sunshades and baseball hats, crowd the sidewalks around the campus. Some are led by the blue and gold clad Naval Academy guides, some by the Historic Annapolis Foundation volunteers with their black and red badges, and some by the eighteenth century costumed guides from a tour service in town. And everybody wants to see the tomb of John Paul Jones.

Women at the Academy

In 1976, women were first admitted to the Naval Academy as students; the first graduating class to include women was in 1980. Their presence created a strong resistance, then an evolving tolerance, and later an acceptance of women as leaders with strengths and qualities that could enhance the effectiveness of military operations. The Naval Academy, first allowing only ten percent of its student body to be female, has had to slowly shake its "Old Boy Network" image.

Having women students in the system changed the tenor of residential life. The Academy realized that these women needed role models, and that the male midshipmen needed to be able to work with and learn to take orders from women, so female officers from the fleet were introduced into the staff of the Academy. Lieutenant Susan H. Stephens was one of the first women officers to work closely with the Brigade in 1976. Mary Seymour (Mrs. Harry A. Seymour, Jr.) detailed her memories of living at the Academy during those transitional years:

> Chip [Captain Harry A. Seymour, Jr., Class of 1965] was deeply involved in the planning and execution of the admission of women, while I was trying to handle the many activities of our two girls, four and one, in 1976, as well as be a dutiful aide's wife! My most indelible memory is the intense anxiety generated by my need to book baby-sitters at least three times a week!
>
> Chip recalls the intensity of the media attention aimed at the women, and they did not want any special treatment.
>
> The first female company officer, Sue Stephens, was very involved with clothing decisions in the sense that I remember a pamphlet in which she was the model for the suggested midshipmen uniforms for the women.
>
> . . . I only remember that I was always in favor of admitting women (since at that time I had two daughters) and there have always been people with the opposite opinion.[326]

By the 1990s, several women officers and their families had been assigned to live in senior officers' quarters on Worden Field. One of the first female senior officers with a major impact on the Brigade was Commander Marsha J. Evans, later Rear Admiral, who was a Brigade Officer. Commander Evans lived in Number 41 Upshur Road from 1986 to 1988. She later returned to the Academy to serve as Chief of Staff with Superintendent Thomas C. Lynch in 1992. Many women officers now live in quarters around the Academy, and serve as administrative staff and instructors.

Women at the Academy became more visible by the 1990s with the assignment of women senior officers. In addition, chosen to lead the Brigade was the first woman midshipman Brigade Commander, Julianne J. Gallina in 1991, and the second, Kristen Culler, in 1992, both of whom received considerable national attention. Gallina was featured as one of *Glamour Magazine's* "Women of the Year."

The "Tailhook Scandal" of 1992 shook the Academy and the entire Navy, providing another chink in the male armor, and serving to heighten the awareness of Navy personnel to sexual harassment issues. Women were also striving for assignment to combat positions, leading to the further integration of women into all aspects of Navy operations.

Just as the traditional roles of women have changed in American society, the activities of the "typical Academy family" have changed. Women who are spouses of officers after the late 1900s are more likely to have their own careers or interests outside of the Academy walls, contrasting greatly to the lifestyle and focus of the "Mrs. Captains" of the late 1800s, who were often devoted to enhancing their husbands' careers. As a consequence, social events among residents have lost some of their former intensity and are less frequent, though the Academy still retains the flavor of a small, homogenous community.

Now that the doors of the Naval Academy are open to women, it is interesting to note the number of daughters who have chosen to continue the family tradition of becoming commissioned here. In the first two decades since admitting women into the Academy, the list of daughters of former graduates is lengthy. Among those with families living on the Yard during their midshipmen years were (then) Lieutenant Commander Wendy B. Lawrence, Class of 1981, whose parents, Vice Admiral and Mrs. William P. Lawrence lived in Buchanan House at the time, and (then) Ensign Kristen B. Fabry, Class of 1991, whose parents, Captain and Mrs. Steven E. Fabry, were residents of Number 9 Porter Road.[327] The women on the Yard as midshipmen and staff members in the 1970s to the 1990s were indeed trailblazers for new Academy traditions.

Yard Traditions in the Late 1990s and Early 2000s

As at any college in America, many of the customary events at the Naval Academy repeat themselves year after year, and reflect the traditional patterns begun at the school's inception in 1845. At the Naval Academy, however, these annual affairs are performed with a ritualistic fervor and strong definition not found at other universities. After over a century and a half, many colorful and festive activities have evolved to enrich the lives of residents and midshipmen each year.

Beginning the annual cycle is Plebe Summer and Induction Day, or "I-Day" in early July. A garden party at the Superintendent's Quarters, followed by the swearing-in ceremony for new midshipmen in Tecumseh Court, is replete with the pomp and circumstance of bands, inspiring speeches, and an ear splitting flyover of airplanes piloted by Naval Academy graduates.

During the summer months, the new plebes are treated to a magnificent Fourth of July fireworks display, which bursts over the serene backdrop of the Annapolis Harbor and the Severn River. For a few years, families from Worden Field celebrated Independence Day with games and a picnic in the hot summer Fourth of July afternoons in the 1990s.

In the late summer, plebes and other "Yard dwellers" are awed by the precision and flair of the Marine Corps at their Sunset Parade, sometimes given at the Academy on Turf Field, but more often seen at the Marine Corps headquarters in Washington, DC at the historic "Eighth and I." The plebes are greatly impressed by the ease with which these consummate showmen perform their elaborate drills.

The beginning of the academic year in the fall brings weekly parades to Worden Field, attended by residents, proud parents, and visiting dignitaries. Like a steady heartbeat, the drums from the Drum and Bugle Corps and the Naval Academy Band mark the time-honored tradition of regimental parades which link the midshipmen of today to their counterparts of more than a century past. Each parade is followed by an elegant garden party in the lush, flower bedecked formal garden behind Buchanan House. Residents and other guests sip wine and nibble delicate hors d'oeuvres. Popular music wafts from the Buchanan House balcony played by professional musicians from the Academy.

Army-Navy Week prior to the annual Army-Navy football clash fills the Academy Yard with pranks, serious frolic, and a chance for midshipmen to let off emotional steam. Children who live on the Yard are entertained by frenzied pep rallies, banners, painted monuments, a fireworks display to rival that of the Fourth of July.

Halloween is the time for small children's fantasies to manifest with masks and costumes, and the midshipmen devote this evening to the children of the Yard. In the late twentieth century, Bancroft Hall was creatively decorated for the local goblins, and raucous, outrageously attired mids led the Academy children through elaborately designed haunted houses. Male mids wearing frilly ballet tutus or superman outfits, and female mids sporting padded football uniforms or pirate disguises handed out candy to the small "Trick or Treaters." Porches of the residents' quarters were decked with witches, skeletons, spider webs, and cleverly carved orange jack o' lanterns lit with candles. In the 1990s, Superintendent Tom Lynch greeted goblins at his door with a bowlful of goodies and tried to guess who was under each mask. And organist James Dale dressed in a black, flowing cape treated the adults to a Halloween concert in the dimly lit, cavernous Chapel.[328]

Christmas season on the Yard is special. With midshipmen studying for semester examinations, the residents add lights, wreaths, and Christmas trees around their homes to bolster spirits of the mids. At the end of the twentieth century, midshipmen and the families of the Yard formed groups singing "Joy to the World" and "We Wish You a Merry Christmas," caroling up and down the sidewalks in front of quarters during the cold and dark December nights. With the blast of a siren, the Yard's large yellow fire truck escorted Santa around the streets of the quarters to assure the children that he would visit the Naval Academy soon.

As part of the Christmas tradition, the Superintendent hosted an Open House for all the Naval Academy families, and the children and parents could glimpse the spectacularly decorated, glitteringly elegant Buchanan House, and speak to Santa who was available to add their last minute wishes to his long list.

The annual *Messiah* concert thrilled residents and townspeople in the Chapel each December. Voices from the large combined choirs of the Naval Academy Glee Club and Hood College resounded in the ethereal stillness of the Chapel while the audience awaited the epiphany of the "Hallelujah Chorus." In 1993, the two choirs performed the *Messiah* together for the forty-seventh year.

And during the dark hours of Christmas Eve, after the midshipmen have gone home and the campus is uncharacteristically serene, the residents and church members gathered at the Chapel to commemorate the symbolic rebirth of the Spirit, and to light candles illuminated from a single flame, shared by all.

The New Year brings more festivity. Officers and spouses donned formal attire to attend the spectacle of the International Ball, also known as the "eye-ball," which brought young men and women from the Washington DC foreign embassies to campus to meet midshipmen. Foreign Exchange Officers assigned to the Academy from other countries were "presented" to the guests in Memorial Hall. Mids who have been practicing ballroom dancing, no longer a mandatory activity, displayed their graceful skills to the accompaniment of orchestral music. Everyone then joined in a jostling Conga line to complete the evening. After staying with the Escude family on Rodgers Road, Julie Sugarman from Bryn Mawr College expressed her delight in the elegance of the 1994 "I" Ball. She wrote:

What an unforgettable night I had at the International Ball! Wearing their dress uniforms or ball gowns, everyone looked like royalty. I felt like a fairy princess gliding in with my escort, who was such a gentleman. As we danced around the ballroom, it felt like nothing else was happening in the world![329]

In the late spring, people from the Academy and Annapolis met on the grassy lawn of St. John's College underneath the ancient Liberty Tree, to witness the annual Croquet Match between the "Johnnies" and the "Middies." Appropriate attire for this outing was spring bonnets and flowing dresses for the ladies, and sporty jackets and bowties for the men. This activity with its

Victorian flavor originated, oddly enough, in 1982. By 1993, the students of St. John's had won eight of these genteel but intense matches.

The end of the academic year in May brought a concentration of activities, enough to strain the social stamina of every resident. Commissioning Week is the culmination of a strenuous and demanding year at the Academy.[330] Plebes enthusiastically race to the Herndon Monument to capture the Dixie cup hat fixed on the top, and to replace it with a regular midshipman's hat. Hundreds of residents and townspeople cheer from the park and the Chapel steps, hoping that the class can climb the slippery, greased-up monument in a reasonably short time.

The second class midshipmen ceremoniously attended the formal Ring Dance under the stars on the Plaza between Michelson and Chauvenet Halls. They dipped their class rings into waters from the "seven seas," and proudly wore them as rising first classmen. Watching from the sidelines, residents could see the midshipmen and their special dates pose beneath a giant ring having their pictures taken to remember this momentous and romantic evening.

With sports and physical fitness being of great importance at the Academy, the athletes who won varsity letters at the Academy were honored at the annual "N" Dance held in the boat house at Hubbard Hall. Students danced in the warm May night air on the dock by College Creek while officers, coaches, and spouses discussed the athletic accomplishments of this academic year on the balcony upstairs.

A Naval Review of sailing skills was seen each year from the deck of the Robert Crown Sailing Center. The show was followed by a blast of Blue Angels performing air acrobatics above the Severn River.

The crowning event of every year, the Commissioning, is one that gives validation to the midshipmen who have studied, trained and developed leadership skills, and have promised to serve our country as Navy officers. As they accept their diplomas on stage at the Navy-Marine Corps Stadium and toss their hats in the air, they are cheered by parents, Naval Academy residents and Annapolitans who have lent hearts, homes, and daily support to these fledgling leaders of the United States Navy.

The experience of living at the Academy among the excitement, traditions, and social activities is focused on a central purpose: to support the midshipmen. As lovingly expressed by a former resident, Ann Snell:

A tour at the Naval Academy was not a typical Navy tour. It was life surrounded by Academia. [It was] filled with the most wonderful opportunities – lecture series, sporting events, college theatrical undertakings, sponsoring of mids, housing their

"dates," listening to "firsties" deciding which car to buy, our children taking sport workshops directed by mids, etc. The best part of all was being involved with the nicest, most hard-working, talented, squared-away young Naval officers-to-be. And, hopefully, feeling that maybe we had just a little something to do with sending them off on the right track.[331]

CHAPTER FOUR: COMPLETING THE CIRCLE

Relationship with Annapolis: A Good Marriage

As always, the people of Annapolis have remained constant in their support of the Academy, though at times they had to stand their ground against military encroachments in their historic town. The bond between the Academy and Annapolis are so close that the genial mayor of Annapolis in the early 1990s, Alfred A. Hopkins, could be seen at nearly every official function on the Yard, demonstrating the town's support of Academy tradition. The Mayor declared May 10, 1991, as the city's "Admiral and Mrs. Virgil Hill Day." **Of this distinction, Superintendent Hill said, "It's very moving and meaningful to us. As you all know, Annapolis and the Naval Academy are . . . inexorably entwined. Always have been and always should be."**[332]

Superintendent Virgil Hill, Jr., in turn, facilitated the mayor's life-time dream of being a midshipman by declaring the 65 year old Hopkins a "plebe," complete with a certificate and a Dixie Cup hat, conferring this honor for the first time in Naval Academy history.

Later in the fall, on October 9, 1991, the gray-haired, jovial gentleman donned a midshipman's uniform, studied his "rates," ate at King Hall, and jauntily marched with the 25th Company across Worden Field as a member of the Class of 1995. Superintendent and Mrs. Thomas C. Lynch hosted the tired mid at a reception and dinner that evening. [333] Mayor Hopkins was so touched by his experience, that he kept his uniform for display in his home as a tribute to this day of honor.

Annapolitans have joined with the residents of the Yard to nurture and groom the midshipmen who will become national leaders, and to mourn any losses in the "family" through the years. This caring was exemplified by the sentiments expressed in a letter to the editor of *The Capital*, the Annapolis newspaper. After several tragic deaths shook the community in 1993, one citizen, James Brianas, wrote:

> Words cannot express the deeply felt sorrow that the residents of Annapolis feel over the loss of six Naval Academy officers and midshipmen.

From their plebe year to when they are 1st classmen, and often beyond graduation, the city of Annapolis is the home away from

home for those who attend the Academy. And many residents treat these young, dedicated, idealistic, and courageous future warriors as their own.

> As residents we value all at the Naval Academy. We are proud of you and share with and stand by you in times of grief as well as times of joy. The bonds between us will soon span a century-and-a-half as you approach your 150th anniversary in 1995.
>
> A memorial should be erected at that time as a special tribute commemorating the close civilian and military ties between the city of Annapolis and the Naval Academy and the triumphs and tragedies that will forever be part of the human experience. . . .[334]

The granddame, Annapolis, though always careful to maintain her own identity, has never failed to embrace the individuals who make up the community on the Yard. Like the changing of the tides, names and faces come and go at the Academy. Like the bride who waits at home for the sailor out to sea, Annapolis remains steadfast, always providing a warm place beside her hearth.

Spiralling Through the Centuries

The people who live on the Yard begin a new cycle of traditional activities each year, closing the loop of time, participating in the constant spiral toward excellence that is the standard of life at the Naval Academy. Many of the familiar events at the Academy have passed in review, and marched on into history. No longer do residents greet each other by "paying calls" or have frequent dinner parties among themselves; spouses working outside the home, and the lack of domestic help make visiting and entertaining less feasible. Midshipmen have fewer hops, do not meet for "tea fights," and no longer look forward to traffic jams of girls crowding into the Academy every weekend; mids now have more liberty, can leave campus, and the women midshipmen provide a balance to the once all-male institution.

With all the changes, there is permanence. For a few years, residents find a sanctuary within these walls by the Severn, a place where time seems to stand still while also adapting to the demands of a changing society. This safe harbor is where youth can be recaptured by watching the midshipmen who never age, by recalling the old homes that never change, and by participating in the time-honored traditions that link the past to the future. Remaining, too, are the eternal sounds of the Yard; the steady swish of the crew-boat paddles and the heartbeat of the parade drums, the heavy-hearted funeral dirge played by the band while "crossing the bridge" and the sharp report of a gun salute. And the children of every decade scurry for pennies from underneath the Tecumseh statue, the "god of 2.5."

The common experiences held by residents of all eras bond them to each other with a sense of family, and to ideals greater than the self. Like one's ever youthful inner core, the Naval Academy matures, yet remains the same. Reminiscent of the old mulberry tree on Windmill Point, the Yard is a constant guidepost to those searching for a home of the heart.

Life at the Naval Academy comes full circle in a grand way, as shown by a story from Colonel James Wesley Hammond, USNA Class of 1951. It seems there was an elderly woman who had a multi-generational association to the Yard, and whose memory dipped into the nineteenth century. In the late 1980s, she asked a young woman what year her brother had graduated from the Academy. The young woman replied, "In '82." The older woman exclaimed, "Well, I remember when the Class of '82 were OLD men!"[335]

THE END

Pictures

Loockerman – Tilton House - Built in the 1700s

Paca House,

Carvel Hall

German Officer's House – Built 1868

The Bungalows – Built 1920s

RADM C.R.P. Rodgers and Naval Academy Officers' Families, 1879

(Courtesy of USNA Archives)

Buchanan House – Occupied as Superintendent's Quarters in 1909

By Superintendent (Captain) John M. Bowyer and family

(Released Official U. S. Navy Photograph)

Blake Row #11 – Interior – Late 1880s

(Photo courtesy of USNA Archives)

Blake Row for Families, #1 Quarters of the Commandant

Called "Rascality Row" by the midshipmen

Completed between 1859 and 1861

(Photo courtesy of USNA Archives)

175

Lovers' Lane – June Week – 1912 Postcard

School for officers' children

Miss Magruder and Students in Mahan Hall – Navy Junior School - Began in 1916

#29 Upshur Road, Used as Temporary Superintendent's Home from 1902 - 1909

#49 & #50 Rodgers Road, Parade Field Homes (Sleeping Porch in 1921)

(Photo Courtesy of USNA Archives)

Commandant's Home - #14 Porter Road

Bowyer Road Homes, Old Marine Quarters

Built 1903

Wood Road Homes, Hospital Point, Built 1911

Perry Circle Apartments, Built in 1939

Quarters A, Experiment Station, Built in 1900

Quarters B, Experiment Station, Built in the 1940s

Quarters E, Experiment Station

Kinkaid Road Homes, Built 1930s

Gardener's House, Built in 1901

(Photo courtesy of USNA Archives)

Stable Keeper's House and Stable, Built in 1904

(Photo Courtesy of the USNA Archives)

Hop, 1957

(Photo Courtesy of USNA Archives)

Porter Road Gang, 1993, by Athletic Director Jack Lengyel

Sally Shapiro with Flowers, Sandy Lengyel with curlers,

Father Hines with Glasses

David Donald Florence

7 June 1965 – 30 May 1969

Memorial Fountain on Parade Field

Parade Field Homes – Rodgers Road

Vicki Escudé, Author, Parade Field Centennial Celebration

In 50 Rodgers Road, 1993

Parade Field Neighborhood

Gathering, 1993

INDEX

About the Author

Vicki H. Escudé lived on the Parade Field at the U.S. Naval Academy from 1990 to 1995 with her husband, Captain Leon R. Escude, Jr., and her children, Laura and Chandler. She was active in the Naval Academy Women's Club, publishing the club's newsletter, as well as organizing the club-sponsored Parade Field Centennial Celebration in 1993. Escude researched names of residents, and created plaques for each Parade Field home listing resident families. She also served as a docent for the Paca House.

Vicki H. Escudé, M.A., Master Certified Coach, Certified Mentor Coach, is CEO of Executive Leadership Coaching, LLC, and has over 20 years experience in executive coaching, business ownership, writing, management and counseling. She was awarded the highest coaching certification offered by the International Coach Federation. She is a Founding Member and Coach Trainer for SECA, and is also a Coach Trainer for Success Unlimited Network, LLC. She was elected to the Board of Directors of the International Coach Federation for 2005-2007. Escudé is also on the faculty of the University of Texas-Dallas School of Management for Coaching Certification.

Escudé graduated from Vanderbilt University, and received her Master's Degree from the University of West Florida in psychology and counseling. Vicki Escudé is the author of the published books – *Create Your Day with Intention! The 30 Day Power Coach*, and *Getting Everything You Want and Going for More! Coaching for Mastery* and *Fast-Track Leader: First, Master Yourself!* - which are masterful tools for executive and personal clarity, focus, and attaining extraordinary results with stretch goals. Vicki has a featured chapter in *The Philosophy and Practice of Coaching*, Wiley Publishers, 2008, entitled, "Creating Corporate Coaching Cultures for Resiliency and Change."

FOOTNOTES and REFERENCES

[1] William Oliver Stevens, Annapolis: *Anne Arundel's Town* (Dodd, Mead and Co., Inc., circa 1937) 238-240.

[2] Elmer M. Jackson, Jr., *Annapolis* (1936) 37.

[3] Elihu S. Riley, *The Ancient City* (Record Printing Office, 1887) 120.

[4] Jackson: 46. One hundred and forty years later, the charred remains of the ship were found at the Academy during a period of reclamation, and some Annapolitans kept pieces of the burned ship in their homes.

[5] Elizabeth B. Anderson, *Annapolis: A Walk Through History* (Centreville, MD: Tidewater Publishers, 1984): 107.

[6] Park Benjamin, *The United States Naval Academy* (New York: Knickerbocker Press, 1900) 146.

[7] Stevens 186-187.

[8] Jackson 134.

[9] Benjamin 23.

[10] Benjamin 157.

[11] James Ford, *History of the Naval Academy*, ms., James Ford papers, 1887. Special Collections, Nimitz Library, United States Naval Academy. 9:34.

[12] Benjamin 23.

[13] Ford 10:8.

[14] Ford 10:8.

[15] Ford 10:8.

[16] Charles Todorich, *The Spirited Years* (Annapolis: Naval Institute Press, 1984) 139.

[17] Todorich 139.

[18] Henry Hayes Lockwood, *Notes of Henry Hayes Lockwood on the founding of the USNA*. Special Collections, Nimitz Library, United States Naval Academy. 3.

[19] Ford 9: 4.

[20] Charles M. Todorich, "Franklin Buchanan: Symbol for Two Navies," *Captains of the Old Steam Navy*, ed. James C. Bradford, (Annapolis: Naval Institute Press. 1986) 96.

[21] Carroll Storrs Alden and Ralph Earle, *Makers of Naval Tradition* (Boston: Ginn and Co., 1925) 248.

[22] Lockwood.

[23] Ford 9: 65.

[24] Officer' Directories, 1893-1899, Nimitz Archives, United States Naval Academy.

[25] Ford 10: 3.

[26] Todorich, *Spirited Years* 52.

[27] Ford 11: 30.

[28] Ford 11: 8-9.

[29] Todorich, *Spirited Years* 54.

[30] Benjamin 180-181.

[31] Todorich, *Spirited Years* 140.

[32] Todorich, *Spirited Years* 140.

[33] Todorich, *Spirited Years* 140 & 184.

[34] Soley 131.

[35] Stevens 168-170.

[36] Soley 131.

[37] This rank was created in 1831 to commission professors in the Navy. Ranking professors, no matter what they taught, held this title. The rank ceased to exist when the last retired officer to hold it died in 1901.

[38] *Edward Seager: Professor of Drawing* (Annapolis: United States Naval Academy, 1986)

[39] Soley 131.

[40] Soley 132.

[41] Soley 130.

[42] Benjamin 262.

[43] Soley 131.

[44] Ford 9: 60-63.

[45] Benjamin 228.

[46] Stevens 256.

[47] Stevens 233-234.

[48] Stevens 234.

[49] Benjamin 262.

[50] Benjamin 262-263.

[51] Tamara Moser Melia, "David Dixon Porter: Fighting Sailor," *Captains of the Old Steam Navy*, ed. James C. Bradford (Annapolis: Naval Institute Press, 1986) 237.

[52] Benjamin 263.

[53] Benjamin 267.

[54] Melia 237.

[55] Benjamin 267.

[56] Jack Sweetman, *The U.S. Naval Academy: An Illustrated History* (Annapolis: Naval Institute Press, 1979) 97.

[57] Edward P. Lull, "Description and History of the U.S. Naval Academy," report for D.D. Porter, 1869: 73.

[58] Melia 238.

[59] Lull 73.

[60] Alden and Earle 210.

[61] "Naval Academy Centennial Edition of the *Evening Capital*," 10 Oct. 1945.

[62] Jackson 134.

[63] Lull 74.

[64] Benjamin 270.

[65] Soley 132-134.

[66] Soley 134.

[67] This creek has been known as Graveyard Creek, Crocus Creek, Stonewall Creek, Robert's Creek, Dorsey Creek, and College Creek.

[68] Ruby R. Duval. "The Naval Academy Cemetery on 'Strawberry Hill,'" *United States Naval Institute Proceedings*, ed. Wells L. Field (Menasha, WI: United States Naval Institute Apr. 1946) 76.

[69] Morris Radoff, "Strawberry Hill," 1976.

[70] Duval 75.

[71] Duval 75.

[72] Radoff.

[73] Jackson 135.

[74] Clarence Marbury White, Sr. and Evangeline Kaiser White, *The Years Between* (New York: Exposition Press, 1957) 109-110.

[75] Lull 60.

[76] Lull 63.

[77] Jackson 130.

[78] Stevens 211.

[79] Jackson 135.

[80] Barton D. Strong, ts., "A History of the Marine Barracks, Annapolis, Maryland," circa 1964. Nimitz Library Archives, United States Naval Academy.

[81] Tilton served at the Naval Academy from 1865 to 1870, from 1873 to 1877, and from 1883 to 1885 as a Captain, USMC. He served from 1892 to 1896 at the Academy as a Lieutenant Colonel, after which he retired. (Strong, p. 15)

[82] Stevens 242-243.

[83] Riley 268.

[84] *The New York Times*, July 24, 1892.

[85] Stevens 215.

[86] Stevens 229-230.

[87] *Army and Navy Register*, 5 Jan. 1884: 11.

[88] Stevens 280.

[89] Alan Moorehead, *The White Nile* (New York: Harper and Row, 1971) 32.

[90] Mary Virginia Ramsay Sease (Mrs. Hugh St. Clare Sease), personal interview, 13 May 1993. Her husband was graduated from the USNA Class of 1917.

[91] White 107.

[92] Riley 268.

[93] *Army and Navy Register, 30* May 1885: 349

[94] White 109.

[95] Michael J. Crosbie, "With Honors," *Historic Preservation* November/December 1993: 74.

[96] Historic Military Quarters Handbook, Legacy Program (R. Christopher Goodwin & Assoc., Inc.) inside cover.

[97] This tour and Celebration was sponsored by the Naval Academy Women's Club. Through extensive research, names of all former residents were found, and a plaque made for each home, also donated by the Women's Club.

[98] Richard Southall Grant, interview, 1942. Special Collections, Nimitz Library, United States Naval Academy.

[99] Jackson 137-138.

[100] Moorehead 114.

[101] Benjamin 377-378.

[102] White 54-55.

[103] Stevens 282.

[104] Stevens 283.

[105] White 68-69.

[106] Board of Visitors' Minutes, 1906. Archives, Nimitz library, United States Naval Academy.

[107] Stevens 266-267.

[108] Stevens 267.

[109] George Schaun, *Annapolis Guide Book* (Annapolis: Greenbury Publications, 1971) 14.

[110] Stevens 241.

[111] Philip B. Cooper, letter to Captain P.H. Cooper, 8 Nov. 1894, Scrapbook of Eleanor B. Cooper, Special Collections, Nimitz Library, United States Naval Academy.

[112] Philip B. Cooper, letter to Captain P.H. Cooper, undated, Scrapbook of Eleanor B. Cooper.

[113] Cooper letters, undated.

[114] Cooper letters, undated.

[115] Michael P. Parker, "A Rose for Miss Lucy (and Miss Hessie): Philip B. Cooper and the Hammond Harwood House," *Anne Arundel County History Notes*, (Jan., 1992) 18. Also, according to Parker, Mr. Cooper helped design Carvel Hall, the portico of the State House, the Cooper Apartments outside of Gate #3, oversaw the construction of the Circle Theatre, and engineered the moving of the Pinkney Callahan House to St. John's campus.

[116] Ken Kimble, "Spanish Prisoners in Annapolis," *TPE* (Aug., 1989) Special Collections, Nimitz Library, 35.

[117] White 108.

[118] P.H. Magruder, "The Spanish Naval Prisoners of War at Annapolis, 1898," *U.S. Naval Institute Proceedings* (Annapolis: Naval Institute Press, Jun. 1930) 495.

[119] Magruder 495.

[120] Kimble 35.

[121] Stevens 217-226.

[122] Stevens 244.

[123] Stevens 243-247.

[124] Board of Visitors' Minutes, 1894, Archives, Nimitz Library, United States Naval Academy.

[125] Board of Visitors' Minutes, 1899, Archives, Nimitz Library, United States Naval Academy.

[126] Board of Visitors' Minutes, 1908, Archives, Nimitz Library, United States Naval Academy.

[127] Board of Visitors' Minutes, 1897, Archives, Nimitz Library, United States Naval Academy.

[128] Board of Visitors' Minutes, 1897, Archives, Nimitz Library, United States Naval Academy.

[129] Philip B. Cooper, letter to Captain Cooper, 25 Apr. 1899. Special Collections, Nimitz Library, United States Naval Academy.

[130] Cooper, letters to Captain Cooper, 25 Apr. 1899. Special Collections, Nimitz Library, United States Naval Academy.

[131] *Army and Navy Register*, 30 Aug. 1902: 14.

[132] Harold N. Burdett, *Yesteryear in Annapolis* (Cambridge, MD: Tidewater Publishers, 1974) 85.

[133] Charles J. Nolan, Jr., and David O. Tomlinson, "Mark Twain's Visit to Annapolis," research paper (circa 1991) Special Collections, Nimitz Library, United States Naval Academy.

[134] Burdett 86.

[135] Board of Visitors' Minutes, 1906. Archives, Nimitz Library, United States Naval Academy.

[136] Jackson 134-135.

[137] Mrs. Roy C. Smith, Jr., *Reminiscences of Mrs. Marc A. Mitscher and Mrs. Roy C. Smith, Jr.,* (Annapolis: Naval Institute, 1986) 70-71.

[138] Michael P. Parker, "Alphabetical (Dis-) Order: The Annapolis Satires of William Oliver Stevens," *Maryland Historical Magazine* Spring, 1990: 33.

[139] Todorich 133.

[140] "Some Things of Interest at the Naval Academy," *The Sun*, Baltimore, 6 Jul. 1907. Special Collections, Buildings and Grounds Vertical File. Nimitz Library, United States Naval Academy.

[141] Memorandum, 1 Jul. 1935. Buildings and Grounds File, Archives, Nimitz Library, United States Naval Academy.

[142] Strong.

[143] William N. Thomas, Jr., letter to the author, 9 Jun. 1993.

[144] Jackson 135.

[145] S.F. Heim, letter to Superintendent Scales, 3 May 1919, Housing File, USNA Archives, Nimitz Library United States Naval Academy.

[146] A.H. Scales, letter to Josephus Daniels, 25 Jun. 1919, Housing File, USNA Archives, Nimitz Library United States Naval Academy.

[147] St. Clair Wright, "The Preservation of Annapolis," *Anne Arundel County, Maryland, A Bicentennial History*, 1649-1977, ed. James C. Bradford (Annapolis: Anne Arundel County and Annapolis Bicentennial Committee, 1977) 185.

[148] Memo, 24 Aug. 1925, Building and Grounds File, Archives, Nimitz Library, USNA.

[149] Mary Greenman Clark, letter to the author, 30 Jun. 1993.

[150] Samuel A. Elder, letter to the author, 30 Jun. 1993.

[151] Elizabeth Dudley, letter to the author, 18 Jul. 1993. Captain John B. Dudley was from the USNA Class of 1939. Rear Admiral Ralph S. Wentworth, Jr. was from USNA Class of 1944.

[152] Susan Forbes Snead, telephone interview, 6 Dec. 1993. Her husband is Commander James C. Snead, USNA Class of 1973. Mrs. Snead was President of the Naval Academy Women's Club from 1993-1994.

[153] "Making Sense Out of Nonsense," *The Centerline,* 14 Jun. 1985: 4. Special Collections, Nimitz Library, USNA.

[154] Paul B. Dungan, "History, Description, and Purpose of the Engineering Experiment Station," 29 Aug. 1925, report to Superintendent. Special Collections, Nimitz Library, USNA.

[155] "Annapolis Shows OIC Quarters," The Centerline 5 Aug. 1983: 4. Special Collections, Nimitz Library, USNA.

[156] #41 Greenlee Road was built in 1942; #104 Church Road apartments were built in 1947; #106 Church Road was built in 1938.

[157] Alice S. Creighton, personal interview, 4 Jan. 1994. Her father was Rear Admiral Liles W. Creighton, USNA Class of 1927. Miss Creighton has worked since 1974 as Assistant Librarian. Special Collections, Archives at the USNA Nimitz Library.

[158] Elizabeth Howell Knorr, personal interview, 26 Apr. 1993. Her husband is Captain David James Knorr, USNA Class of 1960.

[159] Robert S. Cooper, letter to Michael P. Parker, 8 Aug. 1989, Robert S. Cooper Papers, Special Collections, Nimitz Library, USNA.

[160] Eugenia Mandelkorn, "Navy Houseboat on the Severn," c. 1950 *Reine Mercedes* Verticle File, Special Collections, Nimitz Library, USNA.

[161] Mandelkorn.

[162] Board of Visitors' Minutes, 1931. Archives, Nimitz Library, USNA.

[163] Memorandum, 10 Dec. 1939, Buildings and Grounds File. Archives, Nimitz Library, USNA.

[164] Michelle Foley McDaniel (Mrs. Tim McDaniel), letter to the author, 15 Dec. 1993. Her father was Captain Francis J. Foley, USNA Class of 1931.

[165] Cynthia Godman Knapp, personal interview, Sep. 1993. Her husband is Lieutenant Charles I. Knapp, USNA Class of 1980.

[166] Parker, *A Rose for Miss Lucy*, 17.

[167] Tom McCarthy, "Annapolis Guidebooks Ignore Marcellus Hall," *Washington Post*, 7 Oct. 1937: 9.

[168] McCarthy.

[169] Professor Parker has taught at the Naval Academy since 1980, and in 1993 became Chairman of the English Department.

[170] Michael P. Parker, "Alphabetical (Dis-) Order: The Annapolis Satires of William Oliver Stevens," *Maryland Historical Magazine*, vol. 85, No. 1, Spring, 1990: 37-38.

[171] Parker, "Alphabetical," 15-43.

[172] Anne Howard Thomas, letter to the author, 19 Sep. 1993.

[173] Thomas, letter.

[174] Fay Basil Baker, telephone interview, 24 May 1993.

[175] Baker, interview.

[176] Randolph W. King and Mrs. King, personal interview, 15 Apr. 1993.

[177] Stevens, 266.

[178] King, interview.

[179] Naval Academy Women's Club Roster, 1992-1993

[180] Naval Academy Women's Club Roster, 1992-1993

[181] Naval Academy Women's Club Roster, 1992-1993

[182] Rear Admiral Randolph King, USNA Class of 1944, interview.

[183] Jackson, 194-195.

[184] King, interview

[185] Philip Osborn (USNA Class of 1929), letter to author, 22 May 1993.

[186] Colleen Mallgrave, interview, 22 December 1993. Her husband, then-Commander Fred Joseph Mallgrave III, is USNA Class of 1971. They lived at 91 Bowyer Road in the early 1990s.

[187] *Army and Navy Journal*, 26 June 1909: 1228.

[188] Anne Howard Thomas (Mrs. Donald I. Thomas), letter to author, 19 Sep. 1993. Mrs. Thomas's grandfathers are RADM John M. Bowyer, USNA Class of 1874, Superintendent from 1090 to 1911, and RADM Thomas B. Howard, USNA Class of 1873. Her father is CAPT Douglas L. Howard, USNA Class of 1906; her brothers are John M.B. Howard, USNA Class of 1933, and CDR Joseph B. Howard, USNA Class of 1950. Her husband, Donald I. Thomas, is USNA Class of 1932.

[189] Ann S. Roby, "Superintendent's House, U.S. Naval Academy," *Shipmate*, 14. Special Collection, Nimitz Library, USNA.

[190] Roby,14.

[191] Smith, *Reminiscences*, 72-73.

[192] Smith, *Reminiscences*, 190.

[193] Smith, *Reminiscences*, 70.

[194] Smith, *Reminiscences*, 91.

[195] Smith, *Reminiscences*, 98.

[196] Smith, *Reminiscences*, 68.

[197] Smith, *Reminiscences*, 86.

[198] Mary Virginia Ramsay Sease, interview, 13 May 1993.

[199] Sease.

[200] Sease.

[201] Sease.

[202] Sease.

[203] White, pp. 96-97.

[204] Mame Warren, *Then Again. . . Annapolis, 1900-1965* (Annapolis: Time Exposures Limited, 1990) p. xvii.

[205] Sease.

[206] Phyllis Hammond Howard, letter to the author, 19 Aug. 1993.

[207] William T. Dutton, letter to the author, 30 Jul. 1993.

[208] Roy C. Smith III, telephone interview, 25 May 1993.

[209] Margaret Corn King, personal interview, 13 Sep. 1993.

[210] Michael P. Parker, ed., *Good Gouge: An Investigation into the Origins of Naval Academy Slang,* 1982: 19. Special Collections, Nimitz Library, USNA.

[211] Parker, *Good Gouge,* p. 19.

[212] Roy C. Smith III, telephone interview, 25 May 1993.

[213] Roy Smith.

[214] J. B. Rutter, Jr., Captain, letter to the author, 10 Jun. 1992.

[215] Ralph Earle, Jr., letter to the author, 20 Nov. 1992.

[216] Mary Greenman Rae, letter to the author, 30 Jun. 1993.

[217] Rae.

[218] Randolph W. King, Rear Admiral, personal interview, 13 Sep. 1993.

[219] Robert G. Tobin, Jr. Telephone interview, 22 May 1993.

[220] Caryl Sinton Carlson, letter to the author, 19 Jun. 1993.

[221] Carlson.

[222] Louis R. Hird, Commander, letter to the author, 24 Jun. 1992.

[223] Samuel A. Elder, letter to the author, 7 Jun. 1993.

[224] Alister C. Anderson, The Reverend Father, letter to the author, 13 Jun. 1992.

[225] Stevens, 287.

[226] Mary Gale Buchanan, personal interview, 1993.

[227] Hird.

[228] *Lucky Bag,* 1903. Archives, Nimitz Library, USNA.

[229] *San Francisco Chronicle*, 10 Nov. 1902, p. 2:2. Archives, Nimitz Library, USNA.

[230] *Reef Points*, 1940-1941, USNA,

[231] Randolph W. King, Rear Admiral, letter to the author, 30 Sep. 1993.

[232] Eleanor Michelet Mulbry, telephone interview, 9 May 1993.

[233] *Lucky Bag,* 1945, p. XXII.

[234] Carroll S. Alden, "Officers and Gentlemen in the Making," *United States Naval Institute Proceedings* (Annapolis Naval Institute: Vol. 61, Oct. 1935) 1495.

[235] Stevens, 283.

[236] Adelaide Fullinwider, telephone interview, 24 May 1993.

[237] Robert S. Cooper, letter to Professor Michael P. Parker, 8 May 1989. Special Collections, Nimitz Library.

[238] Elizabeth Hill Drake, telephone interview, 24 Jul. 1993.

[239] Patty Wattles Robie (Mrs. Edgar Robie) telephone interview with the author, 23 Nov. 1993.

[240] Margaret Corn King (Mrs. Randolph W. King).

[241] Bane McCormick (Mrs. James H. McCormick, Jr.), personal interview, 1 May 1993.

[242] King.

[243] Irving Hancock, *Dave Darrin's Third Year of Annapolis.* (Philadelphia: Henry Artemus Company, 1911) 49.

[244] Draper L. Kauffman, *Reminiscences of Rear Admiral Draper L. Kauffman* (Annapolis: U. S. Naval Institute, 1982) Volume I: 41.

[245] Alister C. Anderson, The Reverend Father, letter to the author, 13 Jun. 1992.

[246] William N. Thomas, Jr., M.D., letter to the author, 9 Jun. 1993.

[247] Thomas.

[248] Rosemary Rutt, telephone interview, 28 May 1993.

[249] Warren, *Then Again . . . Annapolis 1900-1965, p. 105. Interview with Jane Wilson McWilliams, 17 February 1990.*

[250] Margaret Corn King, (Mrs. Randolph W. King), personal interview, 13 September 1993.

[251] Margaret King.

[252] Sally Marable Camm, telephone interview, 24 May 1993. Mrs. Camm lived in a Perry Circle Apartment in 1943. She lived at 35 Upshur from 1944 to 1945. Her father is Captain Herbert H. Marable, USNA Class of 1930.

[253] Thomas O. Cullins, Jr. Captain USNA Class of 1921 resided at 50 Rodgers Road in 1942.

[254] Adelaide Fullinwider, telephone interviews, 24 May 1993 and 27 Jan. 1994. Her husband is Captain Simon P.J. Fullinwider, USNA Class of 1917, and her son id Professor S. Pendelton Fullinwider, Jr. Class of 1955. Mrs. Fullinwider was President of the Naval Academy Women's Club from 1943-1944. They resided at 11 Porter Road from 1942 to 1943.

[255] John P. Henner, letter to the Housing Officer, 9 Jan. 1945. Buildings and Grounds File, Archives, Nimitz Library, United States Naval Academy.

[256] Notice to residents, 1946. Homoja Village File, Archives, Nimitz Library, United States Naval Academy.

[257] Hanson W. Baldwin, "Annapolis Logs a Hundred Years," *New York Times Magazine*, 7 Oct. 1945:10

[258] *Baltimore Sun*, 8 Oct. 1945, Special Collections, Nimitz Library, United States Naval Academy.

[259] George C. Dorsch, from an article in the *Baltimore Sun*, 11 Oct. 1945:30

[260] Clark, Robert O., Commander, letter to author, 20 Aug. 1993. Commander Clark was from the USNA Class of 1946.

[261] Notice to Residents, Arundel Estates, 15 Nov. 1951. Buildings and Grounds File, Archives, Nimitz Library, USNA.

[262] Elizabeth McDowell Diffie, letter to the author, 31 Jan. 1994. Mrs., Diffie and her husband, LCDR Craig M. Diffie, USNA Class of 1978, lived on Sellers Road from 1991 to 1993.

[263] White 148-149

[264] Wright 185. Mrs. Wright's father is Rear Admiral Arthur St. Clair Smith, Jr., USNA Class of 1897, and the family lived briefly at 4 Porter Road in 1911. This information from a paper by Salvatierra, Daniel. " 'A True and Brave and Downright Honest Man.' – The Life of Arthur St. Clair Smith," 22 Apr. 1993. Special Collections, Nimitz Library, U.S. Naval Academy. Her husband was Captain Joseph M.P. Wright, USNA Class of 1924.

[265] Christopher Raphael and Peggy Wanamaker, *Oyster Shells and Shypokes*, The Faces of Annapolis (ImageAnations, 1988).

[266] Reminiscences of Vice Admiral Eli T. Reich (Annapolis, U.S. Naval Academy, 1982) Vol. 1:264.

[267] Phyllis Hammond Howard, Phyllis Hammond (Mrs. James H. Howard), letter to the author, 3April1993. Her husband is Rear Admiral James H. Howard, Class of 1930. They lived in 39 Upshur from 1947-1950. Her grandfather is Rear Admiral John R. Edwards, Class of 1874, her father is Captain Phillip H. Hammond, Class of 1907, and her son, James H. Howard, Jr., is Class of 1964. Young George Seay's father is Rear Admiral George C. Seay, Class of 1930.

[268] Dorothea Caldwell, letter to the author, 1 Jun. 1993. Her husband is Rear Admiral H. Howard Caldwell, USNA Class of 1927, and they lived in 9 Porter Road from 1948 to 1951. Rear Admiral Walter H. Price is USNA Class of 1927.

[269] Lucille Pauli, letter to the author, 9 Oct. 1992. Her husband is Commander Robert H. Pauli, USNA Class of 1940, and they lived in 47 Rodgers from 1956 to 1959. Rear Admiral Eugene B. Fluckey is a graduate of USNA Class of 1935.

[270] Edith Neese (Mrs. William Gordon Neese), personal interview, 1 Jun. 1992. Captain and Mrs. Neese lived at 31 Upshur from 1956 to 1957.

[271] Ann Snell, letter to the author, 17 Jan. 1994. Rear Admiral and Mrs. William H. Snell lived at D-3 (now 4-C) Perry Circle from 1969 to 1974. Rear Admiral Snell became the 31st Chief of the Navy Dental Corp in 1995.

[272] Snell.

[273] Jean Grkovic, telephone interview, 5 Nov. 1992. Her husband is Captain George Grkovic, USNA Class of 1943, and they lived at 50 Rodgers Road from 1957 to 1959.

[274] Jean Coward Mason, letter to Captain Phillip Ryan, 6 Jul. 1993. Mrs. Mason was formerly married to Captain Asbury Coward III, USNA Class of 1938, and they lived on Perry Circle and 32 Upshur from 1946 to 1949. In 1959, they moved to 16 Porter Road. Her son Asbury Coward IV (Sandy), USNA Class of 1964, and his wife Croom Whitfield Coward, lived on 6 Porter Road from 1992 to 1994. After the death of Asbury Coward III, Jean Coward married Rear Admiral Harry C. Mason, USNA Class of 1938.

[275] Anne C. Madden, letter to the author, 12 Jun. 1993. Her husband is Captain John C. Madden and they lived at 43 Upshur Road from 1961 to 1963.

[276] Roger Staubach, USNA Class of 1965, was a Heisman Trophy winner, and played professional football with the Dallas Cowboys; Rear Admiral Thomas C. Lynch, USNA Class of 1964, was Superintendent from 1991 to 1994. Captain William Patrick Donnelly, Class of 1965, and Edward Andrew Orr, Jr., Class of 1965.

[277] Shirley Childs Pritchard (Mrs. C.A. Pritchard), letter to the author, 11 Oct. 1993. Her former husband, Captain Donald R. Childs, died in 1979. They lived in 35 Upshur Road from 1963 to 1967.

[278] Marjorie Becker, letter to the author, 25 Sep. 1992. Her husband is Rear Admiral Charles Becker, USNA Class of 1944.

[279] John W. Renard, Captain, personal interview, 1993. Captain Renard is from the USNA Class of 1955. Captain and Mrs. Renard lived in 35 Upshur Road from 1972 to 1975. They later lived on Porter Road.

[280] Charles Allen Buchanan, USNA Class of 1926; his son, Charles Allen Buchanan, Jr., (Buck) is from USNA Class of 1956.

[281] Emmie Spalding Hamilton (Mrs. Thomas J. Hamilton).ms. My Story: Second Fiddle to a Pigskin, copyright 1984, 105.

[282] Hamilton 111.

[283] Jean Grkovic (Mrs. George Grkovic), personal interview, 5 Nov. 1992. Rear Admiral William R. Smedberg III, USNA Class of 1926, lived on Porter Road in the late 1940s, and was Superintendent from 1956 to 1958.

[284] Marylee Klunder, e-mail to author, July 29, 2011.

[285] George D. Florence, letter to the author, 4 Feb. 1994. Commander Florence is from the USNA Class of 1949. Commander and Mrs. Florence lived in 34 Upshur Road in the late 1960s.

[286] Philip J. Ryan, Captain, USNA Class of 1950. Captain and Mrs. Ryan lived in 35 Upshur Road in 1969, then moved to Porter Road.

[287] "Dodo Dies," The Evening Capital, 26 Mar. 1971: 2.

[288] Vince Johnson, "Once Over Lightly: Life with the Hamiltons-at Home," circa December, 1948, found in ms. My Story: Second Fiddle to a Pigskin, Emmie Spalding Hamilton, copyright 1984: 116.

[289] Emmie Spalding Hamilton, letter to the author, 4 Jan. 1994.

[290] William S. Busik, Captain, letter to the author, 14 Jun. 1993. Captain Busik is from the USNA Class of 1943.

[291] Sandy Lengyel (Mrs. Jack Lengyel), letter to the author, 4January1994.

[292] Mary Gayle Buchanan, letter to the author, 1 Jun. 1993. Her father is Rear Admiral Charles Allen Buchanan, USNA Class of 1926, who also lived on Upshur road as a child. Her brother, Buck, is Charles Allen Buchanan, Jr., USNA Class of 1956.

[293] Michelle Foley McDaniel, letter to the author, 15 Dec. 1993. Her Father is Captain Francis J. Foley, USNA Class of 1931.

[294] Marylee Klunder (Mrs. Matthew Klunder), from e-mail to author, June 28, 2011.

[295] Elizabeth Rue (Mrs. John Paul Rue), from e-mail to author, June 25, 2011.

[296] Elizabeth Rue (Mrs. John Paul Rue), from e-mail to author, June 25, 2011.

[297] Marylee Klunder (Mrs. Matthew Klunder), from e-mail to author, August 7, 2011.

[298] Elizabeth Hill Drake (Mrs. J.B. Drake), telephone interview, 24 Jul. 1993. Her father is Vice Admiral Harry W. Hill, USNA Class of 1911, who was Superintendent from 1950 to 1952. Rear Admiral Draper L. Kauffman, USNA Class of 1933, was Superintendent from 1965 to 1968.

[299] Draper L. Kauffman, *Reminiscences of Rear Admiral Draper L. Kauffman* (Annapolis: U.S. Naval Institute, 1982) Vol.II: 1129.

[300] Kauffman 787 and 1120-1121.

[301] James F. Calvert, Vice Admiral, letter to the author, 12 May 1993.

[302] Kathleen Quinn Lynch (Mrs. Thomas C. Lynch), personal interview, 7 Oct. 1993.

[303] Thomas C. Lynch, Rear Admiral, personal interview, 7 Oct. 1993. Rear Admiral Lynch is from the USNA Class of 1964.

[304] Thomas C. Lynch.

[305] Fowler, Katie (Mrs. Jeffrey Fowler), from e-mail to author, August 17, 2011.

[306] Sara Friesz, telephone interview, 9June1993. Her husband is Captain Raymond H. Friesz, and they lived at 50 Rodgers Road from 1967 to 1971. Mrs. Friesz was President of the Naval Academy Garden Club in 1969.

[307] James A. Kenney, Captain, letter to the author, 7September1992.

[308] Dr. John Barry Talley was the Director of Musical Activities and worked at the Naval Academy from 1971 to 2006.

[309] Janet Brandquist, letter to the author, 14 Sep. 1992. Her husband id Captain Roland Brandquist, Class of 1960, and they lived at 34 Upshur Road from 1977 to 1980.

[310] Rebecca Caldwell, letter to the author, 14 Sep. 1992. The Caldwell family lived in 34 Upshur from 1982 to 1984, and the Kennard family, lived in 33 Upshur during that time. Mrs. John Kennard was president of the Naval Academy Women's Club in 1985.

[311] Ann Snell, (Mrs. William H. Snell), letter to the author, 17January1994.

[312] Vicki Heath Escude. Captain Leon R. Escude, Jr. and Mrs. Escude lived in 50 Rodgers Road from 1991 to 1995.

[313] Elizabeth Rue (Mrs. John Paul Rue), from e-mail to author, June 25, 2011.

[314] Elizabeth Rue (Mrs. John Paul Rue), from e-mail to author, June 25, 2011.

[315] Marylee Klunder, from e-mail to author, July 30, 2011.

[316] Jennifer John, personal interview, 1993. Commander and Mrs. Michael John lived in 32 Upshur from 1990 to 1993. Mrs. John was president of the Naval Academy Women's Club from 1991 to 1993.

[317] Mary Gale Buchanan, letter to the author, 1 Jun. 1993.

[318] Michele Foley McDaniel, letter to the author, 15 Dec. 1993.

[319] Carol Gebert Bowis, interview with the author, 24 May 1994. Her father is Captain Wesley Robert Gebert, Jr., USNA Class of 1942. Her parents lived at 47 Rodgers Road from 1958 to 1962.

[320] Emmie Spalding Hamilton, letter to the author, 15 May 1993. Her husband is Rear Admiral Thomas J. Hamilton, USNA Class of 1927. The Hamiltons lived at 44 Upshur from 1946 to 1947 and at 7 Porter in 1948.

[321] Carol Baysinger, telephone interview, 4 Jan. 1994. Her husband, Captain Reaves H. Baysinger, Jr., was from USNA Class of 1949.

[322] Gene Bisbee, "Clowning at the Yacht Club," *The Capital*, 24 May 1982.

[323] Michael P. Parker, "Alphabetical (Dis-) Order" 21.

[324] Shirley Childs Pritchard (Mrs. C.A. Pritchard), letter to the author, 11 Oct. 1993. Her former husband, Captain Donald R. Childs, died in 1979. They lived in 35 Upshur Road from 1963 to 1967.

[325] Marylee Klunder, from e-mail to the author, July 29, 2011.

[326] Mary Seymour, letter to the author, 8 Apr. 1994.

[327] Vice Admiral William P. Lawrence, USNA Class of 1951, was Superintendent from 1978 to 1981. Captain Steven E. Fabry, USNA Class of 1965, lived at 9 Porter Road from 1990 to 1993.

[328] James Dale has been an Assistant Director of Musical Activities at the Academy since 1974.

[329] Julie Sugarman, letter to the author, 13Apr. 1994.

[330] "Commissioning Week" was formerly known as "June Week," but the name was changed when graduation began being held in May of each year.

[331] Ann Snell (Mrs. William H. Snell), letter to the author, 17 Jan. 1994.

[332] Deborah Funk, "Mayor Made Honorary Mid," *The Capital* 11 May 1991. Nimitz Library Special Collection, U.S. Naval Academy.

[333] Joanna Sullivan, "Hopkins Becomes Mid for a Day," *The Capital* 10 Oct. 1991: A1 & A12. Nimitz Library, Archives, U.S. Naval Academy.

[334] James Brianas, letter, *Capital*, 29Dec. 1993: A12.

[335] James Wesley Hammond, Jr., Colonel, USMC, personal interview, 1993. Colonel Hammond is from the Class of 1951.

Made in the USA
Columbia, SC
07 June 2021

39374058R00115